Birth of Intelligence

Birth of Intelligence

From RNA to Artificial Intelligence

DAEYEOL LEE

OXFORD
UNIVERSITY PRESS

OXFORD
UNIVERSITY PRESS

Oxford University Press is a department of the University of Oxford. It furthers
the University's objective of excellence in research, scholarship, and education
by publishing worldwide. Oxford is a registered trade mark of Oxford University
Press in the UK and certain other countries.

Published in the United States of America by Oxford University Press
198 Madison Avenue, New York, NY 10016, United States of America.

Library of Congress Cataloging-in-Publication Data
Names: Lee, Daeyeol, author.
Title: Birth of intelligence : From RNA to Artificial Intelligence / by Daeyeol Lee.
Description: New York, NY : Oxford University Press, [2020] | Includes
bibliographical references and index.
Identifiers: LCCN 2019041118 (print) | LCCN 2019041119 (ebook) |
ISBN 9780190908324 (hardback) | ISBN 9780190908348 (epub)
Subjects: LCSH: Intellect. | Brain. | Artificial intelligence.
Classification: LCC BF431 .L43245 2020 (print) | LCC BF431 (ebook) |
DDC 153.9—dc23
LC record available at https://lccn.loc.gov/2019041118
LC ebook record available at https://lccn.loc.gov/2019041119

1 3 5 7 9 8 6 4 2

Printed by Sheridan Books, Inc., United States of America

For Wangbal and Doolie, two intelligent beings

Contents

Preface

We are different from inanimate objects, such as rocks and raindrops, or countless life forms ranging from single-cell organisms to other mammals. Are we humans special and fundamentally different from other animals? If so, how did we come to acquire such a status? What features distinguish humans from other animals? What makes humans "human"? These questions are not new, and since antiquity, many scholars and philosophers have sought to answer them. Perhaps what really distinguishes us from other animals is that we are curious about the origins of our species and the universe and just about everything in our surroundings. What really separates us from other animals is our intelligence. This book explores how that happens.

To explore the origin and limits of human intelligence, we should begin by coming up with a working definition of intelligence. Although many definitions have been proposed, there is still a consensus that intelligence refers to the ability to accomplish a goal in diverse environments. Intelligence is not unique to humans, because all animals have certain abilities to select their actions appropriate to maximize the likelihood of their survival and reproduction in their environments. Nevertheless, compared to other forms of intelligence on Earth, human intelligence has produced more impressive outcomes. For example, only humans have built a spaceship to take them outside the Earth's atmosphere and bring them back safely. Even more amazing is that various technologies are advancing at an accelerating rate. This is probably best illustrated by the technology for digital computers. Only half a century ago, the first computer with the integrated circuit technology was used for flight guidance in the Apollo spacecraft for its journey to the moon. Nowadays, more than 2 billion people in the world carry digital computers hundred thousand times more powerful in their pockets.

Human intelligence has been applied to a vast range of problems, ranging from foraging for food and water to the problems in physics and mathematics. In fact, humans are curious about everything they encounter, including their own intelligence. This book will discuss what role curiosity plays in the intelligence of humans and other animals. In addition, understanding the origin and limitations of our intelligence has practical benefits.

Our intelligence is needed to solve all kinds of problems we face in our society. Therefore, it is critical for us to be aware of potential weaknesses and biases in our intelligence. This metaknowledge is necessary for peaceful resolution of various conflicts within our society, by preventing excessive self-confidence and making us more receptive to the opinions of others.

Human intelligence has many strengths but also has limitations. Many problems in our society, ranging from pollution to traffic accidents, are the consequence of technologies that we developed to solve other, often simpler and more basic, problems. Eventually, more advanced technologies might find solutions to most problems related to the basic material needs for humans. However, advanced technology will also create new sociopolitical problems, which might be the most challenging problems that human intelligence will face. For example, material benefits resulting from new technology will not be distributed immediately and evenly to all the members of our society. It is difficult to make everyone agree about how these material benefits should be distributed, which is often the cause of constant political debate. To resolve these conflicts peacefully, it will be helpful to understand how our intelligence might misguide and prevent us from finding a good compromise. Social conflicts might arise either because people have different motives or because they share a common goal but disagree about what might be the best approach to achieve it. Intelligence plays a key role in both cases. If people have different goals, intelligence will be needed to allow them to find a good compromise. If they have the same goal but still disagree on what might be the best common strategy for them, a close examination of their intelligence and its limitations might be particularly helpful for discovering errors in their reasoning. When we are not aware of the bias in our intelligence, we might be making things worse even with good intentions.

If we have a solid and scientific understanding of our intelligence, this will also prepare us better to deal with societal problems resulting from the rapid development of artificial intelligence (AI). In particular, many authors and scholars have speculated as to whether and when AI will surpass human intelligence. Answers to these questions are possible only when we have good understanding of both AI and human intelligence. This book will demonstrate that intelligence is inseparably intertwined with the history of life. Biological intelligence originated and evolved to enable its owners to survive and reproduce. Even the most primitive life forms can adapt to their environments to some degree, and therefore possess some problem-solving skills. By contrast, the history of AI has taken a very different route. AI is less than 100 years old, but AI and computer industry have been completely transformed during this period, while human intelligence has hardly changed. Especially during the last 10 years, the progress of AI has been startling. AI is now coming up with solutions for many practical problems that used to require extensive human interventions. Increasingly more often, it exceeds the performance of human experts in unexpected domains, such as medical diagnosis and playing complex board games, such as Go, even though until recently many had predicted that human superiority in those domains would continue much longer.

It is not possible to explain everything about intelligence in one book. To understand the nature of intelligence comprehensively, including its origin and future, broad knowledge in multiple disciplines is necessary. Intelligence is not visible and cannot be measured easily. Intelligence is an abstract entity that can be inferred only by observing the behaviors of its owner and interpreting the data according to some theoretical framework. The goal of this book is still to shine some light on all aspects of intelligence. This requires us to become familiar with the methods used to analyze the behaviors of humans and animals. Intelligence is manifested in behaviors, and behaviors are the product of brain functions. Therefore, understanding the structure and function of the brain is a key to understanding intelligence. Neuroscience has made enormous progress during the last several decades and now provides amazing insight into the nature of biological intelligence, including human intelligence. My goal for this book is to share such new insights with the readers.

This book explores several subject areas that are important for understanding the true nature of intelligence. For example, I will introduce many concepts and empirical findings from psychology, which provides rigorous methods to understand the important principles of human and animal behaviors. I will also draw heavily from neuroscience, since behaviors are controlled by the brain and its neurons. To understand how the evolution molded a variety of intelligent behaviors and the nervous systems that support them, we must look into genetics and evolutionary biology. Intelligence is the ability to make good choices in many different contexts, and we will explore some elegant theoretical frameworks developed in economics to sharpen our understanding of what decision making really is. To understand the similarities and differences between biological intelligence and AI, I will briefly explain how digital computers work. I will try to share important insights from each of these areas to present a holistic picture of intelligence, but I am not an expert in all of them. Some statements and claims in this book are based on my speculations and personal opinions, and I have tried to indicate this as much as possible. I think it is better to share tentative and potential answers to important questions rather than omitting them completely.

Here is a brief summary of this book. Intelligence is a function of life. Life is a physical system that replicates itself, but only imperfectly with some errors. Therefore, when life replicates, its copies are at least sometimes slightly different from the original. Although these differences are small and infrequent, when they are repeated many times and accumulated over a long period, this can eventually produce copies that can replicate themselves more efficiently than the original. Exactly which system self-replicates most efficiently depends on the environment, and therefore long-term accumulation of random variation combined with the selection by the environment leads to the process of evolution. Through evolution, different forms of life adapt to their environments. Each lifeform develops the ability to select a course of actions to enhance the likelihood of its survival and replication (i.e., reproduction), and this is the essence of intelligence. Therefore, if we want to evaluate the intelligence of various life forms, it would be reasonable to consider which life form can replicate itself successfully by solving more complex problems in a broader range of environments. In other words, the efficiency of self-replication provides an objective criterion to evaluate intelligence. On the other hand, it is not clear how one can evaluate the level of intelligence without life. When AI programs are designed and managed by humans and deployed to accomplish the goals set by humans, they are surrogates of human intelligence. A machine that merely follows a set of instructions to promote someone else's agenda is not genuinely intelligent. Thus, in this book, I will define intelligence as the ability of life to solve complex problems in a variety of environments for its self-replication. I will refine and defend this definition throughout the book.

Since every life form is a product of evolution, different life forms display a variety of intelligent behaviors customized to enhance the chance of their survival and reproduction in their own environments. To capture the essence of intelligence, therefore, this book will discuss many examples of intelligence and intelligent behaviors, in various animals, such as jellyfish and octopus, as well as in nonanimal lifeforms, such as plants and bacteria. To illustrate the challenges that we face to understand the relationship between the brain and behavior, we will review how such simple behaviors such as eye movements can be controlled by multiple algorithms and neural hardware.

Although eye movements themselves do not move any external objects, they follow many important principles of complex behaviors.

It would be difficult to understand the nature of human intelligence if we completely ignore how human behaviors are controlled by the brain. Brains of all animals, including humans, are, of course, also a product of evolution, and they evolved by contributing to the survival and reproduction of their owners in the past. Many fascinating discoveries in science during the last century have been concerned with how complex and intelligent behavior arise from delicate interactions among many neurons in the brain. Therefore, understanding the basic operations of the brain will be an indispensable part of our efforts to understand intelligence. Biologically speaking, every organ in our body, including the brain, requires valuable energy for maintenance and repair, and would be eliminated through evolution unless its benefit to the organism is greater than its cost. Furthermore, new changes in any bodily organs that arise in one generation would cease to exist in the next generation if they prevent the organism from reproducing, although they might entail beautiful byproducts temporarily. Brains are not exception to this rule. Just as hearts and lungs have evolved to transport various nutrients and metabolites to all the cells in the animal's body, brains are needed to control the animal's behaviors quickly in response to unpredictable changes in the environment. To carry out this mission, the brain must act autonomously without referring to the details of genetic instructions, which would be too slow. This creates a potential conflict between the genes and the brain. On one hand, genes are responsible for maintaining and improving, through evolution, the design of the brain. On the other hand, brains are useless unless they can make decisions autonomously and have the authority to mediate between often opposing demands for survival and reproduction. Of course, the ultimate driver in this relationship is the genes, not the brain. The brain is merely an agent employed by the genes to assist in their replications. Nevertheless, the brain can safeguard the animal's genes from extinction because it can detect unpredictable changes in the animal's environment and produce appropriate behavioral responses without waiting for the instructions coded in the genes to be biochemically translated to physical actions. The brain also provides many ways to learn about the animal's environment, and we will survey multiple solutions based on learning that emerged during the evolution of animal brains. We will see in this book that a higher level of intelligence requires flexibly switching between different learning algorithms.

Human intelligence can be most clearly distinguished from the intelligence of other animals in social contexts. Humans rely on language and other symbols to exchange a large amount of information. Furthermore, they can predict what other humans do and do not do, what they like and dislike, and what they intend to do. Based on such social information, humans have the rare ability in the animal kingdom to create highly sophisticated culture and civilization. The final chapters of this book will examine how this social intelligence ultimately contributes to self-awareness for humans and what problems it might create.

Acknowledgments

I am indebted to numerous colleagues I had the pleasure of interacting with physically or symbolically during the last two decades. None of the ideas contained in this book are mine originally, although I had occasionally thought that some of them were. I would also like to thank Inkook Park, president of the Korea Foundation for Advanced Studies, who organized and invited me to the TEDxKFAS in 2015. The preparation for my talk in that event helped me to come up with the overall organization of this book and triggered the process of writing it. I am also grateful to Gordon Shepherd and Dayk Jang for encouraging me to write this book. Finally, I thank Zhixian Cheng, Alex Kwan, Shanna Murray, Mariann Oemisch, Max Shinn, and Zhihao Zhang for their helpful feedback.

Acknowledgments

1

Levels of Intelligence

Throughout much of history, questions about human nature have been important subjects of philosophical analyses and debates. Now, biology can answer many of these questions. Many disciplines in biology, including cell biology and primatology, are seeking to understand the precise differences between humans and other animals. These inquiries frequently reveal that humans share many similarities with other life forms on Earth after all. Difference in the genetic information for humans and chimpanzees is known to be less than 2 percent. Similarly, the anatomy and neurophysiology of visual systems of many different primates are so similar that it is likely that humans and monkeys experience our visual environment in fundamentally the same manner. In fact, it is difficult to find unique qualities of humans that are absent in other animals. For example, all life forms on Earth, including all plants and animals, consist of cells. They all bequeath their own physical characteristics to offspring by replicating and passing on their genetic materials. Although the behaviors of different animals might look vastly different to us, they mostly arise from contraction and relaxation of muscles in the animal's body that are coordinated spatially and temporally. Muscles contract and relax according to the commands from neurons, and the structure and functions of neurons in all vertebrate animals share many similarities.

Therefore, if you compare humans and other animals in terms of their basic designs and building blocks, it is difficult to find big differences between them. However, humans have many remarkable technological accomplishments. Humans invented and crafted tools, including the hand axe, farming tools, wheels, and weapons. They have used these tools to dominate other animals and even to travel to outer space with rockets. Our planet is about 4.5 billion years old, but no other species that emerged during that time could do all of this. What gave humans such remarkable abilities? Of course, the answer is their intelligence. It is human intelligence that allows humans to acquire scientific knowledge and technologies and to develop unique lifestyles not available to other animals.

That being said, intelligence is also not unique to humans. Intelligence can be found in other animals and even plants. All animals use their intelligence to adapt to changes in their environment. Carefully comparing various forms of intelligence found in the animal kingdom can enable behavioral ecologists and primatologists to understand precisely how human intelligence might be different from the intelligence of other animals. We will follow the same strategy in this chapter. Before we can discuss what is unique about human intelligence, we will first examine intelligence in animals, plants, and even bacteria.

If we want to broaden our discussion on intelligence beyond the familiar circle of human intelligence, we must first re-examine the meaning of the word *intelligence*. In scientific pursuits, colloquial definitions are often not enough, since they do not accurately reflect empirical facts and theoretical ideas. In addition, at least in animals, intelligence is closely tied to the nervous system. This does not mean that life forms without neurons or nervous systems cannot have intelligence. Nevertheless, the type of intelligence most familiar to us belongs to animals and requires coordinated actions of their nervous systems. Therefore, this chapter will also cover the basic terminology useful to discuss important features of the nervous system, such as neuron, action potential, connectome, and so forth, since many of these terms will be used throughout the book. Our goal is to understand the nature of human intelligence better by considering it in the context of evolution.

What Is Intelligence?

In our everyday lives, we tend to describe someone as intelligent when they demonstrate an ability to solve a difficult problem through complex reasoning or quick calculations. However, the concept of intelligence can be applied more broadly to include thinking, imagining, and even sympathizing with others. In other words, intelligence covers all types of mental operations. Furthermore, intelligence is a function of life. It is present in all life forms.

By contrast, an intelligence quotient or IQ is a summary score calculated from the results of a standardized test. Therefore, it is important not to mistake IQ scores for intelligence itself. Tests used to measure IQ are different from other tests or exams in specific subject areas, such as history or physics, in that they do not test the amount of knowledge someone acquired in a particular subject area. Instead, IQ tests are special in that they are designed by psychologists to evaluate the quality of specific cognitive processes, such as memory or analogical reasoning. Such basic cognitive abilities might be needed for a broad range of tasks that people perform daily, such as cooking and shopping. However, they do not capture the entire range of behavioral and mental abilities of humans. IQ tests are also useless in measuring the intelligence of nonhuman animals, since they rely on verbal instructions. Hence, IQ tests are not particularly helpful in understanding the essence of intelligence.

Although IQ scores might not reflect the entire spectrum of human cognitive abilities, they are significant for two reasons. First, whether simple numerical scores can parsimoniously summarize multiple physical and mental abilities of humans is a legitimate scientific question. For example, Francis Galton was one of the first proponents of intelligence tests. In the late 19th century, he hypothesized that intelligence would be correlated with a variety of reflexes and muscle forces, although he didn't find empirical support for his hypothesis. In the beginning of the 20th century, a more successful test was developed by Alfred Binet in France to identify children with mental retardation. At about the same time, Charles Spearman in Britain made an important conceptual advance when he observed that many different academic scores tended to be correlated. Spearman developed a statistical method known as factor analysis and used it to derive a measure of general intelligence, also known as the g factor. However, even Spearman himself did not believe that the g factor could completely capture the individual variability in intelligence.

Second, even if IQ tests might not fully capture the human cognitive abilities, they can still have practical value. Even today, many schools and companies rely on some form of test to select their students and employees, and most of these tests seek to identify individuals not just with special knowledge and experience, but with high intelligence. In fact, in the United States, the popularity of IQ tests owes a lot to the widespread use of alpha and beta intelligence examinations conducted to identify good candidates for officers during World War I. Nevertheless, these tests were merely designed to test specific abilities, such as vocabulary, analogy, and pattern completion. It was well understood that these intelligence ratings were not meant to fully characterize the abilities of draftees and soldiers.

So, what is intelligence? The word intelligence is derived from the Latin verb, *intelligere*, which means to comprehend or perceive. Common dictionary definitions of intelligence include, "the ability to acquire and apply knowledge and skills" (Oxford English Dictionary), and "the ability to learn and understand or to deal with new or trying situations" (Merriam-Wesbter Dictionary). Scholars have defined intelligence in many ways. For example, according to Howard Gardner, "an intelligence is the ability to solve problems, or to create products, that are valued within one or more cultural settings" (Gardner and Hatch, 1989). In contrast, artificial intelligence researchers, Marvin Minsky (1985) and Raymond Kurzweil (1999), defined intelligence as "the ability to solve hard problems," and "the ability to use optimally limited resource—including time—to achieve goals," respectively. Distilling from about 70 different definitions of intelligence, Shane Legg and Marcus Hutter (2007) proposed their definition of intelligence as an agent's ability to "achieve goals in a wide range of environments."

Many of these definitions share something in common. Intelligence is an ability to solve problems. More complex problems require higher levels of intelligence. For example, it requires more intelligence to be able to solve differential equations than simply to be able to add two single-digit numbers. It is more intelligent to excel at the game of Go than to play simpler games like tic-tac-toe. However, the ability to solve one complex problem does not necessarily indicate a high level of intelligence. For example, although electronic calculators can solve very complex arithmetic problems, such as multiplying two large numbers, we do not consider calculators to be highly intelligent. This is because calculators are limited to solving arithmetic problems. They cannot play Go or order your dinner. Therefore, an intelligent person is expected to be good at solving many different problems well. For example, people might think you are intelligent if you are good at chess, can make good weather predictions, and may come up with successful political and military strategies.

Indeed, problems faced by life forms change constantly. You can never reliably predict what problems you might have to deal with next, and therefore it is difficult to develop in advance all the knowledge and skills necessary to solve problems in the future. In addition, it might be important to find something good enough quickly, rather than finding the best possible solution too late. In short, intelligence is the ability to solve a variety of problems to adapt to a constantly changing environment. However, this is still not enough, because, unlike in mathematics, many of the problems we face in our lives do not have objectively correct answers. If you are trying to decide on a dinner menu, for example, the answer depends on who is preparing it and who is eating it. Therefore, intelligence is not merely the ability to solve mathematical or logical problems, but it is the ability to select an option that will produce an outcome most desirable to the subject or agent who is making the choice. Namely, intelligence is the ability to make good decisions from the perspective of the decision maker.

It is important to realize that intelligence requires the preference of the decision maker as a precondition. It is easy to find examples in nature where it is difficult to decide whether a behavior is adaptive and hence intelligent without considering the needs of the decision maker. For example, when we are infected by viruses or other parasites, they produce reactions that interfere with our normal behaviors. The reason why we sneeze and get runny noses when we catch a cold is that such reactions help the cold virus to spread to the next victims before we fully develop an immune response to get rid of them. Therefore, from our own perspective, sneezing or increasing nasal discharge might not be intelligent, while creating such responses in their human host might be adaptive and hence intelligent for the virus. A virus is not considered a life form, because it does not contain all the biochemical machinery necessary for self-replication and requires other life forms for its replication. Therefore, it might be a stretch to talk about the preference and intelligence of virus. Nevertheless, it might be useful to consider the behavior influenced by a virus as a precursor of intelligence, if such behaviors facilitate the replication of virus.

Life is a continuous stream of choices, where we choose a particular action from many possible actions at each moment. In our daily lives, we perform many tasks, such as watching a movie after a dinner. Even for a relatively simple task, such as deciding what to eat and what movie to watch, the number of options can be large. The quality of such choices reflects the underlying intelligence. Therefore, to evaluate someone's intelligence, we also need to examine the entire range of behaviors that can be selected by the intelligent being. We might underestimate the intelligence of someone, if we do not consider the full range of their behavior. For example, we would not fully appreciate someone's communication skills if we do not take into their body language and only listen to their speech.

All life forms make various choices for their survival and reproduction. Moreover, machines created by humans and even computer programs can also make decisions. In this book, we will try to understand such decision-making processes and the expression of intelligence in animals and machines. Intelligence manifests ultimately in behaviors, and we can only infer about the underlying intelligence based on its behavioral expressions.

Therefore, we will first discuss how different types of behaviors can be analyzed. Since animal behaviors are controlled by their neurons and brains, I will also briefly discuss the relationship between the brain and behaviors.

Intelligence Without Neurons: Bacteria to Plants

What is behavior? Generally speaking, behavior refers to the change in a system that is produced in response to an internal or external event. We tend to think that behaviors are unique to animals and that they are not present in other life forms, such as plants. However, this is wrong. Even machines can have behaviors. For example, the action of a thermostat to control a heater to maintain the temperature of a room at a preset level is a behavior. We will come back to discuss the behavior and intelligence of artificial machines in a later chapter. Here, we will focus on various types of biological behaviors.

The methods used by life forms to respond to different events in their environment are diverse. In fact, not all lifeforms rely on neurons to process the information from the environment and control their movements. Even single-cell organisms, such as bacteria, can control movements according to stimuli from their environment. For example, *Escherichia coli*, or *E. coli*, a common bacterium in our intestine, control its behavior to move toward a location with a higher concentration of nutrients. Such behavior is called chemotaxis. *E. coli* can switch between only two different types of movements, running and tumbling. Running allows *E. coli* to move steadily in the same direction, whereas tumbling changes its direction randomly. *E. coli* can choose to run or to tumble, depending on the changes in the concentration of various chemicals. It would continue to run if the concentration of attractive chemicals, such as food, increases or if the concentration of harmful chemicals decreases. By contrast, when the concentration of attractive chemical decreases, *E. coli* will then increase the frequency of tumbling. By repeating this procedure, it can gradually move toward an area with chemical environment most desirable to them. The fact that *E. coli* can determine whether the concentration of a chemical is increasing or decreasing implies that it has a memory of the previous concentration of that chemical and can compare it to the current concentration. Therefore, even in this simple behavior of *E. coli*, we can find the two most basic elements of intelligent behavior: the ability to remember the previous experience and the ability to compare the content of a memory to immediate sensory input.

Chemotaxis is an example of taxis, which is an innate behavior that moves an organism toward or away from a stimulus. In addition to chemotaxis, which is a response to specific chemicals, taxis can be classified into various subtypes, depending on the nature of relevant stimulus. For example, phototaxis refers to movements toward or away from light, whereas thermotaxis refers to movements toward higher or lower temperature. Similar behaviors also exist in plants. Although plants seldom possess the ability to move from one location to another, they can orient their body or change the direction of their growth depending on the direction of light. Plants must also constantly select the direction to grow their roots based on the concentrations of water and other chemicals in the ground. The ability to orient the body of an organism or change the direction of its growth toward light is referred to as phototropism. The chemical basis of phototropism is relatively simple. Its central player is a plant hormone called auxin, which causes cells to swell by weakening their cell wall (Figure 1.1). Auxins tend to concentrate away from light. Therefore, if a plant receives light from one direction, then the cells on the opposite side increase their size and therefore bend the plant toward the light.

In summary, behaviors found in single-cell organisms and plants are limited to relatively simple forms, such as taxis or tropism. By contrast, animals have muscles and neurons that can control movements more rapidly and selectively. As a result, animals have much more diverse patterns of behaviors than plants or bacteria, and this increases the complexity of their decision-making processes. In animals, behaviors are selected and decisions are made

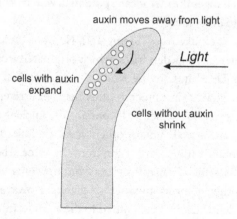

Figure 1.1. Phototropism.

by the coordinated actions of neurons that are organized into the brain and other parts of the nervous system.

How Does a Nervous System Work?

The function of a nervous system is to control muscles based on the sensory signals coming from the external environment and the information stored internally as memory. Many glands throughout the animal's body are also controlled by the nervous system. In other words, the function of a nervous system is decision-making, the ability to choose the most appropriate action in the animal's environment. The intelligence of animals depends on their nervous systems. So, how do neurons and nervous systems work?

A nervous system is made of neurons. Neurons are cells specialized in transmitting information not only within a single cell, but also between multiple cells. They receive chemical, mechanical, and electrical signals from the external environment of the animal or from other neurons. These signals are combined and processed further. Each neuron then passes its outputs to other neurons or muscles adjacent to it. Within each neuron, electrical signals are used for transmitting information across the neuron's different regions and are generated by changes in electrical potential across the cell membrane, called membrane potential. Most cells in animals, plants, and bacteria have more negative charges inside the cells, corresponding to a voltage of about −40 to −80 mV, relative to the cell's immediate surroundings. This is referred to as the resting membrane potential. When a given neuron is stimulated appropriately, this changes the membrane potential, which propagates from the stimulated area to other areas.

Many neurons look like trees (Figure 1.2). Neurons typically have extensive branches referred to as dendrites, which originated from a Greek word for tree, *dentron*. Dendrites are the areas in which physical or chemical signals from the external environment or other neurons arrive. The central part of a neuron is referred to as a soma. It contains the nucleus in which genetic materials are stored, as well as many other types of cellular machinery. Most neurons also contain a thin fiber arising from the soma. These fibers are referred to as axons, which transmit signals from the soma to axon terminals and then onto other neurons, muscles, or glands. However, not all signals received by the dendrites are transmitted to the axon terminal. Decisions as to whether a given neuron will send any signal to the next neurons are made

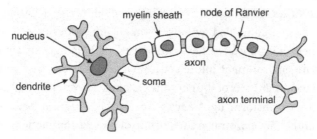

Figure 1.2. Structure of a neuron.

at a transition zone, called the axon hillock, which is where the axon arises. When the membrane potential at the axon hillock becomes sufficiently more positive and reaches a certain threshold, its membrane potential begins to undergo a rapid and explosive change, which is referred to as action potential. For a brief period lasting less than a millisecond, the membrane potential becomes positive. An action potential is all or none. Namely, once it is produced, it can propagate down the axon without much change in voltage. When an action potential arrives at the axon terminal, it triggers the release of specific chemicals, referred to as neurotransmitters. Thus, at the axon terminal, electrical signals are transformed to chemical signals. The site where a signal from one neuron is transmitted to another neuron is called a synapse. The neuron that is transmitting the signal through its axon terminal is referred to as presynaptic, and the neuron receiving this signal is postsynaptic.

Once neurotransmitters are released from the axon terminal, they diffuse across a small space between presynaptic and postsynaptic neurons and bind to specific protein molecules called receptors. The binding of a neurotransmitter to its receptor then determines how the membrane potential of the postsynaptic neuron will change. Depending on how this change occurs, synapses can be divided into two different types. A synapse is called excitatory when the binding of a neurotransmitter with its receptor causes the voltage inside the postsynaptic neuron to become more positive (depolarized) and hence makes it more likely for the postsynaptic neuron to generate an action potential. By contrast, a synapse is called inhibitory when the same event makes the voltage inside the neuron more negative (hyperpolarized), and therefore makes it less likely to generate an action potential.

The intelligence of an animal is ultimately determined by how different neurons are organized inside their nervous system. Neurons in a nervous system can be classified into three major groups, depending on their functions. Accordingly, decision-making in all animals, including humans, results from the combined actions of these three types of neurons. First, sensory neurons transform physical energy, such as light or sound, from the animal's environment into electrical signals that can be rapidly transmitted to the other parts of the nervous system. For example, photoreceptors in the retina transform light energy to electrical signals. Second, motor neurons and their neurotransmitters control muscle contractions and gland secretions. Therefore, in theory, a nervous system consisting of only sensory neurons and motor neurons together with muscles can make decisions and select behaviors that are beneficial to the animal. However, nervous systems also include a third type of neurons, called interneurons, which connect sensory and motor neurons with other neurons.

In late 18th century, Luigi Galvani discovered that the nervous system of animals utilizes electric signals. However, he did not fully understand the nature of such signals. It was Emil du Bois-Reymond who discovered the action potential in 1848. One might still think that action potentials exist only in animals that have nervous systems. However, this is not true, because action potentials also exist in some plants. For example, Venus flytraps (Figure 1.3) can capture small insects or spiders by closing their leaves and then releasing digestive enzymes to slowly extract the nutrients from the prey over several days. Carnivorous plants like Venus flytraps do not have any neurons, but hairs in their leaves can still generate action potentials when they are physically stimulated, and these action potentials quickly propagate throughout the leaves and initiate the closing of the trap. The fact that Venus flytraps produce action potentials was discovered in 1872 by Sir John Burdon-Sanderson (1872). Burdon-Sanderson was an accomplished scientist. In 1871, he had previously discovered that a type of fungi called Penicillium could suppress the growth of bacteria, thereby eventually leading to the discovery of the first antibiotic by Alexander Fleming in 1928.

The fact that some plants, such as Venus flytraps, can close leaves and capture prey after detecting its presence implies that they possess basic abilities to make decisions. Since plants do not have complex nervous systems like animals do, their perceptual and motor functions are relatively limited, and the process of closing their leaves is largely driven by the mechanical stimuli applied to their leaves. Nevertheless, it would be very inefficient if their leaves close every time they are stimulated, since this might trigger a premature closure even before an insect enters the leaves completely. Indeed, the leaves of Venus flytraps close only after they are stimulated at least twice

Figure 1.3. Venus flytrap.

Source: Illustration from *Curtis's Botanical Magazine* by *William Curtis* (1746–1799). Image provided by the National Agricultural Library of the United States Department of Agriculture's Agricultural Research Service. Public domain.

within approximately 20 seconds. This increases the likelihood that prey will be captured when the leaves are closed. This would be similar to float fishing when an angler might not respond to the first movement of the float and wait until the bait is completely taken by the fish. The fact that Venus flytraps can respond differently to the same stimulus depending on whether it was preceded by another stimulus or not also indicates that they have a simple form of memory about their recent experience.

Reflexes: Simple Behavior

Although Venus flytraps and other carnivorous plants can open and close their leaves in response to external physical stimuli, their responses are much slower than animals with muscles. What truly distinguishes animals from plants is muscles. It is estimated that muscle cells emerged about 600 million years ago, which is also when animals first appeared on Earth. Thanks to muscles that can rapidly contract and relax, animals can move to a different location more quickly than bacteria. Muscles also make it easier for animals to steal a large amount of energy by capturing and digesting other organisms.

However, the behaviors resulting from the actions of muscles will not always benefit animals if they are produced randomly. For example, if individual animals simply wander around randomly regardless of what might be going on in their surroundings, this might merely increase the chance of getting captured and eaten by predators. Therefore, muscles are beneficial only when they can be controlled appropriately, and this is the responsibility of neurons and the nervous system. Behaviors controlled by the nervous system can be divided into reflex and learned behaviors. A reflex is a type of behavior predetermined by the stimulus that triggers that behavior, whereas learned behaviors can be modified by the animal's experience. Most human behaviors, including such complex behaviors as speech and playing musical instruments, are learned. Indeed, later chapters in this book will extensively deal with learning. Nevertheless, to understand animal intelligence broadly, we should first understand how a reflex is produced by an animal's nervous system.

The nervous systems of animals underwent dramatic changes during evolution. We can infer this from the fact that the structure of the nervous system varies enormously across different living animals. The brain is a major part of the nervous system in all vertebrate animals, including humans. However, not all animals have brains, and the nervous systems of invertebrate animals have very different appearances. Understanding how the same function can be performed by nervous systems with dramatically different structures gives important insights about the precise relationship between the structure and function of a nervous system. Sometimes, studies of animals with much simpler nervous systems give us important clues about how the human brains might work. A small roundworm called *Caenorhabditis elegans*, or *C. elegans* is a famous example.

C. elegans is a popular experimental animal for neuroscientists because of its relatively simple nervous system with little individual variability. *C. elegans* is a soil-dwelling roundworm or nematode measuring about a millimeter long. An adult *C. elegans* has a total of approximately 3,000 cells. This is vastly simpler than humans, since the number of cells in a human body is approximately 30 to 40 trillion. Cells in *C. elegans* are roughly equally divided into somatic cells, which die with the animals, and germ cells that can reproduce. Only about 100 of the somatic cells are muscle cells, but this is enough to produce all the movements *C. elegans* needs for its survival, including exploratory sideways head movements and choosing between forward and backward swimming.

Although the nervous system of *C. elegans* is extremely simple, there is still a sex difference. A male adult *C. elegans* has 385 neurons in its nervous system, whereas a female has 302 neurons. Within each sex, however, there is no individual variability in the number of neurons. If every neuron in *C. elegans* were to connect with every other neuron, the number of synapses in male and female *C. elegans* would be 147,840 and 90,902, respectively. In reality, the number of synapses in *C. elegans* is estimated to be about 5,600, which corresponds to about 4~6 percent of all possible connections. Consistent with the fact that wiring among different neurons of *C. elegans* is largely fixed, most of its behaviors are reflexes and are determined by the stimuli in its immediate surroundings. If it detects food on the left side, it will turn to the left. If there is a harmful substance on the left side, then it will turn to the right.

Another invertebrate animal that attracts a lot of attention from neuroscientists and evolutionary biologists is the jellyfish, even though they are more challenging to study in a laboratory than *C. elegans*. Jellyfish also have nervous systems in the form of a network of neurons, called a nerve net. Among various species of jellyfish, the box jellyfish have the most advanced nervous systems. They have multiple eyes with lenses and therefore the ability to distinguish different patterns in the visual information they receive from the environment (Figure 1.4). They are also capable of swimming to find an appropriate level of salinity, as well as adjusting the direction of swimming using the position of the sun as a reference. They have the ability to avoid predators and form groups with other jellyfish. However, we do not really know how intelligent jellyfish are. The fact that jellyfish sting people probably does not make it easier for casual observers to get familiar the natural behaviors of jellyfish, either. Nevertheless, scientists have speculated that like *C. elegans*, most behaviors of jellyfish might be reflexes.

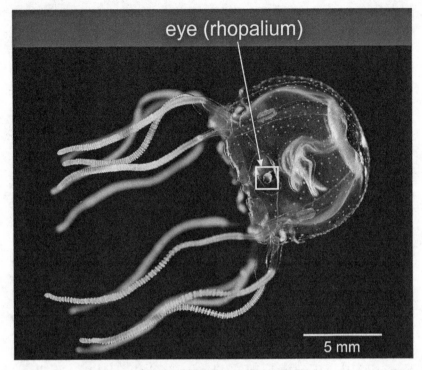

Figure 1.4. A box jellyfish, *Tripedalia cystophora*.

Source: Bielecki J, Zaharoff AK, Leung NY, Garm A, Oakley TH (2014) Ocular and extraocular expression of opsins in the rhopalium of *Tripedalia cystophora* (Cnidaria: Cubozoa). PLoS One. 9: e98870.

Limitations of Reflexes

C. elegans is a popular animal model for neuroscientists, and the jellyfish nervous system is truly exotic. In the animal kingdom, there indeed exist a variety of designs for nervous systems. Another group of animals that are more familiar to us than *C. elegans* and jellyfish is insects. The insect nervous system is more similar to that of vertebrate animals. Nevertheless, just like *C. elegans* and jellyfish, insects mostly rely on reflex to control their behaviors.

To many animals, insects are food. Therefore, an important responsibility of the insect nervous system is to detect predators as soon as possible and escape from them. This must work constantly, day and night. This implies that they should use multiple sensory cues to protect themselves. For example, if cockroaches avoid their predators using only visual information, then they would get eaten by animals that can use chemical or auditory cues to hunt

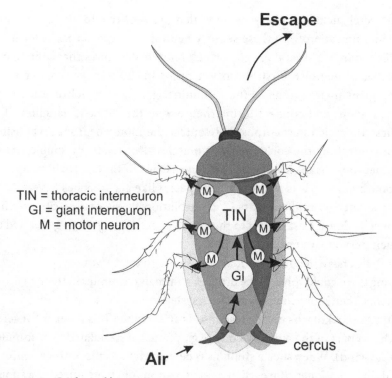

Figure 1.5. Cockroach's nervous system responsible for escape reflex.

cockroaches at night. An important part of the cockroach's defense system is the cerci, which look like a pair of tails (Figure 1.5). Hairs covering the cerci are sensitive to even very small movements of air. When you try to swat a cockroach with a rolled-up paper, it will detect the wind caused by the movement of the paper and immediately start running away in the opposite direction. It takes only 14 millisecond, which is about a seventieth of a second, before a cockroach can begin its escape response after its sensory neurons detect the air movement. This rapid escape behavior must have been optimized by evolution. Animals like cockroaches lacking the ability to escape as quickly as cockroaches would have been more likely to be eaten by their predators and be eliminated.

To produce such a rapid escape response, the nervous system that controls it must be relatively simple. Indeed, if you open the abdomen of a cockroach and inspect its interior, you can easily find many of the neurons that are responsible for the escape response (Figure 1.5). First, hairs in the cerci include sensory neurons that are sensitive to air movements. Communication from these sensory neurons to the cockroach's leg muscles occurs via several ganglia, which refer to structures that contain cell bodies of neurons. First, sensory neurons in the cerci are connected to the giant interneurons in the abdominal ganglion, which in turn send their axons and connect to interneurons in the thoracic ganglion. It is these thoracic interneurons that contact the motor neurons responsible for controlling the cockroach's leg muscles. This relatively simple circuit of neurons makes it possible for cockroaches to initiate their escape response quickly. It is estimated that species like cockroaches have existed for about 360 million years. Such evolutionary success of cockroaches must be due at least in part to the excellent escape responses generated by their nervous systems.

Reflex has a major limitation. If reflexes and the nervous systems underlying them could solve all the problems animals encounter in their environments, then more complex nervous systems would not have evolved. Let's take the cockroach's escape response as an example. This reflex is triggered when a part of the animal's body (e.g., cercus) is stimulated by a stimulus (e.g., wind). When such a stimulus is detected by specific sensory neurons, this information is conveyed by a set of neurons often organized in a simple chain to specific motor neurons controlling the muscles in another part of the body (e.g., legs) in a predetermined manner (e.g., running). This process is largely unaffected by other factors that are potentially relevant for the cockroach's survival, such as the reason why wind was generated, what other goals the cockroach might have had when the stimulus was detected, and so forth. Air movement detected by the cerci automatically leads to the escape response. Imagine a scenario in which cockroaches must tolerate many unpredictable but harmless wind stimuli before entering a large food storage. Automatically triggering escape responses would make it harder for cockroaches to exploit such environments fully. A big advantage of reflex is that it is preprogrammed and therefore can be generated very quickly. This is a good strategy to avoid predators. However, it also has a significant disadvantage. Since reflexes are supported by a relatively simple nervous system that can act quickly, it is often not possible to stop them when they are no longer appropriate. Reflexes are rigid and therefore not a good strategy if the best response to a given stimulus is not fixed, but instead changes according to the animal's previous experience or other changing needs.

Connectome

The size of the animal's nervous system and how it is organized is extremely variable across different animals. Compared to invertebrates like arthropods (e.g., insects) or mollusks (e.g., squid), vertebrates including mammals, birds, reptiles, amphibians, and fish usually have elaborate nervous systems with many neurons. However, what determines different behaviors is not the number of neurons, but rather how they are connected. For example, a cockroach would not be able to produce an escape response without the specific connections among sensory neurons, motor neurons, and interneurons. In vertebrates, most of the connections among neurons that control the animal's behaviors reside within their brains.

When animals move, they tend to orient their heads in the direction of their movement. As a result, new and unexpected sensory information during movement frequently enters the animal's nervous system in the head. During evolution, this would have led to a concentration of sensory neurons in the animal's head where they are most needed. Furthermore, this makes it advantageous to concentrate the neurons involved in the analysis and storage of sensory information in the head as well, because this would reduce the distance among neurons that need to communicate with each other. In vertebrate animals, neurons get highly concentrated in the head and form the brain, which controls complex behaviors. Compared to the brains of vertebrate animals, the brains in invertebrates are often less distinguished from the rest of their nervous systems. It is not possible to recognize anything like the brain of a vertebrate in simple animals like *C. elegans* or jellyfish.

All the behaviors of an animal are determined by the interaction and exchange of information among neurons in its nervous system. Therefore, intelligence of an animal is largely determined by the structure of its nervous system. If we can completely understand the structure and function of the nervous system of a given animal, we might be able to predict how the animal will respond to any stimulus. For example, imagine an animal with an extremely simple nervous system that has only one sensory neuron and one motor neuron. As a first step to understanding the intelligence and behaviors of this animal, we need to find out what stimuli the sensory neuron will respond to. In addition, we also need to find out what behavior results when the motor neuron is activated. Finally, we need to know whether the synapse between the sensory neuron and motor neuron is excitatory or inhibitory. How would this animal behave in response to a light stimulus, if the sensory neuron is sensitive to light, if the motor neuron opens the animal's mouth when it is excited, and if the synapse between these two neurons is excitatory? The answer is that the animal should open its mouth. By contrast, imagine how it might behave, if we genetically modify the synapse between the two neurons so that it becomes inhibitory. Now, the animal would close its mouth in response to a light stimulus.

As the diversity of sensory neurons increases, the animal will respond to a broader range of physical stimuli, such as light, touch, and sound. In addition, as the complexity of muscles and motor neurons that control them increases, the range of possible behaviors will also increase. However, as previously illustrated by the imaginary animal with two neurons, properties of sensory and motor neurons do not entirely determine the animal's behaviors. Rather, direct and indirect connections between the sensory neurons and motor neurons are also important. If the nervous system of a given animal includes only a small number of neurons, then it might be possible to make accurate predictions about how the animal might behave in response to a variety of stimuli, entirely based on the connection or circuit diagram of its neurons. A comprehensive map of all the connections in the nervous system of an animal is referred to as a connectome. It might sound like a simple task to create a connectome for an animal. But this is an extremely difficult task. In addition, predicting behaviors from a connectome is even more difficult. For example, a complete connectome is already available for *C. elegans*, which has only about 300 neurons and 5,000 synapses, but it is still not possible to predict its behavior completely. How accurately we will be able to predict the behaviors of animals with more complex nervous systems, such as insects and vertebrates, is currently not known.

Multiple Controllers for Muscles

Having complex brains, such as the human brain, pays off, because they enable the animal to produce more complex and diverse behaviors and adapt to the ever-changing environment more flexibly than reflexes. However, complex behaviors are harder to study than simple ones. It is relatively easy to understand the functions of behaviors when there is a simple one-to-one relationship between a set of behaviors and their goals. The function of the escape response in cockroaches and its underlying neural mechanism are relatively easy to understand, because the relationship between the behavior and its intended outcome, namely, escape from a potential predator, is straight-forward. However, in general, the relationship between behaviors and their desired outcomes is not simply one-to-one. Humans can generate the same pattern of muscle contractions and hence the same behavior even when their intended consequences are different. For example, if somebody just blinked one of their eyes at you, this could be a signal they intentionally sent to get your attention, or alternatively it could have been a reflex caused by an insect flying too close. Blinking is caused by the increased activity of neurons in the facial nucleus in the brain stem, which triggers the contraction of muscles in the eyelid, called orbicularis oculi. Therefore, to find out the real reason why someone blinked, behavioral observations or measurement of muscle activity would not be enough. We must understand what happened inside their brain.

Of course, we might understand completely how and why somebody produced a particular behavior, such as blinking, if we can record, analyze, and interpret the activity of all the neurons in their brain, but this will not be possible for some time. We can still hope to get some insight about human behavior and intelligence even with much less empirical data. Signals responsible for generating a bodily movement might arise from many different places in the brain. However, regardless of the purpose of a movement, those signals would have to converge somewhere in the brain and flow through the same pathways to muscles. This is referred to as the final common pathway. For example, motor neurons that controlled the hand muscles to produce finger movements for playing piano or guitar is a part of the final common pathways, since they participate in all finger movements. Therefore, to understand the reason why a behavior was generated, we need to understand the source of signals arriving at the final common pathways.

Eye Movements: A Case Study

As we will see throughout this book, animals can use more than one controller to choose its behaviors. This can be probably best illustrated by examining human eye movements, in part because eye muscles are the busiest of all muscles in the human body and in part because they are controlled by several controllers with distinct dynamic properties. Most sensory organs, including eyes, can be dynamically oriented. This is necessary to collect the sensory information most relevant for the animal at each moment. Eye movements are particularly useful for primates like humans, who receive much of the information about their environments through vision. Eye movements must be accurate, because unlike the image on a computer screen or camera, the resolution of the image captured by the retina is not uniform. The center of the retina is called the fovea, and the image projected to this area is captured and analyzed at a much higher resolution than in peripheral vision. Therefore, to identify small differences in the images of different objects, as we do when we are reading a book or trying to understand the facial expressions of other people, the eyes must be oriented accurately so that the brain can analyze the most important details of images (Figure 1.6). Rotating the eyes to redirect the gaze toward an object of interest might sound like a simple task, but the brain utilizes at least five different algorithms that are supported by separate neural circuits in the brain for this purpose. These different types of eye movements are described briefly in the following discussion.

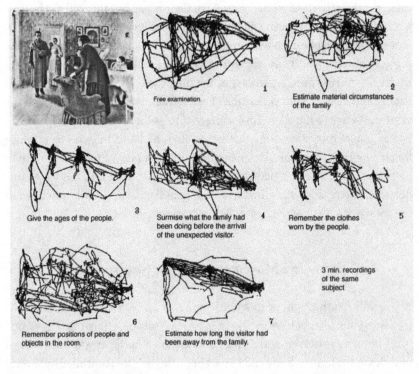

Figure 1.6. Trajectory of eye movements measured by Alfred Yarbus (1967) while a human observer watched the painting, *Unexpected Visitor*, by Ilya Repin.
Source: Public domain.

Vestibulo-Ocular Reflex

Vision requires stable images. Pictures or movies taken by an unstable camera or cell phone are blurry and make it difficult to identify objects in them clearly. Without any compensatory mechanisms, vision would be degraded whenever animals moved their heads. Vestibulo-ocular reflex (VOR) stabilizes images on the retina by rotating eyes in a direction opposite to the direction of head motion. This is accomplished by utilizing signals related to the head velocity and acceleration that the brain receives from the vestibular organs in the inner ear. Rotations and linear accelerations of the head are sensed by two different structures known as the semicircular canals and otolithic organs, respectively. Most of the time, we are not very aware of the information conveyed by vestibular organs or VOR. However, behavioral adjustments based on vestibular inputs, such as VOR and maintaining stable body postures, are extremely important, as evidenced by the fact that dysfunction in the vestibular signals causes vertigo and dizziness.

VOR is the simplest type of eye movement, and it probably evolved earlier than other types of eye movements. Its underlying neural circuitry is also very simple and contains only one layer of interneurons in addition to the vestibular sensory neurons and motor neurons that control the extraocular muscles responsible for rotating the eyes. As a result, it takes only about one hundredth of a second to initiate the VOR following the onset of sudden head rotation. Whenever there is a head motion, regardless of whether this was voluntary or caused by external perturbation, the eyes can be rotated quickly to prevent blurry vision.

Optokinetic Reflex

Like VOR, the optokinetic reflex (OKR) is also an eye movement designed to stabilize an image on the retina when the entire visual field is moving in one direction. For example, in a movie theater, if the entire scene is moving, your eyes will follow it automatically. This is due to OKR. The difference between VOR and OKR is the source of signals used to control eye movements. VOR is driven by vestibular inputs, whereas OKR is driven by the visual motion signals. OKR is primarily controlled by a structure called the accessory optic system.

Saccades

A saccade is a rapid and ballistic eye movement that shifts the direction of stationary gaze from one point to another in the visual field (Figure 1.6). On average, humans produce about three or four saccades per second, even during sleep. Despite such frequent occurrences, saccades are not a reflex. They are not triggered automatically by external stimuli, but generated voluntarily. This means that we are making three or four decisions every second to determine where to look next. The most recent decision made by the reader of this book must be to select another word of this book as the target of their last saccade. Just like VOR and OKR, for each saccade, the brain needs to generate appropriate commands to the extraocular muscles. A structure called the superior colliculus situated underneath the cerebellum is a structure that is mostly dedicated to controlling saccades in the mammalian brain.

Smooth Pursuit Eye Movement

Smooth pursuit is a voluntary eye movement that follows a moving object. To produce a smooth pursuit eye movement, the brain must analyze the speed and direction of a moving object and then control the contraction and relaxation of extraocular muscles so that the retinal image of the moving object remains stable in the fovea. The dynamics of the eye movements and hence the activity of extraocular muscles during OKR and smooth pursuit eye movements are indistinguishable. However, the two different types of eye movements differ in important ways, including the areas of the brain that control them. The most important difference is that smooth pursuit eye movements are generated as a result of selecting a particular object for detailed analysis, such as when we are trying to identify the driver of a moving car. If there are multiple objects moving in different directions in the visual field, we can choose to produce a smooth pursuit eye movement for the object that we are most interested in. By contrast, OKR is produced automatically when a large portion of the visual field moves.

Vergence Eye Movement

The four previously described types of eye movements are all examples of conjugate eye movements in that both eyes move in the same directions. However, when we visually track objects moving toward or away from us, our two eyes will need to move in opposite directions, and these eye movements are referred to as disconjugate or vergence eye movements. To keep the image of an object focused on the retina, the shape of the lenses in our eyes must also change. This coordinated response of eye muscles and lens is referred to as accommodation.

Many Behaviors Are Social

Eye movements have largely evolved to serve one function, which is to optimize the quality of vision. However, your eye movements themselves are visible to others. Therefore, in a social setting, the direction of somebody's gaze can provide valuable information about what they are interested in and even what actions they might choose next. Accordingly, eye movements can be also used as a means of social communication. For example, in primates living in groups with a hierarchy, looking directly at the face of another individual is often interpreted as a sign of aggression and may be punished. In addition, humans also tend to direct their gaze toward an object that other people are looking at. Therefore, we can intentionally direct our gaze to direct the attention of our friends to a particular object.

This implies that when we make voluntary eye movements, such as saccades and smooth pursuit eye movements, many different factors influence the selection of targets. The value and importance of an object determines how soon and how long we will look at it. If that object is another person, the social context will also influence our gaze. Each saccade or smooth pursuit eye movement is therefore a result of elaborate decision-making processes. Although eye movements are relatively simple, the fact that there are multiple algorithms and controllers responsible for choosing different types of eye movements implies that such algorithms and controllers must be closely coordinated. Any potential conflicts among multiple requests to move the eyes need to be quickly resolved. Many of our behaviors, such as finger movements and speech, unfold with more complex temporal and spatial patterns than eye movements. Therefore, understanding precisely how and for what purpose such behaviors are generated can be challenging. Furthermore, the nervous system that controls these behaviors is more complex than the behaviors themselves. A rigorous scientific approach is therefore essential to understand the relationship between the brain and behavior.

So far, we have considered the definition of intelligence and looked at eye movements as a simple example of intelligent behaviors. Intelligence is a tool developed by lifeforms to solve the problems they face in their environment and manifests as various behaviors. However, as the brain becomes more complex, understanding the nature of intelligence based solely on the analysis of behavior alone becomes increasingly more difficult. As demonstrated by studies of eye movements, studying the animal's brain and nervous system can provide valuable insight into the nature of intelligent behavior. In the following chapters, we will review various scientific approaches available to understand intelligent behaviors and their underlying brain mechanisms.

References

Bielecki J, Zaharoff AK, Leung NY, Garm A, Oakley TH (2014) Ocular and extraocular expression of opsins in the rhopalium of *Tripedalia cystophora* (Cnidaria: Cubozoa). PLoS One. 9: e98870.

Gardner H, Hatch T (1989) Multiple intelligences go to school: educational implications of the theory of multiple intelligences. Educational Researcher 8: 4–10.

Kurzweil R (1999) The Age of Spiritual Machine: When Computers Exceed Human Intelligence. New York: Penguin Books. p.304.

Legg S, Hutter M (2007) A collection of definitions of intelligence. In: Advances in Artificial General Intelligence: Concepts, Architectures and AI Algorithms. Goertzel B, Wang P (Eds). Amsterdam: IOS Press. pp.17–24.

Minsky M (1985) The Society of Mind. New York: Simon and Schuster. p.71.

Sanderson JB (1872) Note on the electrical phenomena which accompany irritation of the left of Dionaea muscipula. Proc R Soc Lond. 21: 495–496.

Yarbus AL (1967) Eye Movements and Vision. New York, NY: Plenum Press.

Further Reading

Alcock J (2013) Animal Behavior: an Evolutionary Approach (10th ed.). Sunderland, MA: Sinauer.

Dener E, Kacelink A, Shemesh H (2016) Pea plants show risk sensitivity. Curr Bio. 26: 1763–1767.

Herculano-Houzel S (2016) The Human Advantage: a New Understanding of How Our Brain Became Remarkable. Cambridge, MA: MIT Press.

Leigh JR, Zee DS (2015) The Neurobiology of Eye Movements. New York, NY: Oxford Univ. Press.

Mancuso S, Viola A (2015) Brilliant Green: The Surprising History and Science of Plant Intelligence. Washington, DC: Island Press.

Varshney LR, Chen BL, Paniagua E, Hall DH, Chklovskii DB (2011) Structural properties of the *Caenorhabditis elegans* neural network. PLoS Comput Biol. 7: e1001066.

2

Brain and Decision-Making

In animals with relatively simple nervous systems, like *C. elegans* and cockroaches, most behaviors are genetically determined and automatically triggered by sensory stimuli. Humans also have reflexes, but our relatively large brains allow us to select desirable actions more flexibly so that they can maximize the chance of our survival and reproduction in diverse environments. The ability to select the most appropriate actions flexibly in a variety of environments is the essence of intelligence. For animals with brains, therefore, understanding the brain is a key to understanding intelligence.

However, understanding intelligence requires more than analyzing the genetic, biochemical, and electrophysiological properties of the brain. Intelligence has many dimensions, and its scientific investigation is extremely challenging. Since intelligence is an adaptation of an organism to its environment, the complexity and quality of intelligence must be evaluated in the context of the organism's environment. This makes it difficult to compare the intelligence of different animals that adapted to different environments. We might agree that we face a more complex environment when we are trying to get to a library using a subway than when we are simply lying in bed. However, the complexity of an environment is not always easy to judge, especially across different species of animals. For example, who faces a more challenging environment: a group of ants trying to transport a piece of cookie weighing 100 times more than their bodies, or a human choosing some fruits from a local grocery store? It might be easy to control and measure the complexity of the environment accurately in a laboratory. It is much harder to do this in real life.

Similarly, it is difficult to quantify the complexity of a decision-making problem in real life. For human-made games, such as *Go* or *gomoku* (five-in-a-row), in which the exact rules and the number of allowable moves are clearly defined, it is possible to compare the complexity of different games mathematically. This becomes much more difficult when the number and range of alternative actions available to each person are poorly defined or unknown. For example, it is not easy to determine whether baseball or soccer is more complex, although rules in such sports are specified more accurately than many problems in our daily lives. The complexity of a sport might depend on how many details are included in the analyses of each game, and so the perspective of the observer becomes important. To answer these questions more rigorously and objectively, we need a formal approach.

An important approach used to systematically analyze the process of decision-making is utility theory. Utility theory plays an important role not only in economic studies, but also in the neuroscience of decision-making. An area of neuroscience that studies brain functions related to decision-making according to economic frameworks, such as the utility theory, is referred to as neuroeconomics. Utility is a number reflecting the value or desirability of an option or an action. Utilities are necessary to compare the desirability of qualitatively different options and are useful for quantitative studies of intelligence.

Utility Theory

How do people choose between actions or objects? Although there are many different theories about how people make decisions, almost all of them are based on the concept of utility or value. In theories of decision-making, these two terms, *utility* and *value*, have similar meanings. The term *utility* or *utility function* is often used in the context of axiomatic and mathematical theories of choice in economics. By contrast, value or value function tends to be used more often when its relationship with choice is more approximate or empirically estimated. For our present discussion, this distinction is not that important, so we will focus on utility for now.

Utilities come in two different flavors. Ordinal utilities specify only the ranking of different options so that you can order all available options according to your preference. In other words, it specifies only which of the two options is better, but not by how much. By contrast, cardinal utilities are real numbers assigned to alternative options such that we can specify how much better one option is compared to another. In this chapter, we are going to focus on cardinal utilities, because it is easier to calculate them algebraically than ordinal utilities. Imagine that you are trying to choose between red, yellow, and blue umbrellas and that blue is your favorite color and red is your least favorite color. We might in this case assume that their utilities are 1, 2, and 3, respectively. This implies that your choice would be the blue umbrella, because the blue umbrella maximizes your utility. Similarly, if you see someone selecting the red umbrella, then you know that the utility of the red umbrella is greater than those of yellow and blue umbrellas for that person.

Since cardinal utilities are real numbers, preferences based on cardinal utilities will have all the properties of real numbers. For example, transitivity is a property of real numbers. For any three real numbers, a, b, and c, if a is larger than b (a > b) and b is larger than c (b > c), it follows that a is also larger than c (a > c). Therefore, cardinal utility has the property of transitivity, and this implies that if utilities are assigned to all available options, you can rank order them. Imagine that someone prefers oranges to apples and apples to grapes. Transitivity then implies that the same person also prefers oranges to grapes.

Utilities play an important role in theories about decision-making, because they provide a relatively simple description of how choices can be made. Once utilities are known or determined for all options, any problem of choosing one in any subset of those options is immediately solved. Regardless of how complex a decision-making problems might be, utility theory will always predict that the decision maker will choose the option with the maximum utility. More important, the same theories will also determine what would be chosen even when only a subset of all possible options is available. Imagine that there are four restaurants in your neighborhood. Let us refer to these restaurants as A, B, C, and D. If each of these restaurants can be open or closed independently in a day, then there will be a total 16 different combinations of restaurants that might be open in a day. Imagine that you're trying to choose one of the restaurants that are open. You won't be able to make any choice if they are all closed or if only one restaurant is open. This will exclude five cases, but still leaves 11 different choice problems. For example, today, only restaurants A and B might open, and tomorrow all the restaurants except the restaurant D might open. If there are no utilities for these restaurants, each of these 11 different choice problems will have to be solved separately. By contrast, if the restaurants have utilities, then this will fully determine which restaurant to choose regardless of which subset of restaurants are open. The extent to which utilities simplify decision-making increases tremendously with the number of available options. For example, there are more than 25,000 restaurants in New York City, making the number of choice problems practically infinite. Even relatively simple problems like selecting a place to eat can become hopelessly complicated without utilities.

Utilities also provide convenient tools for characterizing how choices are influenced by multiple properties of different options. Outcomes of our actions are always uncertain, and they are seldom immediately known. For example, when you order something from an online store, nothing arrives instantaneously, and there is always a possibility that you might not receive exactly what you expected. Namely, decision-making in real life always involves uncertainties and delays. If the outcomes of our actions can be predicted without any uncertainty, decision-making problems would be trivial. We would be able to avoid all undesirable accidents and can always buy winning lottery tickets. In real life, however, there are always uncertainties in the outcomes of our actions. Similarly, instant gratification is rare. Outcomes of our actions are almost always delayed, often for hours and sometimes for years. When the desired outcome expected from an action becomes delayed or less certain, we are less likely to take that action. Such changes in behaviors can be described systematically and accurately using the framework of utility.

Time and Uncertainty

The purpose of decision-making is not simply to choose something that might lead to the maximum reward possible. Sometimes, an action that can lead to the best possible outcome might be too risky or too costly. The utility theory is useful in characterizing and understanding how multiple factors such as likelihood and immediacy of reward affect decision-making.

In mathematics, the likelihood that an event may occur is expressed by a probability. An event with a zero probability should never occur, and an event with the probability of 1 should always occur. Therefore, the utility of an uncertain outcome might be naturally considered to be the product of the utility of the same outcome with the probability of that outcome. This product is referred to as the expected utility. However, the expected utility of an uncertain outcome is not always equal to its expected value. Imagine that someone wants to sell you a lottery ticket that can win $100. Will you buy it if this lottery ticket costs you $10? Of course, this depends on the odds of winning the prize. If you know the probability of winning the lottery and the amount of money you can win, the expected value of the lottery ticket is given by the product of these two numbers. For example, if the probability of winning the lottery is just 10 percent, then the expected value of a $100 lottery will be $10. If you are choosing based on the expected value, then you would buy that lottery ticket if the cost is less than $10. But such generous lottery tickets do not exist, because the sellers would lose money. Although real lottery tickets are always more expensive than their expected values, people still buy them, suggesting that they do not base their decisions solely on expected values.

Why do expected utilities differ from expected values? There are largely two reasons for this. First, the objective measure of the outcome is not always a good predictor of its utility. This is true even for the outcomes that have objective numerical values, such as money. For example, the utility of $20 is not necessarily twice the utility of $10. Similarly, numerical ratings attached to the quality of food or music are unlikely to reflect their utilities, since the pleasure expected from such products is subjective. Second, the precise probability of an outcome is often difficult to know. This is especially true for events with relatively low probability. What is the probability that you might have a car accident or power outage today? It would be difficult to answer these questions accurately even if you combine the experience over your entire life. Similarly, accurate estimates for the desirability of many goods that we seek in our lives are often not available.

In addition to probability, there is another factor that has a major influence on utility, and that is the amount of delay. The utility of a desirable but delayed outcome usually decreases with the amount of delay. This is referred to as temporal discounting. As temporal discounting becomes steeper or as the value of future reward depreciates more steeply with the delay, the decision maker would give more weight to the outcomes that are available immediately. What would you choose if someone offers you a choice between $100 available immediately versus $200 available a week later? Unless they need to spend $100 immediately, most people might be willing to wait a week and receive additional $100. A choice between two different outcomes available after unequal delays, like this example, is referred to as intertemporal choice.

In the 1960s, Walter Mischel began to present a simple choice to children at the age of 5 or 6, in a study now commonly referred to as the marshmallow experiment (Mischel et al., 1989). A child could eat one marshmallow located right in front of them and go home or wait until the experimenter returns from a meeting and get two marshmallows. After the experimenter left the room, the amount of time that each child could wait before eating the marshmallow was recorded. Of course, there was individual variability. Some children ate the marshmallow as soon as the experimenter left the room, whereas others successfully waited until the experimenter returned more than 20 minutes later. Walter Mischel and his colleagues studied how the ability of a child to wait and get the second marshmallow might influence their adult life and found that the patience of a child can predict many aspects of their life even several decades later. More patient children had higher IQ and higher SAT scores and were more likely to have high-income jobs, such as doctors and lawyers. They were also healthier and less likely to go to jail.

The ability to delay gratification during intertemporal choice illustrated by the marshmallow study is most prominent in humans. Compared to other animals, humans have extraordinary abilities to forego small rewards at the present moment and instead to wait for a much larger reward in the future. Many studies have measured variability in the ability to wait and receive a larger reward across different animal species. For example, this can be done by determining the longest delay that the animal is willing to wait to receive twice as much reward as immediate reward (Hwang et al., 2009). The results of such comparative studies found that mammals, such as rats, tend to be more patient than birds, such as pigeons. There are differences even among mammals (Rosati et al., 2007). For example, primates are more patient than rodents, and even among primates, apes like chimpanzees are more patient than monkeys. Among all the animals tested so far, humans are more patient than any other. Some people might even prefer to postpone consuming the best reward. For example, when you are eating several small food items, such as sushi or candies, you might prefer to leave the best piece until the end. This is the opposite of temporal discounting, since it implies that the value of a delayed reward increases with delay and is therefore referred to as negative temporal discounting or negative time preference.

We should note that the ability to work toward future rewards is particularly important in a social context. This is because socially desirable behaviors, such as cooperation and following the social norms, often do not produce their full benefits immediately. As we will discuss more in later chapters of this book, people often help each other, and one of the important reasons why people cooperate and display a seemingly altruistic tendency is to earn and maintain good reputation. The benefit of a good reputation is often uncertain and tends to materialize after significant delays. Therefore, such benefits will be attractive only to those willing to give up small immediate rewards and work for larger future rewards.

Indecision: Buridan's Ass

In economic theories, such as the utility theory, every choice is made by comparing the utilities of all available options and choosing the option with the largest utility. What would happen if two alternative options have exactly the same utility? Imagine that a thirsty and hungry donkey exhausted by hard work is offered a choice between food and water. If these two rewards have exactly the same utility and are placed precisely the same distance from the donkey, deciding which has the larger utility would be impossible, and the poor donkey might be dead as a result of hunger and dehydration due to indecision. This hypothetical situation is known as Buridan's ass, named after a 14th-century French philosopher.

Can a Buridan's ass really exist? If one option is substantially better than the other, the choice is easy. If the two available options differ in many ways, but end up being nearly equally attractive, then it becomes very difficult to make a choice. This is the ghost of Buridan's ass. In our daily lives, we often face trivial but difficult choices, as when we are trying to choose between different beverages, such as Coke or Pepsi, or sometimes even between different bottles of the same beverage. When we are trying to order a meal from the menu in a restaurant, most of us have hard time making a choice, even though almost everything on the menu will be probably delicious. In such cases, we frequently spend large amounts of time choosing between items with almost identical values. Although we can eventually make our choices, the time spent on deliberating might be difficult to justify. This is because our brains might lack the ability to calculate the utility values of all available options with infinite precision due to the noisy and stochastic nature of information processing in the brain. When options are equally attractive, we might also change our mind as soon as we begin to consume what we selected. For example, when we choose between different flavors of ice cream, we might wish after we make our choice that we had chosen the other one. This might happen at least in part due to sensory adaptation. The pleasure of eating strawberry ice cream will diminish once it begins to stimulate the sensory receptors in our nose and mouth, thus making us value the vanilla ice cream more.

Limitations of the Utility Theory

The utility theory plays an extremely important role in theories of decision-making. However, this does not necessarily mean that utilities are computed whenever a choice is made between different options. Since choices based on utilities are transitive, any pattern of choices that is not transitive is clearly not based on utilities. For example, transitivity is violated when one prefers A to B, B to C, and C to A, and this is inconsistent with any utilities. Those violating transitivity in their choices can become vulnerable to money pumping, because they would be willing to pay money to get A instead of B, to get B instead of C, to get C instead of A, and so forth.

Although intransitive preference is clearly irrational, choices often violate transitivity when they are made according to multiple criteria. Let me explain this with an example. Imagine that there are three cars, A, B, and C, varying in both price and fuel efficiency. Let us assume that for price, C is preferred to (cheaper than) B, and B is preferred to A, which also implies that C is also preferred to A. Let us also assume that the fuel efficiency of these three cars gets better from C to B and B to A, so that A is preferred to B, and B is preferred to C. Now, a potential buyer who cares more about the fuel efficiency might prefer B when B and C are the two available cars and prefer A when the options are A and B. Now, imagine that car B gets sold and is no longer available, and the same buyer must now choose between A and C. What will they choose? If their choices follow transitivity and if fuel efficiency is still the only important criterion, then they must buy A. However, the price difference between A and C might be greater than the difference between A and B or between B and C, and now this might make the buyer unhappy about the high price of car A and make them now prefer the less expensive car C. This then violates transitivity. As in this example, if the criterion used to compare different options changes when different combinations are presented, transitivity can be violated. Violation of transitivity indicates that such choices cannot be described by any utility function. This might seem fatal to economists who rely on utility theory to predict a specific pattern of choices. You can argue that the utilities are calculated every time a new set of options is presented. For example, we can imagine that the utility for car A changes depending on whether it is compared to car B or car C. However, this is not an attractive solution, since any arbitrary pattern of choices can be fit by some utilities chosen to be consistent with such choices. This is not very parsimonious.

Utility theory has another weakness in that behavioral observations alone do not reveal whether and how utilities are computed and used to make choices. Behaviors that satisfy the conditions necessary for utility functions might emerge without using utility functions explicitly. For example, imagine a sunflower that constantly orients its stalk toward the sun. If we define a utility function of the sunflower as a quantity inversely proportional to the angular deviation of its stalk relative to the direction of the sun, the sunflower's behavior might appear to be the result of maximizing its utility. It might be possible to identify some chemical signal that follows such a hypothetical utility function. However, it is also possible that the sunflower's behavior might be entirely controlled by a mechanism that does not utilize utility functions for solar tracking. For example, if you rotate a sunflower 180 degrees so that it faces west in the morning, it will begin to move from west to east during the day, instead of following the sun. This indicates that the sunflower's movement is not consistent with maximization of the hypothetical utility function designed for solar tracking, but that it results from preprogrammed sequence of mechanical responses. It is not easy to distinguish between these two possible scenarios just by observing the natural behavior of the sunflower.

Indeed, it might be of little interest to economists to determine whether utilities really exist, even though utility theory provides a solid mathematical foundation in many branches of economics, such as game theory. Economists often argue that if the utility theory can provide a parsimonious explanation for the complex behaviors of consumers and companies, then it has a practical value, regardless of whether and how utilities are calculated in our brains. This is an example of as-if theory, since it explains empirical data as if the proposed hypothetical quantities, such as utility, really exist. Clearly, as-if theories are less satisfying than theories that allow their key components to be measured and tested directly.

Until recently, the question of whether utilities are used to make choices was not considered an important scientific question, since no methods were available to study the functions of the human brain accurately. It was not possible to test whether and how the human brain computes the utilities for alternative options and how they were used to make choices, even if utilities are represented in the brain. In the last several decades, however, things have changed a lot. It is now possible to measure signals related to utilities in the human brain while people are making various decisions. The field of neuroeconomics or decision neuroscience has emerged. As a result, it has become possible to predict what people might choose in the future by measuring their brain activity, thus making it possible to empirically test and refine the utility theory biologically.

Findings from research in neuroeconomics can be applied in many areas. What would happen if we could measure the utility of a new product for consumers? In the past, people relied exclusively on surveys and interviews to develop a new product and marketing strategy. These methods are not always reliable, because behaviors of the participants can be influenced by subtle cues from the questioners and might therefore falsely confirm their expectations. Surveys and interviews also assume that the responders are aware of their preferences and can verbally report them, but this may not be always true. Nowadays, it is possible to extract information about the preference of an individual from their brain activity, even if such information could not be verbally described. This is a common method adopted in so-called neuromarketing research.

The most provocative application of neuroeconomics research might be the possibility of manipulating utilities artificially. As early as the 1950s, James Olds and Peter Milner have already conducted an experiment in which rats could electrically stimulate the so-called pleasure centers in their brains by pressing a lever. In these experiments, animals continued to press the lever until they were physically exhausted. Similar experiments have been performed on humans. For example, in the 1970s, Robert Heath was able to induce orgasm in patients by electrically stimulating a brain area known as the septal nucleus (Heath, 1972). It is technically possible for a neurosurgeon to insert an electrode into such brain areas of a patient and to create intensely pleasurable experience whenever they want. In the future, a much simpler nonsurgical method might be invented to accomplish a comparable effect. Once you are equipped with such a device, you will be able to experience pleasure after any arbitrary action. For example, you might be able to increase the utility of any chore like dish washing by using this device. This implies that you can artificially alter your utilities. How then can you determine for which actions you are going to increase utilities, when the utility of that action might be different before and after you perform that action and change its utility? Is it logically possible to calculate the utility of an action, when choosing the same action can alter its utility? In other words, can we assign utilities for different utility functions? It might be useful to think about this logical puzzle before such technologies become a reality.

Happiness

Findings from neuroeconomics research can have implications in many areas of our society. What we learn from neuroeconomics might influence how we try to improve the quality of our lives, since utility is closely related to happiness. The pursuit of happiness is universally considered a fundamental right of all human beings, as stated in the constitutions of some countries as well as in the U.S. Declaration of Independence. Nevertheless, it is not easy to define happiness objectively. In fact, scientists do not necessarily agree whether happiness or subjective well-being can be a topic of scientific inquiry. Despite this complication, it would be helpful to understand the similarities and differences between utility and happiness. To do this, it is important to distinguish at least two different meanings of happiness.

First, happiness might refer to a state in which someone is satisfied with their current condition. This is usually what people have in mind, when someone says "I am happy" or asks other people whether they are happy or not. This kind of happiness is often referred to as "experienced happiness." Since experienced happiness is entirely subjective, the only way to measure it is by asking people directly how happy they are. However, there is no guarantee that people's verbal report or other nonverbal report can reflect truly and accurately how happy they are, so it is challenging to study experienced happiness objectively and quantitatively. Moreover, experience happiness cannot be studied in nonhuman animals without language or while people are performing some tasks that prevent them from making the necessary responses. Neuroeconomics might provide a solution, if experienced happiness is determined by and reflected in the activity of neurons in our brains. Therefore, as we better understand the relationship between neural activity and experienced happiness, it might become possible to study experienced happiness more scientifically.

Second, happiness can also refer to a prediction about how satisfied or pleased someone will feel after accomplishing a specific goal. This can be referred to as "anticipated happiness." Since anticipated happiness is not yet experienced, it is merely a prediction. Nevertheless, anticipated happiness is more closely related to utility in economics. Indeed, if people always behave so as to maximize their anticipated happiness, anticipated happiness would be equivalent to utility, and maximizing utility would mean being as happy as possible.

If people always have accurate knowledge about how happy they would be in the future after every action they take, then experienced happiness would closely match anticipated happiness. Unfortunately, this is not the case, and there is often a large discrepancy between anticipated and experienced happiness (Gilbert, 2006). This is perhaps not surprising, since happiness is a subjective feeling that can change over time. For example, some people might think that they would be happy for their entire lives if they win a multimillion-dollar jackpot. However, empirical studies have shown that such joy is relatively short lasting. Similarly, even when someone is struck by a tragedy, such as becoming quadriplegic from a traffic accident, their subjective well-being—namely, experienced happiness—tends to return to the previous level more quickly than most people might think. These findings suggest that there is a set point in experienced happiness and that experienced happiness tends to return to the same baseline in the long run, even after one experiences extremely joyous or tragic events (Figure 2.1).

The fact that experienced happiness tends to return to a baseline mimics how the brain processes other sensory stimuli from the environment. When the animal experiences the same stimulus repeatedly, this leads to a sensory adaptation and tends to make the animal less sensitive to the same stimulus in the future. This is because the perceptual system in the brain focuses on detecting change or contrast in our environment. For example, the amount of light reflected off of various objects in our environment or their illuminance changes dramatically across different lighting conditions, but the average illuminance provides little information about the identities of the objects we are interested in. Therefore, light and dark adaptation in vision allow us to focus on patterns in our visual inputs, rather than their average brightness. When we move suddenly into a well-lit area, we undergo light adaptation until our vision compensates for excessive illuminance. Conversely, when we

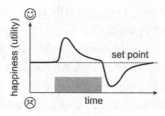

Figure 2.1. Set point in happiness determines how happiness might change over time during and after a pleasurable event (indicated by a gray box).

first enter a dark theater, it takes several minutes before we can begin to identify objects better through dark adaptation.

The same principle applies to happiness and how much pleasure we experience or anticipate in our daily experience. This can be demonstrated even in a well-controlled animal experiment. For example, if you place a hungry rat at one end of a linear track and a food reward at the other end, the animal will easily learn to run along the track and eat the food. You can now divide rats into two experimental groups. For one group, you place two pellets of food at the end of the track, whereas for the other group, you put six pellets. As you might expect, rats tend to run faster when they get six food pellets than when they get only two food pellets. This is not surprising. Once the animals are used to getting a certain number of pellets, now you put four pellets of food in both groups and measure the speed of running. What will happen?

If the amount of food is the only factor determining the motivation of the animal in this experiment, then the running speed will be the same for both groups. However, this is not what researchers found. Instead, they found that the rats who had previously received two food pellets started running faster for the same amount of food than the rats that previous received six food pellets. This result is consistent with the set-point theory. It was not the absolute amount of food the animal was working for, but rather whether the animal was getting more or less food than was received previously that determined their motivation. The fact that animals were more motivated to work harder to receive the same amount of reward when the amount of reward was increased suggests that anticipated happiness or utility was higher when the reward was better than expected. This experiment, which was carried out in 1940, was the first demonstration that the process of adaptation applies not only to sensation, but also to motivation. The phenomenon demonstrated in this experiment is referred to as incentive contrast. Just as our visual system is sensitive mainly to change or contrast, our motivation tends to reflect changes in the expected amount of reward, rather than its absolute amount.

The tendency for happiness to eventually return to a set point or baseline implies that it might be impossible to sustain the feeling of happiness indefinitely after we experience a desirable event. This is referred to as the hedonic treadmill. Just as running on the treadmill doesn't really get you anywhere, getting anything you want might satisfy you only temporarily. Many scholars in both the Eastern and Western cultures had realized for a long time that pleasure arising from accomplishing what was previously desired tends to be short-lasting. For example, it is commonly thought in both Buddhism and

Stoicism that blindly seeking pleasurable sensation does not lead to a better life in the long run. Counterintuitively, the presence of a set point raises a possibility that avoiding the pleasurable experiences might lead to more happiness. This is because abstinence can reduce the level of expectation, and therefore small and even trivially pleasant outcomes might give rise to a feeling of satisfaction and happiness. Later in this book, we will also discuss how our brains have evolved to acquire this seemingly paradoxical property.

Utility Theory and the Brain

Behavioral observations alone cannot determine whether the decision makers made their choices by explicitly calculating and comparing the utilities of alternative options or not. To test this, we need to see what happens inside the brain. Given that decision-making is a function of the brain, if choices are made by choosing the option with the maximum utility, then it might be possible to measure the brain activity directly related to utilities. Moreover, if we can accurately estimate the utilities by measuring the brain activity of someone, then this will allow us to predict their choices. Of course, this will be possible only if we can measure the brain activity with sufficient accuracy and if we have an analytical method to derive the utilities from the brain activity. Economists, such as Francis Edgeworth, who laid the foundation for the utility theory in the 19th century, imagined that such a machine might be possible someday and coined the term *hedonometer* for an imaginary device that can measure the amount of pleasure. It was about 100 years later with the invention of functional magnetic resonance imaging that such experiments became a reality.

Currently, functional magnetic resonance imaging (fMRI) is the most effective method to measure the brain activity of a living person. Originally, magnetic resonance imaging (MRI) was invented to examine the structure of biological tissues, such as the brain. MRI is based on the signals produced by protons after they are briefly excited by a radio wave in a strong magnetic field. Protons are the nuclei of hydrogen atoms, which is a part of a water molecule. Therefore, there are many protons in a human body, including the brain. You can examine the structures of the brain using MRI, because the signals from protons vary depending on the chemical compositions of the tissue surrounding the protons. In the late 1980s, it was also discovered that MRI can be used to measure the level of oxygen contained in the blood, because the magnetic properties of hemoglobin are different depending on whether it is oxygenated or not. Since the level of oxygenated blood in any brain area changes depending on the level of neural activity in that area, this produces the blood–oxygen level-dependent (BOLD) signals that can be measured using MRI. To distinguish it from the MRI used to measure the anatomical structures, this new method is called fMRI. It is still not possible to measure action potentials or the release of neurotransmitters directly from living human brain without invasive surgeries.

Research on the brain functions related to decision-making in humans began to accelerate in the mid-1990s, when researchers started using fMRI to examine how the BOLD signals fluctuate in different brain areas while subjects make various decisions inside MRI machines. As a result, several hundred studies were conducted to identify the brain signals related to utilities. These studies covered very diverse topics. For example, many of these studies examined how the activity in different brain areas changes according to the type and desirability of food. Other studies have tested how brain activity is influenced by the magnitude and probability of monetary reward. Indeed, researchers have characterized the patterns of brain activity related to virtually every type of reward that humans might find pleasurable, including erotic images and funny stories. Many of these studies shared a common goal, which is to identify the brain areas carrying signals related to utilities. As a result of these studies, there is now a consensus that two areas in the human brain display signals most reliably related to utilities: ventromedial prefrontal cortex and ventral striatum (Figure 2.2). In a variety of settings, the BOLD signals in these two brain areas tend to increase with the utility of an option available to human subjects. These two brain areas might be involved in calculating utilities and, hence, in making choices.

The results from fMRI experiments should be interpreted with caution. This is because fMRI experiments do not measure the neural activity directly but are based on the BOLD signals indirectly related to the underlying neural activity (Logothetis and Wandell, 2004). There is a causal relationship between the neural activity and BOLD signals, since neurons require more oxygen and energy as they receive more inputs and become more active. Nevertheless, BOLD signals are relatively slow and do not have the spatial precision to observe the activity of individual neurons. The typical spatial resolution of fMRI is about 1 mm, whereas the soma of a cortical neuron is about 20 μm, about 50 times smaller than the resolution

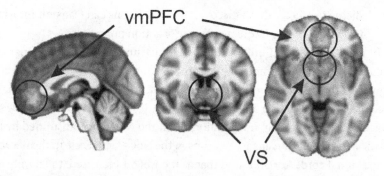

Figure 2.2. Brain areas showing the BOLD signals related to utilities, including the ventromedial prefrontal cortex (vmPFC) and ventral striatum (VS).

Source: Bartra O, McGuire JT, Kable JW (2013) The valuation system: a coordinate-based meta-analysis of BOLD fMRI experiments examining neural correlates of subjective value. NeuroImage. 76: 412–427. Copyright (2013), with permission from Elsevier.

of fMRI. Similarly, the temporal resolution of fMRI is more than 1 second, at least a thousand times greater than the duration of a single action potential. Therefore, to more accurately understand how the brain processes various types of information necessary for decision-making, the findings from fMRI experiments in humans must be complemented by studies in animals. Researchers can measure the neural activity much more precisely in animal experiments.

Meaning of Action Potentials

Measuring the action potentials of individual neurons in the brain provides much more information about brain functions than fMRI. As we discussed in the first chapter, neurons in the brain communicate with each other using action potentials. However, to record the action potentials of a neuron, an electrode must be positioned close to the neuron, so it is technically challenging to make such recordings from neurons that are deep inside the brain. Furthermore, action potentials recorded from most neurons in the brain produce complex stochastic patterns. If you amplify the electric signals from a single neuron and connect it to a loudspeaker, it sounds like the noise from a popcorn machine. An important breakthrough to understanding how to interpret such signals from a single neuron was made by a British physiologist, Edgar Douglas Adrian, who was awarded the Nobel Prize in Physiology or Medicine in 1932. Adrian discovered that neurons can transmit information by modulating the frequency or rate of action potentials.

In the 1920s, Adrian utilized high-tech instruments at that time, namely, vacuum-tube amplifiers and an electrometer to amplify and record the electric signals from the sciatic nerve of a frog (Adrian, 1926; Figure 2.3). He examined the pattern of action potentials in the sciatic nerve as he varied the weight attached to the frog's leg. Information about the weight is transmitted by the sciatic nerve from the sensory neurons in the frog's leg muscle to the neurons in the spinal cord. Adrian found that as the weight increased, the number of action potentials generated in a given temporal interval increased. By contrast,

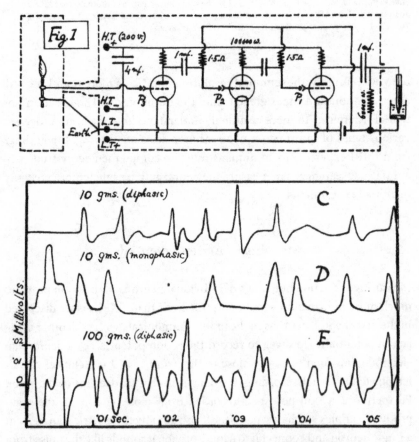

Figure 2.3. Schematic diagram of the amplifier (top) used by Adrian to record the action potentials (bottom) from sensory nerve endings in frog's leg muscles.

Source: Adrian ED (1926) The impulses produced by sensory nerve endings: Part I. J Physiol. 18: 49–72.

the shape or size of each action potential was not altered. Therefore, he concluded that the rate of action potentials must carry the information about how much the frog's leg muscle is stretched by the weight.

Adrian's discovery was extremely important and guided a large portion of the subsequent research in neuroscience. Although the original observation was made in the frog's sciatic nerve, the same principle has been found to be extremely general. For example, neurons in the visual cortex signal the orientation of lines and edges in some region of a visual space by altering the rate of their action potentials. Similarly, neurons in the motor cortex use the same code to signal the intended direction of a reaching movement or how much force needs to be generated in some muscles. Accordingly, the rate of action potential, often referred to as a firing rate, is broadly used to investigate the nature of signals carried by individual neurons through the entire brain.

If individual neurons in the brain independently transmit different types of information, how can such signals be detected by fMRI that does not have enough resolution to detect the activity of individual neurons? Although BOLD signals used in fMRI experiments reflect metabolic changes in a small volume of the brain, this still contains many neurons. Therefore, we can expect to get meaningful result from fMRI experiments only if neurons with similar functional properties are not randomly dispersed, but spatially clustered in the brain. For example, if neurons decreasing their activity in response to a stimulus are intermixed with those increasing their activity, their average activity and hence BOLD signals from that region of the brain might not change although many neurons in this area might change their activity. We can use fMRI to identify neural activity related to certain brain functions because neurons with similar patterns of activity are spatially clustered in the brains. This is especially true for cortical areas that are specialized in sensory and motor functions. It is also easier to characterize the information processed by visual and motor cortical areas, since sensory stimuli and motor responses can be more readily controlled compared to factors related to decision-making or emotions. Accordingly, when fMRI was first invented, many experiments were performed to validate the fMRI method by characterizing the BOLD signals in the visual and motor cortical areas. For example, the visual cortex in the human brain can be localized by determining whether the intensity of BOLD signal from a given region changes depending on whether the subject is presented with some visual stimuli or not. The results from such experiments have repeatedly demonstrated visually evoked BOLD signals in the human visual cortex (Figure 2.4).

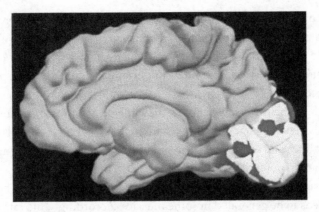

Figure 2.4. BOLD signals measured from the human visual cortex.
Source: Tootell RB, Hadjikhani NK, Vanduffel W, Liu AK, Mendola JD, Sereno MI, Dale AM (1998) Functional analysis of primary visual cortex (V1) in humans. Proc Natl Acad Sci. USA 95: 811–817. Copyright (1998) National Academy of Sciences USA.

Currently, fMRI is undoubtedly a central method used to study the functions of the human brain. In addition to the studies of the brain regions involved in sensory and motor functions, fMRI has been used extensively to study brain activity related to other cognitive functions, such as decision-making. Nevertheless, fMRI is unlikely to provide all the information necessary to understand how individual neurons in various brain areas communicate with each other so that humans and other animals can make appropriate choices. As previously mentioned, numerous fMRI experiments have identified BOLD signals related to utilities, suggesting that the prefrontal cortex and striatum might play an important role in decision-making. However, to understand how such utility signals are generated in these brain areas, and how the activity of individual neurons might be influenced by utilities and other factors related to decision-making, animal experiments are necessary. In particular, recording the activity of individual neurons from the brains of non-human mammals, such as rodents and monkeys, has provided valuable information necessary to advance our understanding about the brain functions related to decision-making. Experiments in monkeys trained to perform a well-controlled decision-making task are even more valuable, because brains of monkeys and humans display many similarities.

For example, monkeys can be trained to choose between a small but more immediate reward or a larger but more delayed reward. In my laboratory, this was accomplished by presenting a green target and a red target in two

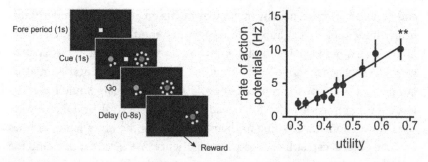

Figure 2.5. Intertemporal choice task performed by monkeys (left) and the firing rate of neuron closely related to the utility of a delayed reward (right).

Source: Reprinted from Cai X, Kim S, Lee D (2011) Heterogenous coding of temporally discounted values in the dorsal and ventral striatum during intertemporal choice. Neuron. 69: 170–182. Copyright (2011), with permission from Elsevier.

different locations on a computer screen (Cai et al., 2011; Figure 2.5, left). If the monkeys shift their gaze toward the red target, they would receive three drops of sweet apple juice, whereas they would receive two drops of juice for selecting the green target. In addition, each of these targets is accompanied by a variable number of small yellow dots, indicating the delay between the animal's choice and juice delivery. Once the animals become familiar with the meaning of the target color and the number of yellow dots, they show a consistent temporal discounting. Namely, when the delays for small and large reward are the same, they always choose the larger reward. However, they tend to increase their preference for the smaller rewards as the delay for the large reward increases or as the delay for the small reward decreases. More important, while the animal makes such intertemporal choices, many neurons in the prefrontal cortex and ventral striatum changed their activity systematically according to the magnitude and delay of the reward expected from a particular target, suggesting that those neurons indeed encode the utility of a particular option (Figure 2.5, right).

Evolution of Utilities

Utilities might underlie all our choices and also shape how happy we are. What then determines utilities? Utilities for some items are determined genetically. This implies that like most physical features of life forms, utilities are selected by evolution. It is difficult to change preference for sweetness and aversion for bitterness by manipulating the environment. Similarly, it is nearly impossible to eat human feces or rotten food. Touching a hot object or getting exposed to a loud noise is always painful. Biologically, the fact that we prefer and hence assign higher utilities to food with nutrients essential for our survival must be the product of evolution. No animals would have survived if they always avoided food needed for their survival, or if they always sought situations threatening to their survival. On the other hand, utilities of some objects can still change with experience. We get tired of eating the same food or listening to the same music repeatedly, even if it was something we greatly enjoyed in the beginning. We might stop liking certain food, if we find out that it contains harmful chemicals. Therefore, utilities are determined not only genetically but also by our experience. Later in this book, we are going to examine more closely how the genes and the environment influence the utilities and our behaviors.

References

Adrian ED (1926) The impulses produced by sensory nerve endings: Part I. J Physiol. 18: 49–72.

Cai X, Kim S, Lee D (2011) Heterogenous coding of temporally discounted values in the dorsal and ventral striatum during intertemporal choice. Neuron. 69: 170–182.

Bartra O, McGuire JT, Kable JW (2013) The valuation system: a coordinate-based meta-analysis of BOLD fMRI experiments examining neural correlates of subjective value. NeuroImage. 76: 412–427.

Gilbert DT (2006) Stumbling on Happiness. New York, NY: Knopf.

Heath RG (1972) Pleasure and brain activity in man. J Nerv Ment Dis. 154: 3–18.

Hwang J, Kim S, Lee D (2009) Temporal discounting and inter-temporal choice in rhesus monkeys. Front Behav Neurosci. 3: 9.

Mischel W, Shoda Y, Rodriguez ML (1989) Delay of gratification in children. Science. 244: 933–938.

Logothetis NK, Wandell BA (2004) Interpreting the BOLD signal. Annu Rev Physiology. 66: 735–769.

Rosati AG, Stevens JR, Hare B, Hauser MD (2007) The evolutionary origins of human patience: temporal preferences in chimpanzees, bonobos, and human adults. Curr Biol. 17: 1663–1668.

Tootell RB, Hadjikhani NK, Vanduffel W, Liu AK, Mendola JD, Sereno MI, Dale AM (1998) Functional analysis of primary visual cortex (V1) in humans. Proc Natl Acad Sci USA 95: 811–817.

Further Reading

Casey BJ, Somerville LH, Gotlib IH, et al. (2011) Behavioral and neural correlates of delay of gratification 40 years later. Proc Nat Acad Sci USA. 108: 14998–15003.

Gallistel CR, King AP (2009) Memory and the Computational Brain: Why Cognitive Science Will Transform Neuroscience. Chichester, England: Wiley-Blackwell.

Glimcher PW, Camerer CF, Fehr E, Poldrack RA (2009) Neuroeconomics: Decision Making and the Brain. New York, NY: Academic Press.

Kahneman D, Diener E, Schwarz N (1999) Well-being: The Foundations of Hedonic Psychology. New York, NY: Russell Sage Foundation.

Kandel ER, Schwartz JH, Jessell TM, Siegelbaum SA, Hudspeth AJ (2013) Principles of Neural Science. 5th ed. New York, NY: McGraw Hill.

Lee D (2006) Neural basis of quasi-rational decision making. Curr Opin Neurobiol. 16: 191–198.

Loewenstein G, Read D, Baumeister RF (2003) Time and Decision: Economic and Psychological Perspectives on Intertemporal Choice. New York, NY: Russell Sage Foundation.

McComas AJ (2011) Galvani's Spark: The Story of the Nerve Impulse. New York, NY: Oxford Univ. Press.

Thaler RH (1991) Quasi Rational Economics. New York, NY: Russel Sage Foundation.

3

Artificial Intelligence

Until the middle of the 20th century, it was taken for granted that intelligence is unique to life. This may not be the case anymore. Combined with the advances in computer science, the progress of artificial intelligence (AI) during the last six decades has created fundamental changes in industries and many aspects of human civilizations. AI is constantly challenging the cognitive abilities of the human mind in areas where many had thought it would be nearly impossible for AI to exceed human performance. For example, in 1997, the AI chess program Deep Blue from IBM beat the world chess champion Garry Kasparov. Even more impressively, in 2016, AlphaGo of Google's DeepMind defeated the former world Go champion Sedol Lee. In 2017, an AI program called Libratus, developed by Noam Brown and Tuomas Sandholm at Carnegie Mellon University, outperformed professional poker players in no-limit Texas hold'em. In early 2019, DeepMind's AI program called AlphaStar has started defeating professional players of StarCraft, which is a sophisticated real-time strategy game. Such phenomenal success worried some scholars. Some of them warned that we should be prepared for AI to exceed human ability not just in abstract games, such as Go and chess, but in every aspect of human cognition. Such AI is often referred to as superintelligence (Bostrom, 2014).

Will superintelligence really emerge and begin to replace humans? Before we can answer this question, we need to understand the nature of human intelligence and how it differs from AI. Otherwise, we might be fooled by superficial similarities or differences between them. For example, digital computers are built using silicon-based semiconductors, whereas brains are cellular structures created with many different types of biopolymers, such as proteins. Nevertheless, the fact that they are made of different materials should not be the sole reason to treat AI as fundamentally different from human intelligence. Although we do not yet fully understand how the human brain functions, it might be possible someday to build a machine that resemble the human brain much more than the computers we know of today.

Present-day AI is still not truly intelligent, not because it is made of materials and building blocks that are different from those of the human brain, but because it is designed to solve the problems chosen by humans. If AI is truly intelligent, it must have its own goals and seek solutions to any problems for its own sake. AI is built to improve the well-being and prosperity of human beings rather than its own. This does not guarantee that AI will never hurt humans, since such outcomes might still occur as a result of AI failure or malevolent human motives. Nevertheless, it is still people who decide the success or failure of an AI program. This is necessary because many real-life problems do not have clear-cut answers, and the best answers might be different depending on who will evaluate the solution. Thus, AI's intelligence can be evaluated differently depending on the preference of its human evaluator.

AI might not be truly intelligent without utility functions that consider its own well-being. Of course, just as decisions can be made without utilities, AI without utilities is possible. However, as we examined in the previous chapter, utilities make decision-making much more efficient. This is also true for AI. When you create an AI robot to solve a set of complex problems, it would be impossible to give a complete set of explicit instructions to all the problems it might face. When the number of alternative options is large and cannot be specified accurately in advance, it would be also difficult to manually define utilities for all possible options. Indeed, in the latest AI technology, such as deep reinforcement learning, AI learns utilities through experience using the criteria provided by humans. If AI begins to discover how to alter its utility functions for its own benefit, will such AI then become truly intelligent?

In the previous chapters, we tried to refine our intuition about intelligence by considering examples of intelligence in humans and other life forms. In this chapter, we will try to further examine the relationship between intelligence and life by comparing biological intelligence and AI. Are there any fundamental differences between human brains and computers? If the computer technology continues to advance, will computers eventually outperform humans at everything? To find answers to these questions, we will turn to Mars rovers. They provide a good example of how robots can make decisions using utility functions set up by humans. We will see why true intelligence requires life.

Brain Versus Computer

We often compare human brains to computers, and this is probably because so far computers perform many of our difficult tasks better than any other man-made machines. Through history, people have often likened the human brain to the most complicated machinery known at the time. For example, in the 17th century, René Descartes compared the brain to a hydraulic automaton in the royal gardens of Saint-Germain-en-Laye outside Paris in which movements of various parts of the machine were controlled by the pressure of water flowing through pipes. Similarly, in the late 19th century, Sigmund Freud was inspired by the steam engines when he developed his psychoanalytic theory. Although we now compare the brain to computers, the accuracy of this analogy is limited by our imagination.

Aside from the fact that we do not understand the brain very well, there are still reasons to view the brain as a type of computer. First, computers are designed to function similarly to the human mind. Originally, they were invented to carry out logical or numerical calculations to improve the speed and accuracy of these computations compared to what humans could accomplish. In many ways, computers are created to mimic the functions of the human brain, and our knowledge about brain functions has been incorporated into the process of building better computers. The brain analyzes and stores the information contained in sensory stimuli. The brain then retrieves such information later when it is needed. Computers work similarly. They receive inputs from devices like a keyboard and mouse, perform various calculations based on such input and additional information retrieved from memory and store the results in memory again. Computers operating in such a manner are often referred to as von Neumann machines (Figure 3.1). Of course, additional mechanical parts like motors and valves can be controlled by such a computer. As the machines become more elegant and sophisticated and their computers become more powerful, AI robots will display more humanlike intelligence.

Similarities between brains and computers do not end there. Building blocks of brains and computers also show functional similarities, although their physical substrates are quite different. This is particularly true for modern-day digital computers. Let us review briefly how the individual neurons in the brain communicate with each other. The dendrites of each neuron in the brain receive signals from thousands of other neurons. These signals tend to come in two different flavors. Some of them reduce the

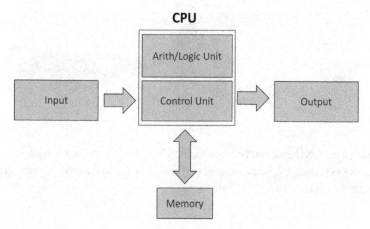

Figure 3.1. Structure of a von Neumann machine.

amount of negative charges inside the neuron, making the neuron more likely to discharge an action potential, whereas others reduce the likelihood of an action potential by increasing the amount of negative charges inside the neuron. The total sum of such excitatory and inhibitory signals determines whether the neuron will produce an action potential or not. Imagine a simple hypothetical neuron that receives only two inputs. Such a neuron might generate an action potential whenever both inputs are active. Alternatively, it might produce an action potential whenever at least one of the inputs is active. These are analogous to logical operations. The former case corresponds to a logical operator AND, whose output value becomes true only when both inputs are true. The latter corresponds to OR, outputting a true value whenever at least one input is true. In computers, these logical operations are used to perform computations on binary numbers, and they are physically implemented using transistors. Using just two transistors, one can build a simple electronic circuit that can perform AND or OR operations (Figure 3.2). Therefore, synapses in the brain and transistors in computers can perform analogous functions.

Many transistors can be concentrated in a relatively small space, which is known as an integrated circuit or chip. A central processing unit (CPU) or processor, which is often likened to the brain of a computer, is a type of integrated circuit and therefore also a collection of transistors. For example, Intel's 8086 CPU released in 1978 included 29,000 transistors (Figure 3.2). By comparison, Apple's A11 Bionic, which was released in 2017 and used in

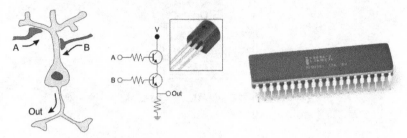

Figure 3.2. AND gate can be implemented by neuron (left) or a pair of transistors (center). A large number of transistors can be combined in integrated circuits like Intel's 8086 chip (right).

the iPhone X, has 4.3 billion transistors. Another processor called Centriq 2400 from Qualcomm, also released in 2017, contains approximately 18 billion transistors. The number of transistors in a CPU, which can be used as a measure of its performance, tends to grow exponentially. For example, Centriq 2400 has 620,000 times as many transistors as 8086, and this is roughly what would be expected if the number of transistors doubled every two years for 39 years from 1978 to 2017. The fact that the number of transistor in a dense integrated circuit roughly doubles every two years is commonly known as Moore's law. It is named after Gordon Moore, who observed this phenomenon originally and was also one of the founders of Intel.

Will Computers Outperform Human Brains?

The fact that computer hardware, such as the CPU, has advanced exponentially for several decades has led to the optimistic prediction that computer performance will continue to grow exponentially in the future. Therefore, if Moore's law continues to hold in the future, then someday performance of computers might exceed that of humans. The similarity between transistors and synapses might provide a way to compare the calculating power of brains and computers. Namely, if we can quantify the complexity of the human brain in terms of the number of transistors, we can predict when the computer will begin to outperform the human brain. There are about 100 billion neurons in the human brain, and each of the neurons includes about 1,000 synapses. Therefore, the total number of synapses in the human brain would be approximately 100 trillion. If we believe that transistors and synapses carry out similar functions, the human brain is equivalent to a digital computer consisting of about 100 trillion transistors. The function of the human brain is then equivalent to the computational power of approximately 23 thousand iPhone Xs. If we extrapolate using Moore's law as a guide, then by 2046, portable computers like the iPhone might contain as many transistors as the number of synapses in our brain. The time when the performance of computers and AI begins to exceed that of humans is referred to as technological singularity. In his book *The Singularity Is Near*, Ray Kurzweil indeed predicted that such singularity would arrive by approximately 2045 (Kurzweil, 2005). However, there are several reasons to suspect that making such a specific prediction might be premature.

First, AI solves problems in special domains with clear boundaries. AI is developed to solve complex problems that are difficult for humans to solve. However, to make AI able to find a solution to any problem, the problems must be clearly defined, as in chess or Go, and it should be possible to determine clearly whether a given answer is correct or not. Moreover, since AI is developed by humans, it is frequently developed to handle specific problems humans are not good at or unwilling to work on. Accordingly, it is difficult for AI to find flexible solutions when its environment changes dramatically. Although AI programs developed by Google's DeepMind can learn to play different video games from scratch, those games still share many similarities. It might be awhile before AI can learn to solve many different types of problems in real life simultaneously.

Second, AI does not solve problems for itself. Since AI is developed to solve problems chosen by humans, it is not required to find solutions to other problems related to its own maintenance, repair, and reproduction. By contrast, survival and reproduction are precisely the primary objectives of animal's nervous system and intelligence. Intelligence cannot be separated from the agent or life form. Currently, most advanced AI programs have been designed to promote the well-being of their human developers. Therefore, the remarkable progress of AI research should be credited to humans and not to AI itself. It's not the intelligence of AI, but rather the intelligence of humans. This is because AI is still a tool. If a violinist plays beautiful music, this is not simply due to the violin, but instead is a product of the skills of the luthier who made the violin and the violinist.

Finally, and perhaps most important, we still do not understand the function of the human brain fully. This makes it difficult to accurately predict how soon the performance of AI will exceed the capacity of the human brain. We may also find that the computer is a poor analogy for the brain and that computers and human brains operate according to fundamentally different principles. This will also make it challenging to compare computers and human brains directly. The prediction that computers and AI will out-perform human brains in the near future relies on the assumption that the basic elements of computers and brains, such as transistors and synapses, are functionally equivalent and perform similar functions. However, as we will discuss now, the structure of a synapse is much more complex than that of a transistor. Transistors largely function as a binary switch, whereas synapses do not.

Synapse Versus Transistor

A synapse is a gap between two neurons that are referred to as presynaptic and postsynaptic neurons. This is where information from the presynaptic neuron is transmitted to the postsynaptic neuron. Such transmission is trig-gered when an action potential arrives at the axon of a presynaptic neuron (Figure 3.3). This causes the opening of calcium channels in the membrane of the presynaptic neurons, allowing calcium ions to flow inside. This activates a cascade of events, eventually leading to the fusion of synaptic vesicles with the membrane of the presynaptic neuron, and the neurotransmitters stored in the synaptic vesicles are then released into the space called synaptic cleft,

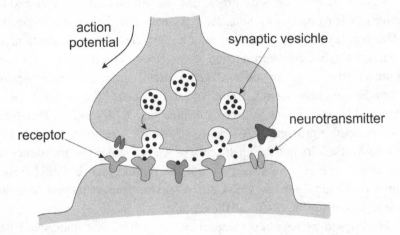

Figure 3.3. Structure of a synapse.

which is only about 20 nanometers wide. Neurotransmitter molecules then diffuse across the synaptic cleft and bind with the receptors in the membrane of the postsynaptic neuron. This then leads to a change in the membrane potential of the postsynaptic neuron. Accordingly, a synapse can be considered as a switch that allows the signal in the presynaptic neuron to ultimately influence the excitability of the postsynaptic neuron. By contrast, the structure and function of a transistor is far simpler. A transistor consists of two different types of silicon with different chemical properties arranged like a sandwich. It has three pins called the base, the emitter, and the collector. A small voltage applied between the base and the emitter can turn on the transistor, which allows a much larger current to flow between the emitter and the collector.

If both a synapse and a transistor mostly function as a switch, then why is the structure of a synapse so much more complicated than that of a transistor? A simple answer is that the complex structure of a synapse makes it possible to change the strength of the signal generated in the postsynaptic neuron depending on the context. Therefore, a synapse should be considered not a single switch, but rather a collection of many switches. A single synapse contains not just one synaptic vesicle, but several hundreds of thousands of vesicles in the presynaptic terminal and tens to hundreds of receptors in the postsynaptic membrane. The number of available synaptic vesicles and receptors in a synapse can vary depending on how often signals passed through it recently. This way, the history of a synapse can influence its function, since the size of the voltage change produced in the postsynaptic neuron depends on the number of synaptic vesicles available in the presynaptic neuron and receptors in the postsynaptic neuron. Such an adaptable property of a synapse is referred to as synaptic plasticity.

Why does the function of a synapse vary depending on the context? If synapses do not always operate consistently in the same manner, this implies that unnecessary noise might be unpredictably introduced during the signal transmission across the synapse. If there were a transistor that changes its function according to its previous experience, they might be thrown away as a defective component in the assembly line of electronic products. On the contrary, plasticity of a synapse is critical for the brain to find solutions to complex problems through learning. Therefore, a synapse is likely to perform a much more complex function than a single transistor. Indeed, a synapse is akin to a hypothetical electrical component, called memristor, whose property can be modified by the history of electrical current passing through the device.

The fact that a synapse is functionally more complex than a transistor does not necessarily mean that computers will never catch up with human brains. If computers and computer chips continue to improve their performance, it might be possible for more advanced computer chips to become functionally equivalent to synapses. For example, developing a novel type of integrated circuit that mimics the functions of synapses and neurons is an active area of research. Such chips are referred to as neuromorphic (Merolla et al., 2016). Moreover, high-end supercomputers include many CPUs and can use them for parallel computing. Some of these computers already contain almost as many transistors as the number of synapses in the human brain. For example, as of June 2018, the fastest computer in the world is IBM's Summit, which includes 9,216 CPUs called Power9. Each Power9 includes 8 billion transistors, and therefore the total transistor count for Summit is about 74 trillion, which is approximately equivalent to the total number of synapses in the human brain.

Hardware Versus Software

Undoubtedly, humans will continue to build increasingly powerful computers, and therefore we cannot predict how computers in the future might operate. For example, computers based on quantum-mechanical phenomena, such as superposition, might be able to carry out some types of calculations much faster than traditional digital computers. Our discussion about the difference between the human brain and computers has been confined to digital computers that exist today. Now let us imagine that we have a computer with computing power equal to or greater than a human brain. For example, if the computation performed by a single synapse in the human brain corresponds to the function of 1,000 transistors, then such computer will have roughly 100 quadrillion (10^{17}) transistors. Does this mean that we would have a computer as intelligent as humans? Probably not. This is because the function of a computer is determined not just by its hardware, such as CPU and memory, but also by its program or software. Even if one has the world's most powerful supercomputer, such as Summit, how well it can play difficult games like Go depends on the program running on that computer, such as AlphaGo. A computer with inferior hardware might be able to find a solution faster than a more powerful computer, if it is running a smarter program.

What is a computer program? A computer program is a set of instructions that determine exactly what calculations a computer is going to perform. Most digital computers follow a design introduced by John von Neumann in 1945. Therefore, digital computers are often referred to as von Neumann computers (Figure 3.1). In von Neumann computers, the CPU of a computer retrieves specific instruction and data from its memory, performs the computations on the data according to the instruction, and stores the results of this computation to a designated location in the computer's memory. This process can be repeated as many times as necessary. A computer program specifies how the data will be processed in each of these steps. Some computers do not follow the same design as von Neumann computers, in that instructions and data might be communicated to the computer CPU through different channels. However, all digital computers will perform functions specified by their programs.

Separation of computer software and hardware is convenient, because this makes it possible to use one computer for a variety of purposes. To perform different tasks, computers need to change only the software, and we do not need to buy a new computer or physically reassemble the entire computer. Unlike computers, however, the brain's hardware is not fixed. For example, the brain can learn to change how it responds to the same sensory stimulus through experience. This is due to changes in the brain's hardware, namely, changes in the structures of synapses in the brain. There is no clean separation between software and hardware in the human brain. Accordingly, it is not possible to compare the functions of computers and human brains by considering only the hardware.

Currently, we do not fully understand how the brain can solve many different types of problems it faces in its various environments. It is not very informative to describe this as switching between different programs, since we do not know how different programs can be chosen in the brain. Nevertheless, before we wrap up our discussion about the analogy between the brain and computers, there is one important question we need to address. In the first chapter of this book, we defined intelligence as the decision-making ability to solve complex problems in a variety of environments. For computers, it is their program that determines what problems they can solve. Therefore, for computers to adapt to different environments and to be truly intelligent, they need the ability to select appropriate programs to solve new problems encountered in different environments. A program capable of solving the problem of selecting a program is referred to as a meta-program. For standard digital computers, a meta-program must be a type of software that forms a bridge between software and hardware. Such meta-programs should recognize the problem the computer hardware has to solve and also possess the knowledge necessary to determine the best program for that problem. Typically, this task is handled by humans. Some specialized software, such as the operating system, can switch between different programs, but this is done only for a limited range of tasks. We humans arrange both the hardware and software of a computer to solve problems we want to solve. A truly intelligent program should be able to function as a meta-program for itself.

The majority of AI programs developed so far perform relatively simple tasks without meta-programs. For example, air conditioners with a thermostat can automatically turn themselves on or off depending on the temperature. Similarly, a robotic vacuum cleaner can return to a charging station automatically after cleaning the entire room. These machines have simple AI in that they can solve the problem they are designed to solve. More recent AI programs, including AlphaGo, are much more powerful, but their ability to select specific problems is similarly limited. If we seriously want to compare human intelligence and AI, then we should compare not only their ability to solve a problem, such as playing Go, but also how they can solve problems arising unexpectedly while they are exploring their environments. Of course, when AI is tested for such abilities, humans should not monitor the AI's performance and provide additional instructions when necessary. AI should be able to perform its task autonomously without communicating with humans. This requirement is essential for AI robots operating far away from Earth.

Computers running AI programs on Earth do not need to worry about their survival, such as power and cooling for normal operation, since these problems can be addressed by their human caretakers or by separate programs. As long as AI requires human caretakers, AI can and will be dedicated to performing tasks specified by humans. Computers and programs not conforming to human desires will be quickly eliminated, although sometimes there may be technical delays. However, AI operating in other planets must be able to take care of its own survival. AI that fails to maintain its normal functions will not be able to solve any other problems.

AI on Mars

If humans colonize another planet in the solar system someday, this will probably be Mars. Venus is not habitable for humans. It is closer to Earth than Mars, but its average surface temperature is about 460°C (860°F), which is hotter than the melting point of lead (327.5°C or 621°F). The atmosphere of Mars is not appropriate for humans, either, since the atmospheric pressure on Mars is less than 1 percent of Earth's. Nevertheless, there is water on Mars. In addition, the duration of a solar day (referred to as sol) for Mars is 24 hours and 40 minutes, so pretty similar to a day on Earth. The fact that Mars might be a relatively habitable environment also implies that there might be or might have been life on Mars.

Human journeys to Mars began in the early 1960s. The exploration of other planets and their moons in the solar system typically proceeds in three stages, from flying by to orbiting and landing. The first fly-by mission to Mars was accomplished by the Mariner 4 spacecraft developed by the U.S. National Aeronautics and Space Administration (NASA; mars.nasa.gov). Mariner 4 left Earth on November 28, 1964 and reached a distance of 9,846 km from Mars on July 15, 1965. It successfully sent 22 digital images of Mars to Earth. The next milestone was Mariner 9, which was launched on May 30, 1971 and became the first successful Mars orbiter. Then, a few years later, in 1975, NASA launched two spacecraft each with an orbiter and a lander. They were Viking 1, which was launched on August 20, 1975 and entered Mars's orbit on June 19, 1976, and Viking 2, which was launched on September 9, 1975 and entered Mars's orbit on August 7, 1976. Their landers arrived successfully on the surface of Mars on July 20 and September 3 in 1976, respectively (Figure 3.4).

Any device sent to explore a celestial body requires many different types of components for a successful mission. This includes machines

Figure 3.4. Photo of a Martian landscape from Viking 1.
Source: Image from the National Aeronautics and Space Administration.

for communication with engineers on Earth as well as batteries or power-generating equipment. For example, Vikings 1 and 2 included radio isotope thermoelectric generators that use plutonium to generate electricity and multiple antennae to communicate with the orbiters or directly with Earth. They included devices to analyze biological, chemical, meteorological, and geological samples. In addition, they also carried a computer and a tape recorder that could store 40 megabits of data. These computers were essential to control the operation of the landers according to the data collected from the on-board sensors and messages received from Earth. However, Viking landers were stationary, so, just like plants, they did not require any of the intelligence necessary for navigation. Eventually, humans started sending robotic vehicles, called rovers, to Mars, opening an era of AI on Mars. We can see some parallel between the development of AI on Mars and the evolution of intelligence in Earth life forms. For example, the ability to move around for survival and reproduction is the most fundamental ability for animals on Earth. This most basic requirement for intelligence applies to Mars rovers as well.

So far, a total of four rovers have landed successfully on Mars (Figure 3.5). The first one was Sojourner, which arrived in July 1997. Therefore, self-driving cars have already existed on Mars for some time. The next two, Spirit and Opportunity, were twins, and they arrived on Mars in January 2004. Curiosity joined them more recently, in August 2012. As of 2019, only Curiosity is still operational. Compared to the stationary landers, these

Figure 3.5. Rovers on Mars.
Source: Image from the National Aeronautics and Space Administration.

rovers must have more complex decision-making abilities, as they must successfully navigate through the unknown Martian terrain. In addition, it is not practical for people on Earth to control the movement of rovers remotely, because they are simply too far away. The distance between Earth and Mars varies between 54.6 million and 401 million km (33.9 million and 249 million miles), with the average distance of 225 million km (139.8 million miles). Therefore, it takes approximately 25 minutes to send and receive a signal between the two planets using radio signals traveling at the speed of light. If a driver on Earth realizes that a rover is about to fall off a cliff on Mars and sends the stop signal as soon as this is detected, the rover will receive that signal about 25 minutes after the potential disaster. Therefore, all rovers sent to Mars require a certain degree of AI, especially for autonomous navigation.

Is Sojourner Still Alive?

Sojourner was the first rover that crisscrossed the surface of Mars, starting in July 1997. It was relatively small, weighing approximately 11.5 kg (25.4 pounds) and included solar panels and a spectrometer. It was equipped with six small wheels with a diameter of 13 cm (about 5 inches). Its top speed was about 1 cm/second (39 yards per hour). The small antenna on Sojourner was too weak to send signals directly to Earth, so they had to be relayed via its companion lander Mars Pathfinder. Sojourner also included three cameras and a computer with 500 kilobytes of memory but did not have the ability to make independent decisions for navigation. Therefore, it navigated according to the following steps. First, Pathfinder collected and sent many photographs of its surrounding area to Earth. Second, based on these images, the engineers on Earth built a detailed three-dimensional model of the area where Pathfinder and Sojourner were located. Third, scientists then sent a set of commands to Sojourner via Pathfinder to drive Sojourner to a new location. This could be done only once a day, which limited the maximum distance of daily travel to about a meter. This is tiny compared to 860 meters or about a half mile that Sojourner could have traveled at its top speed.

Unfortunately, communication with Sojourner ended after about 80 days, which was due to battery failures in Pathfinder, rather than a problem with Sojourner itself. The last command Sojourner received from Earth was to remain stationary for a week and then to circle around Pathfinder. Thus, it is unknown how long Sojourner continued to carry out its final mission, but this was enough to stimulate imagination for many people. It is possible that Pathfinder and Sojourner might still function if their batteries are repaired, as suggested in Hollywood movies like *Red Planet* (2000) and *The Martian* (2015).

Autonomous AI

After losing Pathfinder and Sojourner, NASA launched two more rockets in 2003 to land twin rovers called Spirit and Opportunity. They landed on opposite sides of the planet near its equator on January 4 and 25, 2004, respectively. Like Sojourner, they were also equipped with six wheels, but weighed approximately 180 kg (397 pounds), which was more than 15 times heavier than Sojourner. Sojourner's batteries were not rechargeable, and therefore after they were depleted, Sojourner could operate only during the day using its solar panels, much like ectotherms or cold-blooded animals on Earth that rely on external heat sources in their environment. By contrast, the batteries of the twin rovers were rechargeable, which made it possible to control their body temperature with heaters at night. This is necessary for the rovers to continue their operations at night, when the temperature on Mars can drop to −140°C (−220°F). This also requires an intelligent algorithm to distribute the rover's power between the heater and other devices that consume energy. Endotherms or warm-blooded animals on Earth, such as mammals and birds, face the same problem.

The twin rovers were also equipped with a variety of instruments available to collect high-resolution images and other scientific data. Whereas Sojourner had only three cameras, Spirit and Opportunity each had nine cameras. Of the six cameras used for navigation, four are called hazcams (hazard avoidance cameras). They were mounted on the lower portion of the rover and used for monitoring potential obstacles. Two additional cameras, referred to as navcams (navigation cameras) were mounted on the mast, and provided three-dimensional images to monitor the terrain during navigation. The twin rovers also included a pair of pancams (panoramic cameras), which provided 360° panoramic view of the Martian surface at a resolution similar to that of human vision, as well as a microscopic imager that could take high-resolution (1024 × 1024 pixels) close-up pictures of rocks and soil. The microscopic imager was mounted on the rover's robotic arm, and its position could therefore be controlled more precisely. The robotic arms of Spirit and Opportunity were also equipped with two spectrometers that could ana-lyze the chemical compositions of rocks and soils and the rock abrasion tool (RAT) that could be used to grind away the outer surface of a rock.

To deploy these devices and instruments appropriately, the rovers need AI to address important problems related to navigation and data management. In fact, these are the two most basic problems that all intelligent agents must deal with. First, to explore Mars more efficiently than Sojourner, the new rovers needed the ability to select the trajectory through the Martian terrain autonomously and maneuver themselves safely to the destination chosen by the scientists on Earth. Second, the twin rovers also needed to make constant decisions about which images to send to Earth, because the amount of data collected from nine cameras was simply too much to transmit without ed-iting and curating. These two tasks were handled by specialized AI programs of the rovers.

Autonomous Planetary Mobility (APM) is the name of the AI program responsible for driving the twin rovers to the daily destination chosen by humans on Earth. Without this program, the mobility of the twin rovers would not have been much better than Sojourner, which was limited to about 1 m/day. The limiting factor in the rover's mobility was not its motors or wheels, but rather its ability to control its navigational system. APM allowed the rovers to drive themselves for about 10 seconds at the speed of 5 cm/second, before stopping and analyzing the new images collected by the hazcams and navcams. APM could adjust the trajectory of the rover if it discovered any obstacles. Because of APM, the twin rovers could travel at a speed of 36 m/hour or about a half mile a day, approximately 800 times faster than Sojourner. Most of this improvement was due to APM, rather than to improvement in hardware such as wheels or motors.

Another AI program in twin rovers was Autonomous Exploration for Gathering Increased Science (AEGIS), which controlled the rover's cameras. Although APM and AEGIS might appear to have completely different goals—namely, navigation and image analysis, respectively—their functions were intimately related. First, APM needed the results of image analyses from AEGIS to select its navigational path efficiently. The rover must slow down, for example, if the AEGIS cannot identify the shape and type of objects in its path. Second, the number of images that the AEGIS needs to analyze increases with the speed of the rover. Therefore, AEGIS's task became more challenging and its complexity increased with the efficiency of the APM. AEGIS also played a key role in analyzing and evaluating the images collected by the rover's pancams and microscopic imager. What would happen if the rover cannot evaluate any of the images it collects for their scientific significance? What if only humans on Earth could evaluate them? Without AEGIS, the rovers would simply continue their journey toward the chosen daily destination, even if some of their cameras have captured images of rocks or landscapes of extremely high scientific value. By the time these images are sent to Earth and analyzed by scientists, the rovers would have moved to a completely new location and might have to be sent back to their previous location if additional images are required. If the original images contained evidence of some shy Martian life forms, the opportunity to study them further might be permanently lost. To exploit such opportunities appropriately, AEGIS was provided with knowledge about the type of rocks and landscapes sought by Earth scientists and was capable of making autonomous decisions as to when to stop the rovers to take additional photographs.

The navigation system (APM) and the image analysis program (AEGIS) of the Mars rovers nicely illustrate that the performance of the sensory and motor systems fundamentally constraints each other. Such co-evolution of sensory and motor systems is often seen through evolution of animal nervous systems. This is because the nature of information received by the animal's sensory system changes according to its movement through the environment. For example, images collected by birds and fish while they are flying and swimming, respectively, are fundamentally different, which would be reflected in how those images are analyzed and processed in their nervous systems.

Spirit and Opportunity far exceeded the original expectations of NASA scientists. The expected duration of their original mission was about 90 solar days. However, until communication was lost on March 22, 2010, Spirit lasted 2,210 solar days and drove 7.73 km (4.8 miles). Last communication with Opportunity was on June 10, 2018, after it operated for 5,111 solar days and its odometer read 45.16 km (28.1 miles), more than the distance of a marathon. On February 13, 2019, NASA declared that it lost Opportunity. Currently, there is only one Mars rover, named Curiosity, which landed in August 2012. Curiosity weighs about 900 kg (1,984 pounds), five times the weight of Opportunity. Curiosity's hardware is far superior to that of Opportunity. Curiosity derives its power from a radioisotope thermoelectric generator, which continues to operate even at night. It has better antennae than Opportunity and a total of 17 cameras, almost twice as many as Opportunity. It even includes a backup computer, so it can continue to carry out its task if the main computer fails. Perhaps the most impressive fact is that Curiosity has an infrared laser to vaporize a small portion of Mars surface. After applying the laser, it can identify elements in the rock samples based on the wavelengths of light emitted from them. Interestingly, despite such huge improvement in the hardware, the AI programs for Opportunity and Curiosity are quite similar.

AI was crucial for the success of Mars rovers. Ironically, this success required that humans give up direct control of the rovers. The primary reason for building rovers was to explore Mars. However, once equipped with AI, rovers could begin to make their own decisions independently. For example, imagine that Opportunity discovered a rock that AEGIS indicated to be of high significance and decided to abort its journey to the destination selected by human controllers, instead choosing to spend the rest of the day taking many more pictures to transmit to Earth. This would incur a large amount of cost both in time and electricity. The contents of images might be trivial, and the rover's decision might not have been a good one. However, once the rovers begin acting independently, it is not possible for humans to correct their behavior immediately. Even if humans on Earth are monitoring the behaviors of the rovers continuously, it will take many minutes to discover such unwise behaviors and override the rover's decision. This is an example of the principal–agent problem, in which a principal assigns a task to an agent. In economics, the principal–agent problem arises when the principal tries to control the actions of an agent so as to maximize the principal's interest, after delegating the power to make autonomous decisions to the agent. This problem is common in human societies and is not unique to the relationship between humans and AI. For example, when an employer hires an employee, a principal–agent problem is created. What kind of arrangement should the employer make to provide the employee with a sufficient incentive not to shirk? Fundamentally the same problem exists for the brain. The human brain is a biological machine that evolved to facilitate the process of replicating our genes. From the perspective of genes, the human brain is an agent deputized to find more efficient strategies for genetic self-replication.

AI and Utilities

In the previous chapter, we saw that the problem of decision-making can be simplified if we can assume that all choices are rational and always maximize utility. This is true not only for humans and animals, but also for AI programs, including those used in Mars rovers. For example, the number of possible trajectories a rover can choose between its current position and its destination could be infinite. If the rover is lucky and is placed on a flat surface without any obstacles, then it can choose the straight line between its current location and the destination to minimize the time and energy of relocation. However, if there are multiple obstacles, then the problem of selecting the best route is not trivial. A common technique in such cases is to define a utility function that can be computed for each possible trajectory, so that the rover can select the trajectory that maximizes the utility function. Without using a utility function, engineers would have to preselect the rover's trajectory for each of all possible obstacle locations. Instead, the rover can receive an algorithm to calculate the utility not only according to the information about the obstacles, but also using the distance to the destination, time allowed for the travel, the amount of available energy, the acceptable risk or probability of physical damage, and so forth. With such utility functions, the rover has the AI to select its pathway autonomously according to the current condition of its environment. Indeed, computations based on utilities or values are common in the field of AI. For example, AlphaGo learned to play Go better than humans using the deep reinforcement learning algorithm that updates the values of various moves through simulation. As we will examine more closely in the second half of this book, such algorithms improve their decision-making strategies iteratively by updating quantities like utilities according to new and unexpected information from real or simulated environments. In short, utility plays an important role in a variety of fields ranging from economics and psychology to AI.

Robot Society and Swarm Intelligence

It is not possible to understand human intelligence and behavior adequately without considering social contexts. Virtually all human behaviors occur in social domains. This includes even such simple movements such as saccades, as we saw in the first chapter of this book. Currently, the largest discrepancies between human intelligence and AI might also be in the social domain. Nevertheless, as AI technology continues to improve and as the amount of communication between AI robots begins to increase, the nature of social communication among machines will become more complicated. Once AI robots begin to interact among themselves more efficiently than humans do, this will have monumental impact on our society.

Even if Opportunity is still operating, it is unlikely that Opportunity and Curiosity would make any direct physical contact, since they were more than 8,000 km (5,000 miles) away from each other. Besides, their AI programs focus on the image analysis and autonomous navigation. Therefore, we would not expect any meaningful communication or inter-action between them, such as cooperating to accomplish some missions more efficiently. Nevertheless, we can still speculate that as the number of rovers and other robots on Mars increases, the frequency and intensity of social communications and physical cooperation will increase. As a simple example, if sharing weather information among different rovers and robots becomes possible, this would allow them to seek shelter more efficiently for their safety. If one of them discovers important information about the Mars landscape or possible life forms and needs additional memory to store new image files, they might share their storage space. However, to make such co-operation possible, there should be a set of rules that determine the priority of various tasks. For example, if two rovers both require additional memory at the same time, who decides which images are more important? Resolving such conflicts might not be easy. As humans never stop arguing about whose preferences and opinions are more important, we might someday see AI robots on Mars arguing about the importance of the data and knowledge they have acquired.

Once AI robots begin to interact physically, even more interesting social problems related to cooperation will occur. For example, once rovers begin to share their energy, some rovers might be expected to donate energy to others engaged in a more important task. In some cases, we might expect a rover to sacrifice itself to save another rover. To fulfill any complex mis-sion, robots must have the ability to protect themselves from unexpected harm. Namely, robots should be selfish. Without direct orders from humans, it might be tricky to induce such selfish robots to sacrifice themselves to save other robots. Humans have not yet learned to resolve such conflicts com-pletely. We do not fully understand why and when humans choose to behave altruistically and cooperate with others.

If the number of active robots on Mars continues to increase someday, this might lead to swarm intelligence. Swarm intelligence refers to the emergence of well-organized behaviors in a large group of agents each communicating only with a relatively small number of other agents, even without a central leader who directs everyone else on how to behave. Swarm intelligence is common in biological systems, such as ant or bee colonies.

In animal and human societies, hierarchical structures are also common. It is therefore possible that someday many Mars rovers might be controlled by a rover leader with superior AI and hardware. Indeed, in the science fiction "Catch That Rabbit" by Isaac Asimov, a robot named Dave controls six subsidiary robots called "fingers" to carry out a mining project. Unfortunately, Dave begins to order other robots to perform strange marches or dances whenever it faces unexpected situations without humans around. Eventually, humans come up with the hypothesis that this might result from overburdening Dave with managerial responsibility and fix the problem by blowing up one of the fingers. As suggested in this story, AI robots in the future will face significant challenges in dealing with many different types of social dilemmas with other robots and humans. Similarly, to fully understand the human brain and intelligence, it is essential to consider how animals have found solutions in problems they face in social settings through evolution.

In the future, we might witness the arrival of AI robots with the ability to make decisions to improve their own well-being. It is difficult to accurately predict how they would behave, but this frequently stimulates our imagination. Such robots are more likely to arise once they acquire the ability to replicate or repair themselves, like humans and animals. To be able to predict the behavior of such robots more accurately, we must analyze the basic questions related to life. We have defined intelligence as the ability of life forms to find solutions to complex problems encountered in a variety of complex environments. In the next chapter, we will examine more closely how the brain and its intelligence emerged during the evolution of life.

References

Bostrom N (2014) Superintelligence: Paths, Dangers, Strategies. New York, NY: Oxford Univ. Press.

Kurzweil R (2005) The Singularity is Near: When Humans Transcend Biology. New York, NY: Penguin Books.

Merolla PA, Arthur JV, Alvarez-Icaza R, et al. (2016) A million spiking-neuron integrated circuit with a scalable communication network and interface. Science. 345: 668–673.

Further Reading

Horowitz P, Hill W (2015) The Art of Electronics. 3rd ed. Cambridge, England: Cambridge Univ. Press.

Koch C (1999) Biophysics of Computation: Information Processing in Single Neurons. New York, NY: Oxford Univ. Press.

Pyle R, Manning R (2012) Destination Mars: New Explorations of the Red Planet. Amherst, NY: Prometheus.

Stone P, Brooks R, Brynjolfsson E, et al. (2016) Artificial Intelligence and Life in 2030: One Hundred Year Study on Artificial Intelligence: Report of the 2015–2016 Study Panel, Stanford University, Stanford, CA. http://ai100.stanford.edu/2016-report. Accessed September 6, 2016.

4

Self-Replicating Machines

If an animal is eaten by another animal, its most likely outcome is death. However, this is not always the case. For example, parasitic or intestinal worms like helminths would welcome the opportunity to be eaten by their hosts, since they need to steal nutrients from inside the host's body. These parasitic worms must have evolved from ancestors who were lucky enough to survive and reproduce even after they were unintentionally eaten by their predators. During evolution, they must have gradually developed more efficient means by which they could protect themselves from the stomach acid and other digestive enzymes of their hosts. Now, what happens to these parasites when their hosts themselves are eaten by other predators? The parasites might have to transform their bodies to survive more effectively inside the body of the new hosts. However, if the parasites can adapt, the body of the new host might present an even better opportunity. The new host is almost certainly higher in the food pyramid and is likely to provide more nutrients and space for the parasites to grow and multiply.

Many parasites not only steal nutrients from their hosts, but also change the brain and behaviors of their hosts to benefit themselves. For example, nematomorph hairworms, called *Spinochordodes tellinii*, grow inside the body of insects like grasshoppers and crickets. When they are ready to reproduce, the worms can cause their hosts to jump into water by manipulating the proteins in the host nervous system. This usually drowns the hosts, but allows the worms to leave the host's body and reproduce in water. The strategies used by parasites become even more sophisticated when they need to move to new hosts for reproduction. For some helminths, this means that their current hosts must be eaten by new hosts, and it would be beneficial to make their hosts attracted to predators. For example, parasitic flatworms called *Leucochloridium paradoxum* live inside snails, but when they are ready to reproduce, they make the hosts less sensitive to light, thereby encouraging the snails to get exposed to predators, often birds, who will become new hosts for the worm. To make the infected snails more visible to predators, the worms will invade the snail's eyestalk and produce a colorful pulsating

Figure 4.1. Leucochloridium paradoxum penetrating the left eyestalk of a land snail.

Source: Image from Wikipedia under the terms of the GNU free documentation license.

display, making the eyestalk look like a caterpillar (Figure 4.1). Another example is an intracellular protozoan parasite called *Toxoplasma gondii*, which infects many types of warm-blooded animals, including humans. *Toxoplasma gondii* can reproduce only inside cats. Nevertheless, they often infest rodents and can alter rats' behavior to make them more likely to get captured by their predators. Normally, rats are averse to cat urine. However, rats infected with *Toxoplasma gondii* become attracted to cats' urine. *Toxoplasma gondii* increase their numbers inside the rat's digestive tract and then invade the rat's brain via the bloodstream. Once inside the brain, *Toxoplasma gondii* form cysts and begin to manipulate the expression of a chemical called vasopressin to reduce the rat's fear of cats (Berdoy et al., 2000).

A host might lose the ability to select the behaviors most beneficial to it, when its brain is controlled by parasites. Such hosts might even choose suicidal behaviors. Clearly, such self-destructive behavior does not reflect the intelligence of the host. Instead, they are the product of the parasite's intelligence. Intelligence can be properly assessed only with respect to a subject or agent who both chooses specific behaviors and is affected by the outcomes of their choices. For example, intelligent rats must be good at escaping from cats, whereas intelligent *Toxoplasma gondii* must be good at controlling infected rats to follow cats. Similarly, when AlphaGo defeated Sedol Lee, it might be inappropriate to attribute this feat to the intelligence of AlphaGo. This remarkable accomplishment clearly belongs to the scientists and programmers at DeepMind. The problem they faced was to develop a program that can defeat the best human Go player, and the success of their mission attests to their intelligence.

Intelligence is closely related to the goals of the life forms that own it. However, this does not mean that intelligent animals can choose any arbitrary goal. There are at least two important requirements for the goals that can be adopted by intelligent agents. First, the goals of intelligent agents should be temporally stable. If the goals change every moment, they cannot be accomplished. The more complex and more difficult a goal gets, the longer it is necessary to maintain the same goal. Second, the goal of any intelligent behavior should include self-preservation. Self-destruction cannot be an ultimate goal of any intelligent agent, since agents with successful self-destructive skills will cease to exist quickly.

How can an intelligent agent preserve itself? As time passes, everything breaks down into an orderless state. According to the second law of thermodynamics, all complex buildings and human artifacts will eventually crumble to dust after enough time passes. A machine with more complex internal structure would be broken more easily and stop functioning, since the probability that an important part would be broken increases with the number of such parts. By contrast, living organisms appear to maintain their complex internal structures almost indefinitely. However, this is not a violation of the second law of thermodynamics. Life forms can resist the passage of time and maintain their appearance, because they replicate themselves and multiply in number. The best possible strategy for an intelligent agent to preserve itself is to replicate as much as possible. Self-replication is the essence of life. This suggests that intelligence might be a feature of life. Living things require intelligence to preserve themselves. This is also why intelligence can be found only in living things. In this chapter, we will review how self-replicating machines have emerged, and how such machines have become more and more efficient through evolution. The history and evolution of life includes everything ranging from ribonucleic acid (RNA) and deoxyribonucleic acid (DNA) to cells and the brain. The brain and its intelligence might be the most amazing device invented by genes for their replication during evolution.

Self-Replicating Machines

All life forms on Earth consist of cells whose outer surface consists of two layers (bilayers) of lipid molecules. These cells can divide under appropriate conditions and therefore they can increase their number exponentially. Cells contain genetic material in the form of DNA, which is replicated and transferred to newly formed cells after each cell division. Although this is how all living cells on Earth divide, it would be unjustifiable to define life as a physical system surrounded by lipid bilayers that replicates its DNA. For example, life forms demarcated by something other than lipid bilayers and replicating genetic materials other than DNA might exist on other planets. The essence of life is not specific chemicals like DNA, but the process of self-replication. Life can be defined as a physical system or machine that replicates itself (Figure 4.2).

Self-replicating machines inevitably have other properties we commonly associate with life. First, all self-replicating machines will have heredity. This necessarily follows from successful self-replication. Self-replication should lead to another copy of the original, so self-replicating life forms should produce offspring closely resembling their parents in their physical traits. A second property of life expected from self-replication is a set of complex chemical processes collectively referred to as metabolism. A self-replicating

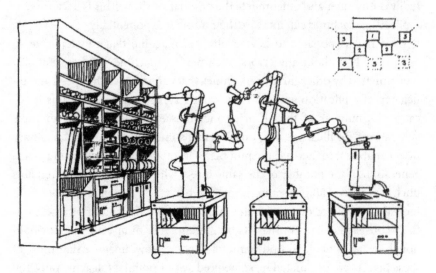

Figure 4.2. A simple imaginary self-replicating machine.
Source: From a National Aeronautics and Space Administration conference publication (1982). Public domain.

machine must collect all the necessary raw materials or parts from its environment and assemble them appropriately. This process requires energy from the environment. Most plants use light energy from the sun for this purpose, but other life forms, including animals, steal chemical energy from plants or other life forms. There are other less common strategies to obtain energy. For example, microorganisms known as archaebacteria live in deep sea and support their metabolism using thermal and chemical energy emanating from openings in the sea floor, known as hydrothermal vents. One way or another, self-replicating machines must get the necessary energy from their environment.

The third property of life is evolution. Evolution results from errors in the process of self-replication. No physical system can be completely safe from unexpected perturbations from its environment, and self-replicating machines are no exception. There will always be some probability that self-replicating machines will make errors. Since these errors will occur randomly, they usually diminish the efficiency and accuracy of replications. Most such harmful errors would be outnumbered and gradually eliminated by other correct copies of the machines that can replicate better. However, these random errors will occasionally produce copies that can replicate themselves better than the original. Even though there would be fewer such new machines in the beginning, machines that can replicate better will eventually outnumber and outcompete the original versions. This is because self-replicating machines can increase their number exponentially.

Even if it is possible to have a physical machine that can replicate itself perfectly without any errors, such perfect machine will be eventually outcompeted by other inferior machines that can improve the speed and efficiency of replication gradually by making some errors. Again, this is because the number of the offspring increases exponentially over multiple generations. To illustrate this, imagine that some mutation in an imaginary insect enables it to increase the number of its offspring by 20 percent in each generation. If the number of the same insect without this mutation remains unchanged, after 50 generations, the number of the mutated insects would increase by a factor of more than 9,000. If the population of this insect initially consisted equally of these two different types of insects, then it would now be very difficult to find unmutated ones. Now, imagine that most of these insects are decimated by some predator or pollutant, leaving only 100 lucky insects alive. In this case, the probability that the remaining population would include any slowly replicating, original strain of insects is only about

1 percent. Furthermore, the environment for any life form is likely to change over time. This is also likely to favor life forms that replicate themselves with some errors over perfect self-replicating machines. Evolution is a process in which life continuously adapts to its environment.

Natural History of Self-Replicating Machines

How life first emerged on Earth is still a mystery. Nevertheless, from the basic requirements for self-replicating machines, it is possible to make some inferences about what very early forms of life might have looked like. For example, it is reasonable to assume that early life forms had much simpler structures than those living today, since they would have lacked sophisticated cellular machinery necessary for precise self-replication. Speed and accuracy of self-replication must have improved gradually through evolution.

Perhaps the most important first step in unlocking the secrets of the origin of life is to find out the simplest chemical structure that can replicate itself in a laboratory. Such a chemical should have the following properties. First, the number of parts required for self-replication should be relatively small, and it should be relatively simple to assemble all the parts to complete the replication. It is likely that all the parts in very early life forms were similar in their size and physical properties, since this would be easier to handle than having many heterogeneous parts. Second, the shape and structure of these early life forms should be relatively easy to build using their parts. Third, they should be durable, and ideally they should be able to maintain their structural integrity during multiple cycles of replication. In chemistry, a polymer is a relatively large molecule made of many smaller subunits, so is a good candidate for a self-replicating chemical. Indeed, all life forms on Earth use two polymers, RNA and DNA, as their genetic materials. These two polymers are examples of polynucleotides, because their subunits are molecules known as nucleotides (Figure 4.3). There are important differences between RNA and DNA. As we will see in the following discussion, some of these differences have led many biologists to speculate that RNA might have played a critical role in the origin of life (Higgs and Lehman, 2015).

The chemical units comprising RNA are called ribonucleotides (Figure 4.3), so RNA is a string of ribonucleotides. Each ribonucleotide consists of three smaller units, including a type of sugar called ribose, a phosphate, and a nitrogenous base. The nitrogenous base included in RNA, which is often

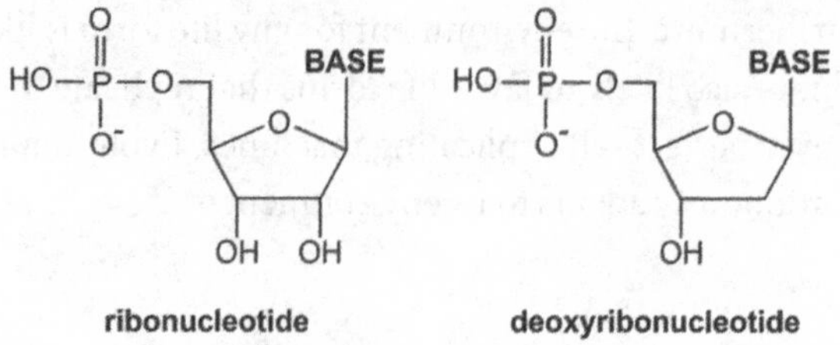

Figure 4.3. Ribonucleotide (left) and deoxyribonucleotide (right) are the building blocks of RNA and DNA, respectively.

just referred to as base, can be one of four different types: guanine, uracil, adenine, and cytosine. These four different bases then give rise to four different ribonucleotides, which are referred to as guanosine, uridine, adenosine, and cytidine monophosphates, respectively. Accordingly, RNA can be specified using a string of letters each indicating the base of the ribonucleotide, such as G (guanosine), U (uridine), A (adenosine), and C (cytidine). For example, RNA consisting of five guanosines can be written as GGGGG.

One important property of RNA useful for self-replication is that ribonucleotides tend to form specific pairs. Namely, A and U tend to form pairs, while G and C tend to form pairs. This gives RNA the ability to produce its complementary copy. For example, an RNA segment consisting of AACUGA will produce UUGACU. If this new RNA segment produces its complementary copy, this will correspond to the replica of the origin RNA. RNA can replicate itself.

However, successful self-replication requires more than just the presence of hereditary materials like RNA. If every step of replication relied on a chance encounter with the correct nucleotide, the speed of RNA replication would be extremely low. In fact, in addition to these hereditary materials that must be copied and transmitted to the next generation, all living things on Earth possess machinery to facilitate their replication. For most life forms, self-replication is accomplished by an enormously complex sequence of chemical reactions, and they are accelerated by various catalysts. Catalysts must have appropriate three-dimensional shapes to arrange individual chemical ingredients in precise locations.

It is extremely unlikely that a particular hereditary substance and a matching catalyst capable of copying that substance would find each other by chance, if they were randomly mixed with many other chemicals. It is far more likely that the first self-replicating chemical had dual functions and worked both as genetic material and as a catalyst for its own replication. A chemical facilitating the very same chemical reaction that produces it is called an autocatalyst. Therefore, the first life forms might have been autocatalysts. RNA can function as an autocatalyst, which is why RNA is often thought to be ancestors to all life forms on Earth. Not only can RNA store genetic information like a string of letters using four different types of ribonucleotides, its three-dimensional structure can change depending on the order of different ribonucleotides. Using such unique three-dimensional structures, some RNA might facilitate the assembly of its parts. RNA that functions as a catalyst is referred to as a ribozyme. For example, a ligase is a type of ribozyme that can combine two short RNA segments to create a longer RNA (Figure 4.4). In fact, a system of ligase ribozymes that can replicate itself has been constructed in a laboratory (Lincoln and Joyce, 2009).

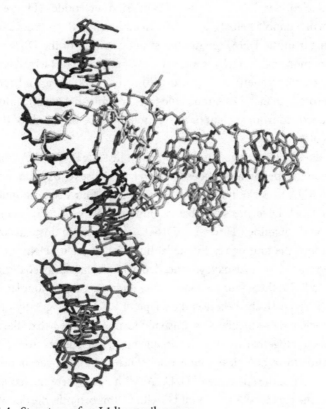

Figure 4.4. Structure of an L1 ligase ribozyme.

Source: Robertson MP, Scott WG (2007) The structural basis of ribozyme-catalyzed RNA assembly. Science 315: 1549–1553. Reprinted with permission from AAAS.

This demonstrated the feasibility of the idea that life might have originally emerged as a self-replicating system of ligase ribozymes.

It is easy to imagine that once multiple self-replicating systems of RNA emerged, they would immediately begin to compete with each other to secure the parts necessary for replication, such as ribonucleotides or short RNA segments. This would have gradually increased the number of RNA with a higher rate of replication compared to slowly replicating RNA. Through such natural selection, the rate of RNA replication would have slowly increased. However, RNA is not ideal for information storage, because it is not a stable medium. For example, ribose sugar in RNA makes RNA chemically less stable than deoxyribose sugar, which is used in DNA. Therefore, at some point during RNA evolution, self-replicating ribozymes might have started adopting a strategy of writing and storing their genetic information more safely using DNA. Whereas RNA typically takes the form of a single strand of ribonucleotides, DNA consists of deoxyribonucleotides (Figure 4.3) and often form a double helix (Figure 4.5). In addition to the presence of a more stable sugar in the DNA, the double-stranded shape of the DNA makes its structure more stable. DNA is indeed very stable, which is why it is still possible to recover genetic information from the 40,000-year-old remains of Neanderthals. In fact, DNA molecules are so stable that genetic information can be decoded from ancient bacteria thought to be hundreds of thousands of years old.

How does DNA store genetic information? Just like RNA, DNA is built from four different types of nucleotides. However, DNA uses deoxyribonucleotides, whereas RNA uses ribonucleotides. Three of the four deoxyribonucleotides used in DNA have the same bases found in RNA, namely, adenine, cytosine, and guanine. However, DNA uses thymine instead of uracil. Accordingly, the four deoxyribonucleotides that make up DNA are referred to as deoxyadenosine, deoxycytidine, deoxyguanosine, and deoxythymidine. Similar to RNA, these four nucleotides are often denoted by four letters: A, C, G, and T, respectively. Whereas the shape of RNA varies greatly depending on its nucleotide sequence, DNA usually form a double helix, like a pair of wires twisted together. Within the double helix, nucleotides from two opposite strands form chemical connections, known as hydrogen bonds, which further stabilize the structure of DNA. As with RNA, these nucleotides bond with specific partners: A with T and C with G. Importantly, the double helical structure of DNA provides a very convenient way to replicate itself. During self-replication, the double helix of DNA opens like a zipper, and each strand

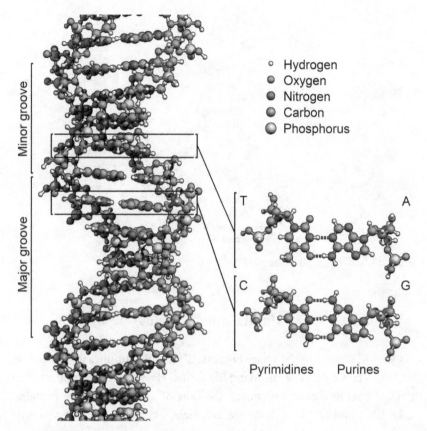

Figure 4.5. Structure of DNA.
Source: Image from Wikipedia under the terms of the GNU free documentation license.

of DNA then attracts new nucleotides that are complementary to the old nucleotides in the original DNA (Figure 4.6). Self-replication is complete when the new nucleotides are chemically bonded and get separated to form two copies of the original DNA.

The period before DNA emerged as the storage medium of genetic information is referred to as the RNA world (Figure 4.7). Currently, we live in the DNA world, in which DNA is the primary genetic material and RNA assists in the replication of genetic material. All current life forms on Earth store their genetic information in DNA. However, RNA is still used as genetic material in some viruses. These so-called RNA viruses are responsible for many diseases, including Ebola, hepatitis C, polio, measles, and even the common cold.

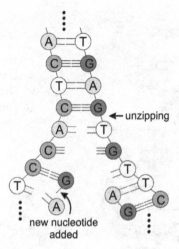

Figure 4.6. DNA replication.

Multitalented Proteins

As we will discuss in the following text, RNA still continues to function as an important catalyst in all living life forms. However, most catalysts that control chemical reactions inside the cells of all life forms are proteins. Like RNA and DNA, proteins are polymers, but they are made of amino

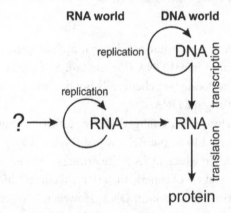

Figure 4.7. Replication in RNA world and DNA world. In the RNA world, RNA functions as an autocatalyst. In the DNA world, genetic information is stored in DNA, whereas proteins work as catalysts.

acids. Proteins are versatile, and they perform many different functions. Some proteins provide structural support in our body, such as keratin in our hairs and collagen in our skin. Therefore, not all proteins are catalysts, and those that functions as catalysts are referred to as enzymes. Just as the three-dimensional structure of RNA can change with the sequence of its nucleotides, the shape and function of a protein can vary according to the sequence of its amino acids. Whereas RNA and DNA use only four different types of nucleotides, proteins are created from 20 different amino acids. Accordingly, proteins with complex forms or functions can be created much more easily than RNA or DNA.

Proteins and enzymes carry out countless jobs inside cells. They are responsible for replicating DNA, producing the chemical fuel necessary for various cellular functions, and removing chemical wastes from cells. How are proteins with so many functions then created? Interestingly, it is RNA that still plays a central role in protein synthesis. This is another reason why many scientists speculate that RNA and ribozymes might have been catalysts for all chemical reactions necessary for the replication of RNA and even DNA before proteins took up such responsibilities.

Proteins are not produced directly from DNA, but rather indirectly from a type of RNA called messenger RNA (mRNA), which is created by an enzyme called RNA polymerase. RNA polymerase assembles different ribonucleotides according to the base sequence of DNA. This process is referred to as transcription. Once mRNA is synthesized, it exits the nucleus and docks with a chemical factory called ribosome, in which protein synthesis takes place according to the information written in the mRNA (Figure 4.8). This process is referred to as translation.

There is a major problem in translating the sequence of nucleotides in RNA to a protein, in that the number of different amino acids used in protein is much greater than the number of different nucleotides. There are only four different nucleotides in RNA, whereas proteins are created using 20 different amino acids. Therefore, it is not possible to translate each nucleotide to a single amino acid in a one-to-one fashion. Interestingly, all life forms on Earth adopted the same solution to this problem, suggesting that this solution was adopted very early in the history of life. This universal solution is to specify each amino acid in a protein using a sequence of three nucleotides. A sequence of three nucleotides that specifies a single amino acid is referred to as a codon. Since a sequence of three nucleotides can create 4^3 or 64 different patterns, most amino acids can be coded by more than one codon.

For example, one of the amino acids, glutamine, is coded by two different codons, CAA and CAG.

During translation, the amino acid corresponding to each codon in the mRNA has to be transported to the ribosome and attached to a new growing protein. Interestingly, this important step in translation is also handled by a type of RNA known as the transfer RNA (tRNA). A part of a tRNA binds to a codon in mRNA, while another region carrying an amino acid (Figure 4.8). tRNA works like a shuttle for protein production. After donating an amino acid to the ribosome, it undocks, finds another amino acid that matches its anticodon with the help of an enzyme called aminoacyl tRNA transferase, and returns to the ribosome again to deliver it.

Translation always starts from the start codon, a special code signaling the start of the protein. There are also three so-called nonsense codons, UAA, UGA, and UAG, which do not have corresponding amino acids. These nonsense codons terminate the translation and release the newly completed protein from the ribosome. These nonsense codons are also referred to as stop codons. A gene refers to a region in the DNA that encodes a protein and corresponds to the interval between the start and stop codons. The entire collection of genes for a life form is referred to as a genome.

It is likely that life on Earth started as an RNA system. Self-replicating systems of RNA must have evolved to become more complex life forms through a division of labor by which DNA and proteins become the media for storing genetic information and catalysts, respectively. In this scenario, RNA delegates some of its responsibilities to DNA and proteins. During evolution,

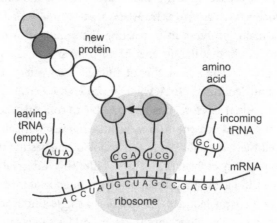

Figure 4.8. Protein synthesis at ribosome.

efficiency of self-replication improved. Such an increase in efficiency is often accomplished by a division of labor and specialization. The transition from the RNA world to the DNA world is a good example, and as we will see next, emergence of multicellular organisms is another.

In addition to proteins and genetic materials, all living life forms on Earth include another important component, which is the membrane surrounding individual cells. All life forms are made of cells, and cellular membranes create the physical barriers between the interior and exterior of a cell. Without cellular membranes, all the chemicals necessary for the replication of DNA, such as RNA and proteins, would be constantly diluted with other chemicals in the environment, severely limiting the efficiency of self-replication. Therefore, the emergence of cells and cellular membranes mark another major event in the evolution of life. In all life forms, the climax of self-replication is cell division, which takes place after the replication of DNA and other chemical components inside the mother cell is completed.

Multicellular Organisms

Another groundbreaking event during the evolution of life was the emergence of multicellular organisms (Figure 4.9). Although cellular membrane can protect a life form and facilitates the process of self-replication, it introduces a limit on how large a cell can be. This is because the amount of

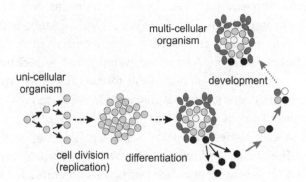

Figure 4.9. Self-replication in unicellular and multicellular organisms. Light gray disks indicate undifferentiated cells, whereas black disks indicate germ cells.

materials that must be imported and exported through the cell membrane increases proportionally with its volume. However, since the ratio between its surface area and volume decreases with the cell size, the efficiency of cellular metabolism would also decrease with the cell size. A physical limit in cell size then implies a limit in its structure and function and, most important, in the ability of a single cell to solve complex problems for its replication, limiting the intelligence of a single-cell organism. By contrast, multicellular organisms can maintain a more complex structure by producing multiple types of cells specialized in different functions through the process referred to as differentiation. To develop a sophisticated control center, such as the brain, some cells need to specialize for communication with other cells in the body. Multicellularity is a prerequisite for a higher level of intelligence.

During evolution, division of labor plays a key role in improving the efficiency of self-replication. In essence, the transition from the RNA world to the DNA world is also an example of specialization. In the RNA world, RNA was responsible for all the functions of life, and it transitioned to the DNA world through division of labor among RNA, DNA, and protein. Similarly, it is the division of labor and specialization that makes multicellular organisms possible. Multicellular organisms can have different organs dedicated to various functions, such as immune response and circulation, only because they can produce different types of cells with special functions, such as immune cells and blood cells. In a multicellular organism that reproduces sexually, all cells of an organism are derived from a single cell, namely, a fertilized egg. They can be grouped into germ cells and somatic cells. Germ cells maintain the ability to produce sperms and eggs and can contribute to producing new life forms. By contrast, somatic cells die with the individual organism. In most animals, including humans, the vast majority of cells in our body are somatic cells. The brain is entirely composed of somatic cells, so all the memory of an individual perishes with the death of the individual. As Richard Dawkins pointed out, somatic cells are responsible for assisting in the maintenance and replication of genetic material contained in the germ cells and can be viewed as their temporary survival machines (Dawkins, 2006).

How can cells derived from the same fertilized egg have different functions? This can happen because individual cells are capable of producing different set of proteins appropriate for the function of each cell. A gene determines which protein will be produced but does not specify how much should be produced. Since the space inside a cell is limited and many different types of proteins are needed for normal metabolism, the amount of each protein that is synthesized should be strictly controlled. This important task is again accomplished by a collaboration between DNA and proteins. DNA includes two different components; the coding regions that contain information about the sequences of amino acids for various proteins and the noncoding regions called regulatory elements that control the level of transcription. Therefore, not all nucleotides in DNA are used to encode the sequence of amino acids. Noncoding DNA was once referred to as junk DNA, because it did not appear to have any function at all. It is now understood that a substantial portion of noncoding DNA plays an important role in controlling the quantity of various proteins that should be produced in a given cell.

A special group of proteins referred to as transcription factors can bind to the regulatory elements of DNA segments that code other proteins. Namely, the rate of protein production can increase or decrease depending on whether appropriate transcription factors are bound to a regulatory element or not. As a fertilized egg undergoes many cell divisions and the resulting cells differentiate and acquire distinct structures and functions, numerous transcription factors direct individual cells to produce the right amount of each protein. If transcription factors are responsible for developing specific organs in different parts of the animal's body, then the concentration of transcription factors critically involved in the development of an animal should vary systematically across different areas of the body. For example, a transcription factor called Bicoid is present in a high concentration in the part of the developing animal that will eventually become the animal's head. Similarly, Hox transcription factors are expressed in specific segments of the body, such as the head and limbs, and control the development of specific body parts in correct positions along the head–tail axis. Therefore, different cells can acquire specialized functions as a result of signals delivered by various transcription factors.

Brain Evolution

We can now turn our attention to how the brains of animals might have evolved. Among the many different types of cells in multicellular organisms, muscle cells are particularly important for the evolution of intelligence, because they allow animals to change their position rapidly. To harness the full power of muscle cells, however, they must be controlled accurately according to the condition of the animal's environment as well as their internal state.

This requires a special group of cells that can rapidly transmit information from one part of the animal's body to another. This is precisely the function of neurons and nervous systems. As we already observed in earlier chapters of this book, the shape and complexity of nervous systems vary greatly, from *C. elegans* to jellyfish and cockroaches and to mammals. Unfortunately, fossils of nervous systems are extremely rare, which makes it very challenging to study their evolution. Nevertheless, it is possible to make some inference about the evolution of nervous systems by comparing how their structure and function vary across today's animal kingdom. Recently, it also became possible to estimate when different species of the animal kingdom diverged from common ancestors based on the analysis of DNA sequences.

What did the first animals on Earth look like? It is estimated that animals first appeared on Earth approximately 600 million years ago. Could they have had nervous systems? If so, how might they have worked? Many paleobiologists speculate that the earliest animals might have looked similar to sponges and other animals that belong to the group Porifera (Figure 4.10). Unlike most animals, sponges do not have any muscle cells or neurons and live most of their lives attached to rocks and other surfaces. Despite this sedentary lifestyle, sponges are not plants. Unlike plant cells, sponges' cells do not have cell walls, and they derive the nutrients they need from other living things, such as bacteria. Although sponges do not have any muscle cells, their bodies are covered by a group of cells called pinacocytes, which are capable of some contraction that leads to slow movements. Like sponges,

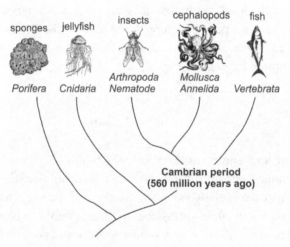

Figure 4.10. Evolutionary tree for animals.

it is possible that the earliest animals might have lacked muscle cells and neurons. However, not everyone agrees with this view, and some scientists believe another group of animals called Ctenophora, similar to comb jellies, might have been the first animals and even evolved neurons independently from other animals.

All animals must steal the energy and nutrients they need from other living things, since they are incapable of photosynthesis. Therefore, muscles and neurons must have been valuable inventions for animals. Even if the function of the earliest muscles and neurons might not have been sophisticated by today's standards, they would have still given the animal a substantial advantage in hunting compared to other sedentary animals. Among animals living today, the simplest nervous systems can be found in a group of animals called Cnidaria that includes jellyfish. Accordingly, some paleobiologists believe neurons appeared first in the ancestors of jellyfish, although others believe that the ancestors of a different group of animals called comb jellies might have developed nervous systems earlier. The nervous system of jellyfish and comb jellies do not have a centralized structure like the brain. Instead, neurons in their nervous system are arranged in a more diffuse structure called a nerve net. It is likely that neurons in the earliest nervous system were similarly decentralized and mostly controlled the contraction of nearby muscle cells only.

It is thought that the prototypes of all existing animal species emerged during the early Cambrian period, which began about 540 million years ago and lasted 60 million years (Figure 4.10). Because so many species emerged during the first 20 million years or so of the Cambrian period, this time is often referred to as the Cambrian explosion. All life forms of the animal kingdom are divided into about 35 different groups known as phyla. For example, all vertebrates, including humans, belong to the phylum called Chordata. The phylum Arthropoda includes such animals as insects and shrimps, whereas the phylum Mollusca includes animals like squid and octopus. All of these phyla appeared during the Cambrian period. Nevertheless, some types of multicellular animals probably existed even before the Cambrian period, so the true explosive nature of the Cambrian explosion is still somewhat controversial.

Given that animals as diverse as arthropods, mollusks, and vertebrates already started evolving independently more than 500 million years ago, it is perhaps not too surprising that there is a huge difference in the structure of nervous systems throughout the animal kingdom. For example, in all animals that belong to the phyla Chordata (chordates), neurons are concentrated in the form of a tube at the upper side of the animal's body. This tube-like structure, called the dorsal neural tube, is thought to be a prototype of the vertebrate nervous system. During evolution of vertebrate animals, the mouth and multiple sensory organs as well as the neurons functionally related to these sensory organs gradually became concentrated at the front of the animal that eventually became the head. This process is referred to as cephalization.

In vertebrates, visual, auditory, and olfactory information is all collected from the sensory organs in the animal's head. It is more efficient to place all the neurons involved in analyzing and storing the sensory information close to the sensory organs themselves. Placing all these neurons close together has another advantage: this also makes it easier to synthesize the information from multiple sensory organs for the purpose of detecting important changes in the animal's environment and using that information to make important decisions. This is how the brain evolved. Thus, the brain of vertebrate is like a centralized government. In all vertebrate animals, the brain and the spinal cord together form the central nervous system. Almost all complex decisions about the animal's behavior take place inside the brain, whereas the spinal cord is largely responsible for transmitting a variety of sensory and motor signals between the brain and the rest of the body.

Some animals have nervous systems that look very different from those of vertebrates. For example, the nervous systems of many arthropods and mollusks consist of multiple clusters of neurons, called ganglia, which are connected by nerve cords or fibers. Even without a brain, neurons in a ganglion can still make necessary decisions, depending on where they are located within the animal's body. Figuratively speaking, the nervous system of invertebrate animals is a like a decentralized government.

The human brain has amazing abilities. In addition, most animals we often consider smart and highly intelligent, such as dogs and monkeys, are all vertebrate animals. It is tempting to conclude that the brains of vertebrate animals make them more intelligent than invertebrate animals. However, it is difficult to justify this claim. As a counterexample, we can consider the octopus, which is arguably one of the most intelligent animals in the invertebrate world. First, octopuses have eyes that resemble a camera, in that it has a pupil, lens, and retina. These sophisticated eyes provide octopuses the ability to analyze the details of different objects in their environments. Interestingly, camera-type eyes of octopuses have evolved independently from the eyes of the vertebrate animals. Second, octopuses display highly complex behaviors. For example, in a laboratory setting, an octopus can shoot water selectively toward some people, suggesting that they can distinguish between different human individuals and might even dislike some of them. It is well known that octopuses can manipulate complex objects and, for example, can learn to open a bottle. They are also excellent escape artists. This is likely due to many neurons in their nervous systems. It is estimated that the nervous system of an octopus contains about 500 million neurons, which is more than the number of neurons in many vertebrate animals, such as pigeons or rats. It is a prejudice to think that all invertebrate animals are less intelligent than vertebrates. Nevertheless, we know very little about the nervous systems of octopuses and other invertebrate animals with complex nervous systems and hence about the nature of their intelligence.

Evolution and Development

Many things must happen in the right place at the right time before a fertilized egg can fully develop and form such a complicated structure as the brain. A huge number of neurons must be produced, they must relocate accurately to their final locations from where they are generated, and they must also produce many synapses between their axons and dendrites of other neurons. All these processes rely on proteins, and each cell along the way must initiate the production of various proteins necessary for each stage of brain development and turn it off when those proteins are no longer needed. Not surprisingly, like any other aspects of cell differentiation, brain development involves a large number of transcription factors.

As an example of transcription factors involved in brain development, we can look at the development of corticospinal tract. The corticospinal tract is a bundle of nerve fibers consisting of axons of neurons in the cortex that project to the motor neurons in the spinal cord. These fibers play a very important role in fine control of hand and finger movements. Damage in the corticospinal cord leads to the loss of the ability to accurately control the movements of affected body parts. The development of the corticospinal tract is triggered by a transcription factor called *Fezf2*. If this transcription factor is removed from a developing animal, the animal grows up without the corticospinal tract.

Transcription factors and their genes are involved in nearly every stage of brain development. However, it is not just genes that determine the structure and function of the brain. Precisely how different neurons are wired in the brain of an adult animal is not controlled exclusively by genes, but rather also reflects the entire experience of the animal throughout its development. Remember that animals need brains because genes cannot control behaviors quickly in real time. This is analogous to the fact that rovers on Mars need artificial intelligence to control their movement because remote control by humans on Earth is too slow. Although much of the information necessary to build the brain comes from the genes, the brain must be able to select the animal's action based on its current knowledge of the environment, which the genes do not possess. To figure out which action might produce the most desirable outcome, the animal often has to combine the information coming from its sensory organs about the current condition of the external environment with the memory of its past experience. Namely, the brain must be capable of learning the most appropriate actions through experience. If genes completely determine the functions of the brain, an animal would always produce stereotypical behaviors, regardless of important yet unpredictable changes in its environment. Such senseless brains would be useless to the genes. As we will examine more closely in later chapters of this book, the essence of intelligence lies in learning, which continues during the entire life of the brain.

The fact that brain functions can be modified by experience implies that genes do not fully control the brain. However, this does not mean that the brain is completely free from genes, either. If the behaviors selected by the brain prevent the self-replication of its own genes, such brains would be eliminated during evolution. Thus, the brain interacts with the genes bidirectionally. On one hand, the brain is a subsidiary organization within a multicellular organism designed to improve the efficiency of gene replication. On the other hand, it is also an agent capable of autonomous decision-making without direct orders from the genes. Economically speaking, the owner or principal of an organism is still its genes, not its brain. The brain is an agent responsible for the safety and reproduction of the organism. Now, let us examine the details of this contract between the brain and the genes.

References

Berdoy M, Webster JP, Macdonald DW (2000) Fatal attraction in rats infected with Toxoplasma gondii. Proc R Soc Lond B. 267: 1591–1594.

Dawkins R (2006) The Selfish Gene. 30th anniversary ed. New York, NY: Oxford Univ. Press.

Higgs PG, Lehman N (2015) The RNA world: molecular cooperation at the origins of life. Nature Rev Genet. 16: 7–17.

Lincoln TA, Joyce GF (2009) Self-sustained replication of an RNA enzyme. Science. 323: 1229–1232.

Robertson MP, Scott WG (2007) The structural basis of ribozyme-catalyzed RNA assembly. Science. 315: 1549–1553.

Further Reading

Alberts B, Johnson A, Lewis J, et al. (2015) Molecular Biology of the Cell. 6th ed. New York, NY: Garland Science.

Biron DG, Loxdale HD (2013) Host-parasite molecular cross-talk during the manipulative process of a host by its parasite. J Exp Biol. 216: 148–160.

Kaplan HS, Robson AJ (2009) We age because we grow. Proc R Soc B. 276: 1837–1844.

Kosman D, Mizutani CM, Lemons D, Cox WG, McGinnis W, Bier E (2004) Multiplex detection of RNA expression in Drosophila embryos. Science. 305: 846.

McAuliffe K (2016) This Is Your Brain on Parasites. Boston, MA: Houghton Mifflin Harcourt.

Mlot C (1989) On the trail of transfer RNA identity. BioScience. 39: 756–759.

Moore J (2002) Parasites and the Behavior of Animals. New York, NY: Oxford Univ. Press.

Parker GA, Chubb JC, Ball MA, Roberts GN (2003) Evolution of complex life cycles in helminth parasites. Nature. 425: 480–484.

Robertson MP, Joyce GF (2014) Highly efficient self-replicating RNA enzymes. Chem Biol. 21: 238–245.

Taylor AI, Pinheiro VB, Smola MJ, et al. (2015) Catalysts from synthetic genetic polymers. Nature. 518: 427–430.

5

Brain and Genes

How did life end up needing such a complex organs as the brain? How did the brain evolve? These are the two main questions we are going to explore in this chapter. In seeking answers to these questions, we will notice again that diversity and complexity are often how life improves the efficiency of its replication. Through evolution, life becomes more diverse, while the structure and functions of individual life forms tend to become more complex. The same patterns can be observed during the course of brain evolution.

Life becomes more diverse over time, because evolution is ultimately driven by the diverse properties of the environment. It is likely that the most primitive life forms could replicate themselves only under rare and special circumstances when there were enough nutrients that were needed for replication. However, over time, newer life forms emerged and continued their self-replication despite unfavorable changes in their environment, and this would have pushed the evolution of subsequent life forms into multiple directions, further increasing the diversity of life.

Evolution tends to increase the complexity of living things, and perhaps the best example of increasing complexity can be found in brain evolution. As reviewed in the previous chapter, the nervous systems of animals have become more and more sophisticated through evolution, and eventually led to the evolution of the brain. However, the structure of life forms does not always become more complex during evolution. We should expect that a more complex structure will emerge only when this allows a life form to replicate itself more efficiently in its environment. When life forms with unnecessarily large or complex structures are penalized by the environment, animals might decrease the size of their bodies and simplify their body plans through evolution. Indeed, some insects, such as the fairy wasp (Figure 5.1), are comparable in size to single-cell organisms like amoeba or paramecia. Therefore, complexity should be viewed as a byproduct of increasing diversity. In other

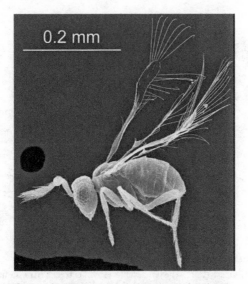

Figure 5.1. *Megaphragma mymaripenne*, a wasp, is the third smallest insect alive and has only about 4,600 neurons in its brain.

Source: Polilov AA (2012) The smallest insects evolve anucleate neurons. Arthropod Struct Dev. 41: 27–32. Copyright (2012), with permission from Elsevier.

words, through evolution, life can become more diverse, and some life forms will end up with greater complexity.

The brains of humans and other mammals are a good example of extreme complexity that resulted from evolution (Figure 5.2). As mentioned in previous chapters of this book, the evolution of complex structures in life is based on division of labor and delegation. In fact, successfully delegating some tasks to other individuals is a hallmark of cooperation in human society in which people divide their labor and specialize. In economics, how the division of labor and delegation can be successfully accomplished is analyzed by the principal–agent theory. Since the division of labor occurs not only among different people but also among different elements of life forms, the principal–agent theory is relevant to biology and might help us better understand the relationship between the genes and the brain. This chapter will examine what role the division of labor and delegation played during biological evolution.

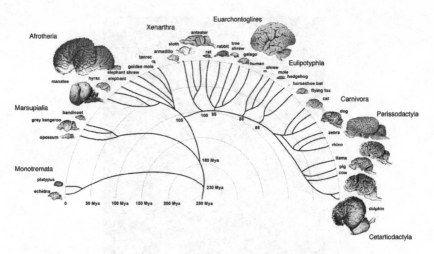

Figure 5.2. Brain evolution.

Source: Herculano-Houzel S (2012) The remarkable, yet not extraordinary, human brain as a scaled-up primate brain and its associated cost. Proc Natl Acad Sci USA. 109: 10661–10668. Copyright (2012), National Academy of Sciences USA. Brain images are from the University of Wisconsin and Michigan State Comparative Mammalian Brain Collections (www.brainmuseum.org).

Division of Labor and Delegation

Division of labor and delegation took place during several key stages of evolution and contributed fundamentally to increasing complexity of life and intelligence. The following describes most noticeable examples.

From the RNA World to the DNA World

As we discussed in the last chapter, the earliest life forms might have started replicating themselves using RNA, rather than DNA and proteins. The transition to the DNA world might correspond to the first major division of labor and delegation during the history of life on earth. In the RNA world, RNA was responsible for the entire process of self-replication. By contrast, in the DNA world, DNA is the primary medium for storing genetic materials, while proteins are responsible for controlling chemical reactions inside cells. RNA has delegated these two functions to DNA and proteins and therefore does not have to be involved in every aspect of self-replication anymore.

Despite this division of labor, RNA did not disappear completely. This is important. In every cell, RNA continues to play central roles in synthesizing all proteins according to the genetic information stored in DNA. mRNA delivers a copy of the genetic information from the DNA to ribosomes outside the cell's nucleus, where tRNA delivers amino acids necessary for protein synthesis.

From Single-Cell Organisms to Multicellular Organisms

The emergence of multicellular organisms is another major event that can be characterized as a division of labor and delegation. All organisms must be able to complete the process of self-replication inside each one of their cells. For single-cell organisms, cell division is equivalent to reproduction, and resulting daughter cells are functionally equivalent to and indistinguishable from the parent cells. By contrast, cells within a multicellular organism become differentiated and specialize in a variety of functions, such as movement, circulation, digestion, and reproduction.

Perhaps, the most surprising consequence of multicellularity is the division of labor between germ cells and somatic cells. In many multicellular life forms, germ cells specialize in reproduction, whereas somatic cells perform all other functions. Only the germ cells can produce both germ cells and somatic cells, thereby reproducing the entire organism. Therefore, germ cells can be considered immortal. By contrast, somatic cells typically lose the ability to create germ cells and therefore cannot recreate the entire organism. Somatic cells delegate the responsibility of self-replication to germ cells, whereas germ cells have delegated all other functions except for reproduction to somatic cells.

Evolution of the Brain

Somatic cells in a multicellular organism are specialized to carry out many different functions and make many decisions necessary for these functions. For animals, most important decisions are made by their muscles and the nervous systems controlling those muscles. Muscle cells can contract or expand rapidly and therefore can be used to quickly change the bodily shape of the animal or move the entire animal to a new location. Accordingly, the safety of the entire animal often relies on the decisions made by the nervous system and the execution by the muscles. If the brain makes the unfortunate decision to commit suicide, all the cells in the same individual organism, including germ cells and somatic cells, cannot escape the fatal consequence of that decision.

To function as a control center, the brain requires authority over other cells in the animal's body. With this power, animals with brains can rapidly select actions appropriate for their survival and reproduction. These decisions must be made carefully based on all available information, which is often delivered by sound and light from the animal's environment. Information received by sensory neurons must then be quickly transmitted to appropriate locations of the animal's body where the information can be utilized. Therefore, without neurons capable of relaying information quickly over a long distance, much of the impressive array of animal behavior would not exist. There would not be any high-speed races between predators and prey. Similarly, without complex nervous systems, humans would not be able to play beautiful music or solve complex mathematical puzzles. However, all neurons are somatic cells. Therefore, the individual's unique memory and knowledge end with the life of that individual. Humans are aware of their mortality and disappointed by it. Nevertheless, this is inevitable. Our thoughts are functions of our brain, which is entirely made up of somatic cells. Somatic cells make up the survival machine that exists solely to assist in the reproduction of germ cells.

Social Cooperation

Division of labor and delegation occur not only within a single organism but also form the basis of cooperation and symbiotic relationship among multiple organisms. For example, flowering plants and insects have a symbiotic relationship in which plants provide insects with nutrients while insects distribute the plants' pollens broadly and therefore facilitate their pollination. This is called mutualistic symbiosis, since both parties benefit from the relationship. Agriculture is another example. By breeding various domesticated animals and plants, humans assist in reproduction of domesticated species and secure reliable food source for themselves. Thanks to humans, chickens have been quite successful as a species, since there are approximately 20 billion chickens in the world. Perhaps, the most complex division of labor and delegation might be the one among humans. Among 7.7 billion people on earth, few can produce everything they need by themselves. With the invention of money, division of labor became much more efficient, and the market-based economy provides accurate signals that are necessary to determine the amount of production and consumption for many different goods. This process has become so efficient that nearly everything we consume in our daily lives is now getting produced by people we have never encountered.

The reason why division of labor is universally adopted by life is simple. As eloquently illustrated by Adam Smith in his pin factory example, division of labor improves the efficiency of the task. However, there is also a danger. Completion of a complex task through division of labor requires appropriate cooperation among the participants. Cooperation is needed because everyone must fulfill their minimum responsibility necessary for the larger task. This implies that all the participants must be rewarded appropriately, because otherwise they would not have the crucial incentive to cooperate.

The same danger lurks in any type of division of labor, including the division of labor inside a single cell. As an example, we can consider the division of labor between DNA and proteins. The protein that plays the most critical role in DNA replication is DNA polymerase, which is responsible for synthesizing DNA using deoxyribonucleotides. Thus, this enzyme is responsible for replicating the very gene that encodes itself. If the sequence of this gene in a given cell is mistakenly altered by the errors of the DNA polymerase and results in a gene coding a less efficient enzyme, then the entire process of self-replication for this cell will be compromised. Similarly, the division of labor among different types of cells in a multicellular organism is vulnerable to multiple risks, including cancer cells that continue to divide in an uncontrolled manner and exploit the resources generated by other cells in the organism. Division of labor cannot be sustained unless the fruits of cooperation are fairly shared among the participants. If some individuals or groups take a disproportionate share of the payoff at the cost of others, this is referred to as parasitic symbiosis and would compel the hosts to expel such parasites. Of course, cooperation fails sometimes in human societies as well, as when manufacturers knowingly sell defective products or when some people free-ride and enjoy the benefits of public goods supported by taxes, such as parks and museums. Cooperation in human societies can also fail due to lies and fraud. Therefore, there must be some mechanisms to ensure that individuals participating in a cooperative project perform their duties reliably. Various forms of social norms and legal systems serve such purpose.

Principal–Agent Relationship

When there is a division of labor, some responsibilities can be delegated by one individual to another. The person who transfers his or her responsibility to another is referred to as a principal, whereas the person who accepts this new responsibility is referred to as an agent. When a principal delegates a responsibility to an agent, the agent needs to be properly incentivized. Otherwise, the agent will pursue their selfish goals, ignore the principal's demand, and the cooperation will fail. In economics, the principal–agent theory tries to find an optimal incentive for the agent so as to bring the best possible outcome to the principal. In this framework, it is the principal who presents the contract. By contrast, the agent does not have the power to modify the contract. It can only accept or reject the proposal from the principal. Therefore, the principal–agent theory can give us an insight as to the nature of contract that might exist between a principal and an agent with specific interests.

The principal–agent theory has been intensely studied since the 1970s and was originally applied to various economic problems arising from the relationship between an employer and employees in a company, between a landlord and tenants, and between an insurance company and its customers. What these examples have in common is the fact that the agent has much more information about their own behavior and the potential outcomes from their behaviors than the principal. In other words, asymmetry in information is the essence of the problem analyzed in the principal–agent theory. This makes the principal–agent theory relevant for problems in biology in which information is not equally distributed during division of labor. Similarly, as artificial intelligence finds more applications in human societies, the principal–agent theory is also relevant for the relationship between humans and AI. However, how well the theoretical framework developed in economics can be applied to problems in biology and AI research and how much insight can be obtained from this needs to be tested. We will examine the key assumptions underlying the principal–agent theory. If these assumptions apply to the relationship between two biological entities, the lessons from the principal–agent theory will help us understand how such entities might behave and how any potential conflict of interest between them might get resolved. For example, if the genes of an animal and its brain satisfy the assumptions of the principal–agent theory, then the principal–agent theory might help us understand the nature of their relationship more accurately (Figure 5.3). The principal–agent theory makes the following five assumptions (Miller, 2005).

First, *the actions of the agent must affect the payoff to the principal*. This is a critical assumption in the principal–agent theory because otherwise the principal will simply not care about the actions of the agent. For example, an employer would be interested in the work of his or her employees because it affects the employer's income. Similarly, many chemicals inside a cell influences the rate of synthesis for other chemicals. For example, the actions of DNA and proteins influence how successfully RNA in the same cell can be replicated. Therefore, the principal–agent theory might be applicable to describe the relationship between RNA and other elements inside a cell, such as DNA and proteins, if the rate of RNA replication can be viewed as the payoff to the RNA. Alternatively, if we define the rate of DNA replication as the payoff to the DNA, then genes and brain can be viewed as the principal and agents, respectively, because decisions made by the brain and the consequent actions of muscle cells can significantly influence the preservation and replication of the genes.

Second, *the agent should have the information not available to the principal*. In the principal–agent theory, the principal is unable to observe all the actions of the agent and can only observe the final outcomes of the agent's actions. The solution to the principal–agent problem would be trivial if the principal and agent share all the information, because this would allow the principal to reward the agent only when the agent produces the actions wanted by the principal. If the employer always has the perfect and accurate knowledge about how much work an employee has done, then the employer could maximize its profit by paying the employee according to the exact amount of work performed. However, when there is a division of labor, it is often impossible for anyone to constantly observe the behaviors of other people. The objective of the principal–agent theory is to find the best possible contract and compromise between the principal and agent despite such asymmetry of information.

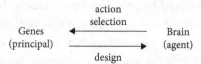

Figure 5.3. The brain can be viewed as an agent selected to select actions for its genes.

The problem of the information asymmetry would become extreme if the agent specialized in collecting and exploiting all the information. This is what happens for the brain. The brain is responsible for receiving nearly all the important information about the animal's environment and, based on this information, decides which actions to take. The amount of information analyzed by the brain is simply too much for germ cells or genes to process. This information asymmetry gives rise to the possibility that the actions selected by the brain might not always contribute to the replication of genes in the best possible way. A similar irony exists for the branch of a government that specializes in collecting and analyzing all types of intelligence information for national security. It is not always easy to implement appropriate countermeasures to prevent such agencies from acting against the public's interest, because they are often much better informed about important domestic and foreign affairs than the public and other government offices.

Third, *the principal controls the contract between the principal and agent.* In the principal–agent theory, the principal unilaterally and ultimately determines the contents of the contract between the principal and agent, and the agent can only decide whether to accept the contract or veto it. This distinguishes the principal–agent problem from other decision-making in social settings in which multiple rounds of negotiations can occur allowing the possibility of finding more equitable solutions. The assumption about the ultimatum in the principal–agent theory applies to many real-life examples, as when the insurance company specifies the exact contents of the insurance available to customers. Similarly, genes specify how various cells are differentiated to perform various subtasks necessary for the entire organism. Except for rare genetic experiments, the brain does not have the ability to rearrange the base sequence of DNA, whereas the genetic information encoded in the DNA contains detailed programs about the brain's development.

Fourth, *interests of the principal and agent do not agree.* In other words, there is a potential conflict of interest. What benefits the agent does not always benefit the principal, and vice versa. Otherwise, there would not be any problem to be solved by principal–agent theory. In almost all human societies with economic division of labor, conflicts of interest occur. In fact, whenever there is any interpersonal conflict, this results from an underlying principal–agent problem. For example, the relationship between parents and their child might have an element of the principal–agent problem, when they are trying to decide what the child should do. For the parents, the safety of the child might be the utmost priority, whereas the child might be more interested in having as much fun as possible.

Division of labor introduced during biological evolution can also produce a conflict of interest. Sometimes, division of labor can occur peacefully and trivially without any conflict. For example, DNA and DNA polymerase influence each other through a positive feedback loop, and therefore they have vested interest in each other. Any mutation in the DNA that reduces the efficiency of DNA polymerase critical for its replication is unlikely to propagate and will be gradually removed. The relationship between DNA and proteins is not always perfect, though. Some proteins encoded in the genes mainly affect the structure and function of the brain. Some of these proteins might be involved in determining how the brain remembers and learns from previous experience. In such cases, how some changes in the genes coding these proteins ultimately affect the efficiency of DNA replication would be difficult to predict. This can potentially lead to a conflict of interest between the brain and genes. For example, some genes might tune the brain of an animal to become attached to the first moving object seen by the animal, thereby making it more likely for the young animal to follow their parents. However, this might become maladaptive in an environment with many harmful moving objects.

Compared to the division of labor among different chemical components inside a cell, the division of labor among different cells in a multicellular organism takes an even more complex form. Somatic cells give up the ability to reproduce themselves and take up the responsibility of protecting germ cells specialized in reproduction. Whereas self-replication is the defining feature of all life forms, somatic cells abandon their own reproduction, precisely because they share the same genes with the germ cells. Therefore, if germ cells with the same DNA sequence multiply in a large number, so does the DNA sequence in the somatic cells of the same individual. This implies that there is no real conflict of interest between somatic cells and germ cells and hence no real principal–agent problem. This is true, however, only when somatic cells perform their assigned duties appropriately. For example, unregulated proliferation of cancer cells would pose a threat to all cells in the same individual.

Given that various cells inside a multicellular organism tend to cooperate successfully most of the time, it might come as a surprise that the interests of the brain and its genes may not always go hand in hand. Ironically, this is because of the rules and instructions set by the genes for the brain. The behaviors specified by the genes might be firmly fixed and genetically programmed, especially when they are directly related to the animal's survival and reproduction and therefore do not need to change. For example, most animals avoid contacting very hot objects. They are attracted to sweet things and repelled by bitter things. For many animals, behaviors involved in mating are often under the direct control of appropriate genes. This implies that the values of utilities assigned to those behaviors can be set much higher than the utility values assigned to other less critical behaviors, such as resting or playing, so that the correct behaviors are always chosen. This is why food and sex provide much pleasure. However, benefits of some behaviors can be more subtle and variable. Accordingly, behaviors controlled directly by the genes do not always produce the most desirable outcomes for the animal and its genes. For example, it would be extremely difficult for genes to specify optimal behaviors for humans living in a complex social network. As we will discuss more in subsequent chapters of this book, deciding whether and when someone should cooperate with another member in society is a very hard problem. All genes are selfish but still delegate the responsibility of their replication to the brain, because they are not well equipped to solve such complex problems. If the brains pursue only the most immediate pleasures explicitly and directly specified for survival and reproduction, this would ultimately limit the interest of the genes and reduce their ability to replicate.

Finally, *the principal and agent both act rationally*. This is a common assumption in most economic theories. Rationality in economics implies that choices are made consistently to maximize the self-interest of the decision maker, namely, their utility function. In the context of principal–agent theory, this means that both the principal and agent are choosing their actions to maximize their own interests individually. However, this assumption needs to be interpreted differently depending on whether we are dealing with division of labor among human decision makers or among different components inside a single life form. As we discussed earlier, human behaviors are not always consistent with utility maximization. Nevertheless, rationality is still a good approximation to account for many choices people make. By contrast, for chemical reactions taking place inside a cell, it is difficult to argue that chemicals like DNA and proteins are making rational choices to maximize their utility functions. Therefore, applying the principal–agent theory to explain division of labor among multiple chemical elements inside a cell may not be meaningful.

The assumption of rationality might be more relevant to the relationship between the brain and the genes. Genes do not make choices in the way that humans and other animals do. Nevertheless, evolutionary biologists often quantify the efficiency of gene replication based on the concept of fitness, defined as the expected growth potential of offspring. Therefore, genes can be seen as making choices to maximize their fitness and considered rational if fitness is substituted for utility. This is also why Richard Dawkins considered genes as selfish. At least to a first approximation, the decisions made by the brain can be also considered rational. Given that most choices made by the genes and brain are rational, we can apply the principal–agent theory to understand their relationship better.

In summary, although divisions of labor commonly occur in many different forms in biology, the principal–agent theory is not applicable to all of them. One exception to this might be the relationship between the brain and genes, since both of them can be considered to make rational choices consistent with the maximization of some theoretical quantities, such as fitness and utility. In addition, the interests of genes and brain do not always agree. Therefore, the brain of an animal and its genes satisfy all the assumptions of the principal–agent theory.

Brain's Incentive

To understand the behavior and intelligence of humans and animals, we need to analyze how the conflict of interest resulting from the principal–agent relationship between the brain and genes might be resolved. Optimal solutions to principal–agent problems often include some incentive given by the principal to the agent so that the utility function of the agent becomes better aligned with the principal's utility function. In economic divisions of labor, financial incentives are often provided to sustain the necessary cooperation. As examples, we will examine two classical principal–agent problems. They cover relationships between a landlord and a tenant farmer and between an insurance company and its customer.

In the first example, a tenant farmer receives a payment for his farming activity from a landlord who owns the land used for farming (Shappingon, 1991). A rational landlord would seek the maximum profit from his land, which would correspond to the value of the total yield from the land minus the payment to the tenant. Similarly, a rational tenant would try to maximize their income and minimize the labor. Therefore, the tenant would work more only if this increases their income. Although it is obvious that the landlord must pay the tenant something, it is not trivial to determine the tenant's optimal wage, namely, the wage that maximizes the landlord's profit.

In principal–agent theory, it is assumed that the landlord has only incomplete information about the amount and quality of the tenant's work. This also implies that the tenant's labor cannot be determined precisely based on the total yield either, because otherwise the landlord would calculate the amount of the tenant's work based on their yield. The lack of such knowledge is a realistic assumption, since many other factors unknown to the landlord, such as the local weather, can unpredictably influence the crop. If the landlord obtains an unexpectedly small crop, this could have been due to bad weather or a lazy tenant. A potential solution to this problem might be for the landlord to pay the tenant a bonus when the crop exceeds a certain criterion. However, this is not an optimal strategy, because the tenant would have no desire to maximize the yield if they expected a yield higher than the criterion without additional work, for example, due to unexpectedly nice weather. This is an example of moral hazard. Moral hazard happens when a person has no incentive to work diligently or avoid risks because their actions are decoupled from their consequences. An optimal solution from principal–agent theory is for the landlord to collect a fixed franchise fee from the tenant, which is calculated as the crop expected by the tenant from their work minus their labor. This allows both the landlord and tenant to maximize their incomes. The tenant will continue to work as long as they expect to increase the crop, since the additional revenue will not be shared with the landlord. We can learn an important lesson from this example. When a principal cannot fully observe the behavior of an agent, the amount of incentive the principal provides to the agent should be tightly linked to the outcome of the agent's behavior.

Another example of the principal–agent problem is insurance. When there is a relatively small possibility of a very costly accident, such as a cancer or a car accident, insurance is an attractive solution. By paying a relatively small premium, an insured individual can be protected from a large expense, as this will be covered by the insurance company if an accident strikes. However, after purchasing the insurance policy, the insured individual can now be less careful, since the real cost of the accident is now completely removed or at least significantly reduced. After getting medical insurance, for example, people might increase unhealthy behaviors, such as smoking and drinking, and with car insurance, they might start driving more recklessly. Such behaviors are also examples of moral hazard, as they stem from the inability of the insurance company to obtain full information about the behavior of its customers, making it impossible for them to raise the insurance premium for people with undesirable habits. An effective solution for insurance companies to prevent such moral hazard is a deductible that the insured individual must pay out of their own pocket before receiving the payment from the insurance. This provides the insured individual with some incentive to avoid the accidents or other losses covered by the insurance, since the insurance no longer fully covers such losses. This can benefit the insured individuals as well as the insurance company, since a deductible also lowers the insurance premium.

When the landlord receives a fixed franchise fee from the tenant, or when the insurance policy includes a deductible, the landlord and insurance company (principals) can induce the tenants and insured individuals (agents) to behave in such a way as to promote the principal's interest. When chosen optimally, such incentives are much more effective than constantly inspecting and micromanaging the agent's behaviors. However, this also requires that agents act rationally and maximize their self-interest. By creating additional incentives for the agents, the principal is effectively modifying the shape of the agent's utility function.

The fact that brains of different animals vary greatly in their shape and size implies that animal's environments create diverse solutions to the principal–agent problem between the genes and brain. For some animals, the nervous system might be hardwired and built directly according to the instructions in the animal's genes. This might not be the best solution, however, since the animal's environment can unpredictably change. Since the brain interacts with the animal's environment more closely, it tends to have more information about the environment than its genes. Therefore, innate behaviors or reflexes that do not take into account the latest changes in the animal's environment do not always produce the most desirable outcomes for the genes.

For animals with complex brains, these utility functions can be tuned by the animal's experience. This implies that the brains become more autonomous and acquire the ability to control behavior more independently from the genes over time. Nevertheless, the genes can still specify the main constraints of the animal's utility functions, analogous to the incentives the principal provides to the agents. The initial parameters of the utility functions set by the genes might correspond to the desirability or value of different outcomes resulting from the animal's behavior, such as food or mates. However, setting the desirability of outcomes is not enough for controlling behavior accurately, because the outcome of a behavior is not always pre-dictable in a constantly changing environment. The brain must determine the utilities of different actions through experience by learning which actions are likely to produce the most desirable outcomes. The brain has to learn the solutions to the problem that the genes cannot handle. This is why learning lies at the heart of intelligence.

References

Herculano-Houzel S (2012) The remarkable, yet not extraordinary, human brain as a scaled-up primate brain and its associated cost. Proc Natl Acad Sci USA. 109: 10661–10668.

Miller GJ (2005) The political evolution of principal–agent models. Annu Rev Polit Sci. 8: 203–225.

Polilov AA (2012) The smallest insects evolve anucleate neurons. Arthropod Struct Dev. 41: 27–32.

Shappington DEM (1991) Incentives in principal–agent relationships. J Econ Perspect. 5: 45–66.

Further Reading

Robson AJ (2001) The biological basis of economic behavior. J Econ Lit. 39: 11–33.

Polilov AA (2015) Small is beautiful: features of the smallest insects and limits to minia-turization. Annu Rev Entomol. 60: 103–121.

Varian HR (1992) Microeconomic Analysis. 3rd ed. New York, NY: W. W. Norton.

6
Why Learning?

Humans can learn. We can change our behavior through experience. But can animals with much simpler nervous systems learn, such as *C. elegans*, which has only about 300 neurons? Indeed, even animals with such simple nervous system can learn and modify their behavior through experience. For example, if *C. elegans* bumps its head unexpectedly into a hard object while moving forward, it immediately reverses the direction of its movement. This is called head withdrawal reflex, and it protects the animal from a potentially harmful object in its path. However, if the animal experiences the same mechanical stimulus repeatedly, it will gradually reduce the magnitude of this reflex. This is a simple form of learning called habituation. It is easy to understand why such habituation would be beneficial to *C. elegans*. If the object *C. elegans* first bumped into were indeed a predator, it is unlikely that *C. elegans* would be bumping its head into the same object again and again without getting eaten. If the same stimulus were repeated multiple times, it would be reasonable to assume that it is safe, since a real predator would have eaten the animal sooner. It would not be efficient for *C. elegans* to keep moving backwards when it is running into a completely harmless object, especially when it is hungry and needs to aggressively explore its surroundings for food to avoid starvation. Without the ability to habituate, animals like *C. elegans* might repeat the same withdrawal reflex unnecessarily.

Almost all animals have nervous systems, and all animals with nervous systems can learn. This is not surprising, given that nervous systems evolved to do something genes cannot do, which is to make decisions in real time while the animal's environment changes unpredictably. Even if animals do not have the ability to learn, their nervous systems might still allow them to make appropriate decisions according to their environment, but this would be very inefficient. Without learning, animals can still produce appropriate behavior through mutations in genes that control the development of their nervous systems. If the animal's environment changes unpredictably, many mutations over multiple generations must accumulate to modify the developmental programs so that neurons can be rewired to generate appropriate behaviors in the new environment. During such a trial-and-error process, many animals with inappropriate behavior would die from starvation or predation. By contrast, learning allows animals to modify their behavior more quickly within the lifespan of an individual. Learning makes the division of labor between genes and brains much more efficient.

A human brain has 300 million times more neurons than *C. elegans*. This gives humans a much greater ability to learn, and human learning is much more complex and diverse than learning in *C. elegans*. Almost all voluntary human behaviors are selected and refined by learning. The sophisticated finger movements of a guitarist that create beautiful music or a surgeon's skillful movements that save many patients' lives are both products of learning. It would not be possible to discuss human intelligence without understanding how humans learn. Learning is an essential feature of intelligence. In this chapter, we will understand that learning is not a unitary process. There are multiple learning mechanisms, and their interplay is at the heart of intelligent behavior.

Diversity of Learning

When humans and animals learn, exactly what are they learning? Psychologists have debated this topic vigorously throughout the last century. Obviously, the exact content of learning will change depending on the task the animals face, and therefore, the contents of learning theory have often varied depending on the task scientists used to study learning. Nevertheless, if there are multiple ways animals can learn, the performance of individual animals of the same species might diverge even for a relatively simple behavioral task depending on which learning strategy was chosen by individual animals. One of the most famous examples of such variation comes from a series of behavioral experiments performed by Edward Tolman (1948). In the 1940s, Tolman was trying to elucidate the nature of information acquired by rats during learning. He and his colleagues frequently used a T-maze task (Figure 6.1), which is still a popular method for studies of learning. During a T-maze task, a rat is first placed at the stem of a T-shaped maze and then allowed to run forward. Eventually, the animal arrives at the T-junction and will choose to turn rightward or leftward. In most cases, only one side of the arm is baited with reward like a food pellet. When this is repeated many times, the animal usually learns which side has food and begins to turn

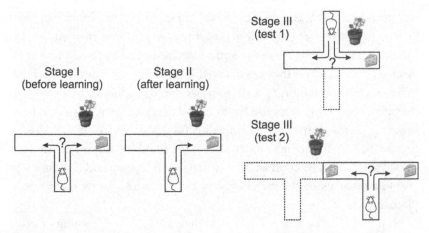

Figure 6.1. A series of experiments performed by Tolman to distinguish between place learning and response learning.

toward that location most of the time. This is one way learning can be measured and quantified in a laboratory.

How can such a simple task tell us what is learned? Let's imagine that we trained a rat in a T-maze while repeatedly baiting the right arm of the maze. The rat will eventually begin to turn toward the right arm (Figure 6.1, Stages I and II). When this happens, what could the animal have possibly learned? One possibility is that the rat might have learned to make a specific behavioral response when it arrives at the junction, namely, just to turn rightward. Tolman named this type of learning response learning (Tolman et al., 1946). The goal of response learning is to learn the precise pattern of body movements necessary to accomplish the goal. However, there is an alternative possibility, which is to learn the location of the destination the animal has to reach to collect its food. According to this scenario, the rat begins to turn rightward, not because it learned to produce specific bodily movements, but because it learned the location of the food. The animal can use a variety of cues to learn the location of the food, such as the position of food relative to other salient landmarks in the surroundings. Since it knows where the food is located through learning, it can later use this information to select the body movements that will bring the animal to that location. This is referred to as place learning. For example, if the rat notices a flowerpot close to the right arm of the T-maze, it might learn that the food is close to the flowerpot, rather than simply learning to turn right at the junction. Whether response learning or place learning is more convenient depends on the accessibility of the information necessary for learning. For place learning, the learner must acquire two pieces of information. First, they need to know their current location, that is, where they are currently. Second, they also need to know their desired location, where they can obtain the outcome they want, such as food. When we give directions to a stranger, we can use either of two strategies that are analogous to response learning and place learning. For example, if someone points their finger in some direction, and says "Walk this way for 5 minutes, turn to the right, and walk 5 more minutes," this is analogous to response learning. By contrast, if someone points to a tall building, and says "Go to a place about 200 meters east of that building," that is analogous to place learning.

So, if you train a rat in a T-maze, do they use response learning or place learning? It is not possible to answer this question using only one T-maze, because the results expected from response learning and place learning are identical. To distinguish between these two possibilities, you must expose the rats to a new condition after they learn the original T-maze. For example, once a rat begins to run toward the right arm of the T-maze reliably, we can test the rat's behavior after rotating the entire T-maze 180 degrees (Figure 6.1, stage III, test 1). If the animal used response learning, it would still turn to its right side, using the same bodily movements learned previously. By contrast, if the animal used place learning, then they might now turn leftward after noticing that the flowerpot associated with the food is now on the left side of the animal. Another way to test what the animal learned is to move the maze to the right so that the end of the right arm in the original T-maze now corresponds to the end of the left arm (Figure 6.1, stage III, test 2). Again, only the rat who used place learning would now turn to the left after realizing that its starting position has changed.

The logic of these two experiments is straightforward, so these experiments were expected to provide a clear answer to the question of what animals learn in a T-maze. Unfortunately, the results from many experiments using the previously described paradigms described varied across different studies. Some investigators found that the rats used response learning, whereas others found evidence for place learning. This was confusing and frustrating at first. Ultimately, however, scientists realized that the animals have access to multiple learning strategies and might be choosing the most appropriate way to learn depending on the animal's previous experience and exactly how the task was set up. As a result, during the last several decades, the focus of research on learning has gradually shifted from the question of what animals learn to the question of how animals choose between different learning strategies or algorithms.

Scientific research on animal learning began more than 100 years ago. Tolman's research was preceded by the work of Edward Thorndike and Burrhus F. Skinner in the United States, who discovered an important principle of animal learning, now commonly referred to as instrumental or operant conditioning. The two types of learning Tolman identified, namely, response learning and place learning, are both examples of instrumental conditioning. In the beginning of the 20th century in Russia, Ivan Pavlov also discovered a principle of learning completely different from instrumental learning, which is now referred to as classical or Pavlovian conditioning. Our goal in this chapter is to understand precisely how these multiple principles of learning differ from one another, so that in the next chapter, we can examine how they are implemented in the brain. Therefore, we will now examine the difference between classical conditioning and instrumental conditioning.

Classical Conditioning: A Salivating Dog

As any dog owner knows, dogs slobber easily. They salivate not only at the sight of food, but also when food is anticipated. For example, a dog might begin salivating as soon as its owner touches a drawer that contains its favorite food. The dog begins to fill its mouth with saliva to prepare the digestive process, since the owner's hand approaching the drawer predicts the upcoming delivery of food. This is a learned response, because dogs are not born with the knowledge that food is stored in a piece of furniture. Canine genes do not contain precise information about where people might store pet food. Dogs salivate in response to a food-predicting cue, because they have previously learned that the same cue tends to be followed by food. By studying the process of this learning, Pavlov discovered the principle of classical conditioning, which is one of the most fundamental and universal principles in animal learning. To honor its discoverer, it is also referred to as Pavlovian conditioning. The fact that dogs salivate a lot must have been quite convenient for Pavlov, since this makes it easy to measure the amount of saliva accurately even with relatively imprecise instrument of his time.

What is classical conditioning, and how does it work? There are several requirements for classical conditioning. First, there must be a behavioral response, such as salivating, that can be triggered by some stimulus without any previous learning. For example, the smell of a delicious food might trigger salivating, even without having smelled the same food previously. A behavioral response that doesn't depend on prior learning is referred to as an unconditioned response, and the stimulus that can trigger a response prior to learning is referred to as an unconditioned stimulus. Any unconditioned stimulus requires a corresponding unconditioned response. Classical conditioning cannot occur without an unconditioned response.

A second requirement for classical conditioning is that a neutral sensory stimulus should be presented some time before an unconditioned stimulus is delivered, and these two stimuli must be presented successively multiple times. The neutral stimulus should be unrelated to the unconditioned stimulus and should not by itself produce the unconditioned response. In Pavlov's original experiment, the sound of a bell often served as a neutral stimulus. Once a dog learned that the sound of a bell would be followed by food, the animal would begin to salivate as soon as it heard the bell, even before the food was presented. This behavioral response to a previously neutral stimulus is referred to as a conditioned response, and the neutral stimulus responsible for the conditioned response is referred to as a conditioned stimulus.

In classical conditioning, a conditioned stimulus evoking the conditioned response can be arbitrary and quite different from the unconditioned stimulus. By contrast, a conditioned response resulting from learning is fundamentally the same type of behavioral response as the unconditioned response. This important feature of classical conditioning makes it unique and distinguishes it from other types of learning. For example, in Pavlov's original experiment, a conditioned stimulus paired with food does not generate any arbitrary behavioral response, such as sitting or giving a paw. Instead, both conditioned and unconditioned stimuli produce salivation. In other words, classical conditioning enables a conditioned stimulus to trigger a conditioned response that closely resembles the unconditioned response. Accordingly, the range of behavior that can be learned through classical conditioning is rather limited.

Behaviors that can be learned through classical conditioning are mostly reflexes or other relatively simple innate behaviors. For example, prey animals tend to stop all voluntary movements at the sight of their predators, which is referred to as freezing. Predators are usually unconditioned stimuli, suggesting that the genes might code information about sensory features of the most common predators an animal may encounter. Therefore, prey animals can be trained to freeze in response to other conditioned stimuli. Unconditioned responses frequently include actions of the autonomous nervous systems, such as salivation and changes in blood pressure or breathing. Although conditioned responses are similar to unconditioned responses, they are not identical. The strength and magnitude of conditioned responses are usually less than those of unconditioned responses. For example, when presented with a conditioned stimulus associated with food, dogs will not salivate as much as when they are actually eating the food.

Law of Effect and Instrumental Conditioning: A Curious Cat

At about the same time that Pavlov was investigating classical conditioning using dogs at the Imperial Institute of Experimental Medicine in St. Petersburg, Russia, a psychologist named Edward Thorndike at Columbia University in the United States was studying a completely different form of learning in his New York apartment. In his experiments, Thorndike was measuring the amount of time it takes a cat to escape from a puzzle box (Figure 6.2). To escape from the box, the cat had to learn arbitrary behavioral

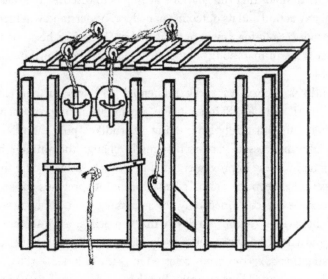

Figure 6.2. Thorndike's puzzle box.
Source: Public domain.

responses, such as pulling a string or pressing a lever, and was rewarded with his favorite food after the escape. Thorndike placed the same cat repeatedly in the same puzzle box and measured how the time to escape changed. Somewhat not surprisingly to us today, he found that the cats were able to escape within less and less time, indicating that the cats learned to produce behavioral responses necessary for the escape.

Even though the results from Thorndike's experiment might seem trivial, these observations provided the basis for one of the most influential laws in psychology, called the law of effect (Thorndike, 1911). This law states that if an animal's action produces an outcome desirable to the animal, the animal is likely to repeat the same action. By contrast, if the outcome of an action is aversive to the animal, then the animal is less likely to repeat the same action. For example, if the cat was fed fish after successfully escaping from a puzzle box by producing a series of actions, the cat is more likely to produce the same sequence of actions when it is placed in the same box again later. By contrast, if the cat gets punished with a painful stimulus, such as electric shock, whenever it escapes from the box, then the same law would predict that the cat would be less and less likely to try to escape from the box. In the context of Thorndike's experiment, a stimulus or event, such as food, that strengthens a preceding action is referred to as reinforcement, whereas anything that reduces the likelihood of a preceding action is referred to as punishment. Thorndike thought that the goal of learning is to discover the relationship between any action and its outcome, namely, to understand whether a given action produces reinforcement or punishment. Therefore, he argued that intelligence is the animal's ability to identify many such relationships as quickly as possible.

Thorndike's theory was very influential and was further elaborated by Burrhus F. Skinner. Skinner made an important improvement in his experiments by drastically simplifying Thorndike's puzzle box and eliminating any unnecessary factors that might change the animal's behavior unpredictably. These improvements made it much easier to find the lawful relationship between the animal's behavior and its previous consequences. His testing device contained only the necessary elements to measure the animal's behavioral response: a device that can deliver a reinforcement such as food and a device that can deliver a simple sensory stimulus, such as a light bulb. Using this box, commonly referred to as the Skinner box, Skinner and his colleagues studied how an animal's behavior changes as they manipulate the timing and frequency of reinforcement (Ferster and Skinner, 1957).

Despite this simplification in the experimental setup, the type of learning Skinner studied is fundamentally the same as described by Thorndike's law of effect and so differs from classical conditioning. Skinner referred to the behavioral response the animal must produce to receive reward as operant behavior or simply operant. Strengthening or weakening of an operant behavior by reinforcement or punishment is referred to as operant conditioning or instrumental conditioning. Instrumental conditioning is fundamentally different from classical conditioning. Understanding the precise difference between them is important, because this provides insight into why these two different forms of learning might have evolved.

Classical conditioning requires repeated pairing of an unconditioned stimulus and a conditioned stimulus. Once an arbitrary conditioned stimulus, such as the sound of a bell, is repeatedly followed by a much more behaviorally meaningful unconditioned stimulus, such as food, the animal can begin to predict that upon detecting the conditioned stimulus, the unconditioned stimulus would follow soon. Therefore, the animal can begin to prepare an appropriate behavioral response. This is especially useful if the unconditioned stimulus requires an immediate reaction for the safety and survival of the animal. For example, if there are warning signs available to the animal's sensory systems about the imminent attack of a predator, learning this relationship would be extremely valuable. In classical conditioning, an appropriate behavioral response can be chosen easily, since this is the same as the unconditioned responses.

Instrumental conditioning is more complicated and flexible, because the animal has to find out by trial and error what appropriate behavioral responses are required to obtain reinforcement or to avoid punishment. For example, a naive cat that had never seen the puzzle box in Thorndike's experiment before would not have any clue as to how it could escape from the box. What does it take for an unexperienced cat to eventually figure out that pressing a lever and pulling a string inside the box might lead to door opening? The answer is the curiosity and playfulness of the cat. The essential ingredient in instrumental conditioning is the ability to generate seemingly random behaviors, even when it is not obvious that they might be helpful in solving any real problems. When the animals do not have complete knowledge of their environment and optimal behavioral responses, exploring possible solutions by trying seemingly random behaviors might be useful sometimes. Presumably, this is why many young mammals spend so much time playing with their peers while they are still protected by their parents.

For classical conditioning, learning is limited to the same behavioral repertoires, a set of the unconditioned responses available to the animal, whereas instrumental conditioning is applicable to any behavior that is physically possible. It is for this reason that Skinner claimed that he could modify any animal or human behaviors he wanted. Language might be arguably the most complex animal behavior we can think of, but Skinner did not think that language would be an exception. Skinner caused a lot of controversy by arguing that learning a language was also a type of instrumental conditioning. During the Second World War, Skinner even proposed that he could train pigeons as pilots to control the trajectory of missiles to improve the accuracy of their targeting. This project was supported by the U.S. government. Skinner believed that all human and animal behaviors are determined by their environments, especially by the relationship between actions and their outcomes and therefore argued that it would be possible to grow humans to be far more intelligent and emotionally stable by carefully applying the principle of instrumental conditioning continuously from the time of birth. He wrote a novel titled *Walden Two* to describe a utopian society in which all children are raised in an optimized educational system based on instrumental conditioning (Skinner, 1948).

By today's standards, Skinner's view that human behaviors are entirely determined by the environment is too radical and not consistent with empirical evidence. Skinner might have erred because in the first half of the 20th century not much was known about how genes can influence the development of the nervous system and promote behaviors that are specific to individual species. Moreover, psychologists that came after Skinner, such as Edward Tolman, also discovered many examples of behaviors that require explanations based on cognitive processes that Skinner strongly rejected, such as cognitive map or internal representations. Skinner also thought that human creativity was entirely based on random mutation of behaviors, which were merely building blocks in instrumental conditioning. Skinner was not always right. However, he made many contributions to the progress of psychological research in the 20th century. In particular, his emphasis on the quantification of behaviors and rigorous experimental control still play a very important role in all areas of behavioral sciences.

Instrumental Meets Classical

How animals learn new behavioral responses is fundamentally different for classical conditioning and instrumental conditioning. In addition, these two types of learning are usually applied to movements generated by different types of muscles. For example, voluntary movements are always produced by skeletal muscles and are usually subject to instrumental conditioning. By contrast, classical conditioning tends to work for smooth muscles that are largely involved in respiratory and digestive functions of the body. The fact that humans and animals can employ multiple types of learning is advantageous in that this makes them more likely to find the most appropriate actions in various environments. At the same time, this comes with the risk of running into conflict between different learning strategies.

One might think classical conditioning and instrumental conditioning work independently for different types of behaviors without any conflict. Interestingly, this is not always the case, because these two types of learning can sometimes influence the same behavior. In fact, we can easily find examples in our daily lives where a combination of classical conditioning and instrumental conditioning produces a desirable effect. Clicker training for dogs is one of them. If a dog trainer feeds the dog whenever it produces an action, such as handshake or rolling, such behavior will be reinforced, and the dog is likely to repeat the behavior whenever it receives a signal from the trainer. During training, however, it might not be easy to feed the dog quickly whenever it produces a desired behavior. Therefore, dog trainers often use clickers to give immediate auditory feedback to signal to the dog that it has produced the correct behavior. How then would a dog learn to associate the sound of a clicker with food and get motivated to work for the click? This can be done separately through classical conditioning. Namely, the trainer can sound the clicker shortly before he or she feeds the dog. If this procedure is repeated, the dog will begin to expect to get food whenever it hears the click. Once this is accomplished and the click has become the conditioned stimulus, the click acquires the ability to reinforce the operant behavior. This makes it much more efficient to train the dog for a variety of behaviors, because any behavior can now be reinforced more easily using a clicker without food. A stimulus that acquires a reinforcing property as a result of classical conditioning is referred to as a secondary or conditioned reinforcer. Conditioned reinforcers are usually conditioned stimuli as defined in the context of classical conditioning. By contrast, a stimulus that can be used as a reinforcer without such conditioning is referred to as a primary reinforcer. A primary reinforcer in instrumental conditioning, such as food, can be also an unconditioned stimulus in classical conditioning.

One of the reasons why Skinner believed that any human or animal behavior could be arbitrarily modified is because classical conditioning and instrumental conditioning can be combined flexibly in many different ways. For example, classical conditioning does not always have to occur directly between a conditioned stimulus and an unconditioned stimulus. Once the animal learns that a particular conditioned stimulus, such as the sound of a clicker, predicts the imminent food delivery, we can put the animal in another training paradigm, in which the animal will be presented with another neutral stimulus, such as a picture of a tree, followed by the click, but without the food. The animal will now learn that the picture of a tree is predictive of the conditioned stimulus previously associated with food, and therefore begins to produce the conditioned response whenever it sees the picture of a tree. A chain of classical conditioning like this is referred to as higher-order conditioning. Sometimes, a stimulus that predicts a secondary reinforcer might become a tertiary reinforcer through high-order conditioning. Human behaviors include many examples of such high-order conditioning. For example, most people would work for money and fame, which can be considered as high-order reinforcers, since they are a means to obtain many other desirable goods or conditioned stimuli. Often, high-order reinforcers like money that can be exchanged with many different types of reinforcers are referred to generalized reinforcers.

Advertisement combines the power of classical conditioning and instrumental conditioning for commercial purposes. The importance of advertising cannot be emphasized enough in a capitalist society. In 2017, the worldwide advertising market was thought to be an approximately $550 billion industry, whereas the spending on advertising in the United States alone is estimated to be about $200 billion. The cost of a 30-second TV ad during the Super Bowl game in 2018 was more than $5 million, resulting in a total revenue of $414 million for NBC. Whenever a manufacturer releases a new product, this information must be conveyed to potential consumers. However, the purpose of an advertisement is not restricted to conveying information about the product. If that were the case, most ads would be very boring to watch. Ads are made to stimulate the consumers to buy the product. How does this work? To make customers spend their money, classical conditioning by itself would not be enough. Many TV or Internet ads show some symbolic images of the product, such as the company logo, and the product together. If they relied only on classical conditioning, this would not lead to the act of purchasing the product. After watching an ad for a steak with delightful music and attractive images, the viewer might salivate like Pavlov's dog whenever they hear the same music or image, but they would not necessarily order the steak. The problem is more complicated for products that are not unconditioned stimuli or primary reinforcers. For example, how do you make an ad for a refrigerator? The physical appearance of a refrigerator does not usually tell you a lot about its function. Nevertheless, watching a refrigerator with an appealing design often creates a strong desire to buy it. When the ad plays a sweet music and features an attractive model, this might induce a potential buyer to imagine a future pleasurable experience with such music and an attractive partner. This is why many companies spend an astronomical amount of money to feature famous stars in their ads. After viewing such an advertisement, how do the consumers associate such positive stimuli with the act of paying for the advertised goods?

The powerful effect of advertising depends a lot on a phenomenon called Pavlovian-instrumental transfer (PIT), which has been studied extensively in laboratory animals. Like high-order conditioning, PIT also requires classical conditioning. Let's consider again the case where a dog has undergone repeated pairing of the sound of a bell and food, so that it salivates whenever it hears the bell. Now, imagine that the same dog is trained to perform another action with instrumental conditioning where the same food from the classical conditioning is used as the reinforcer. Any action can be used since there is little restriction to the range of behaviors that can be learned through instrumental conditioning. For example, covering its eye with its right paw will work. After instrumental conditioning, the dog would be more likely to perform that action anytime.

Now, what will this dog do when it hears the sound of the bell that was used as a conditioned stimulus in classical conditioning? This should induce the dog to salivate, which corresponds to the conditioned response. However, if the effects of classical conditioning and instrumental conditioning are completely independent, the sound of the bell should not induce the animal to produce the behavior acquired by instrumental conditioning, such as covering its eye with the right paw. Although the same food is used in both types of conditioning, they involve different behavioral responses, so one would not necessarily affect the other. Interestingly, the dog in this hypothetical scenario would perform the act learned through instrumental conditioning more frequently when it hears the bell. This would be an example of PIT, which refers to strengthening of an operant behavior in the presence of a conditioned stimulus when this conditioned stimulus is also associated with the reinforcer for the same operant behavior.

When people pay money to buy something, this behavior is always the outcome of instrumental conditioning, because paying money is not an unconditioned response and therefore cannot be learned through classical conditioning. The fact that ads tend to make people remember certain products and anticipate the pleasure that can be derived by their consumption suggests that ads function as conditioned stimuli for the advertised products. Ads often include beautiful faces and other pleasant images, because they make the ads more effective conditioned stimuli. Such ads might induce some conditioned responses, such as dilation of pupils, an increasing heart rate, or salivation, but not paying money for an item. Buying something is an operant behavior, so it is through PIT that ads can induce consumers to pay for the products.

Instrumental and Classical Clash

Conditioned reinforcer and PIT are two examples in which classical conditioning and instrumental conditioning work together harmoniously without any conflict. However, the presence of two different learning principles can cause a problem if the operant behavior acquired through instrumental conditioning is incompatible with the conditioned response learned through classical conditioning. This implies that instrumental conditioning might not be applicable to all behaviors, since it might not work for behaviors incompatible with unconditioned responses for the reinforcer used in instrumental conditioning. Ironically, Keller Breland and Marian Breland, who reported a series of such conflicts between classical conditioning and instrumental conditioning, were Skinner's students. The Brelands applied the principle of learning established by Skinner and his colleagues to many different species of animals and developed an entertainment business called Animal Behavior Enterprises. Their enterprise included interesting animal behaviors, such as a hen playing a piano and a pig using a vacuum cleaner. During their extensive experience in animal training, the Brelands realized that, contrary to Skinner's claim, it was nearly impossible to apply instrumental conditioning to some behaviors because of their undesirable conflict with classical conditioning (Breland and Breland, 1961). For example, the Brelands tried to train raccoons to put coins into a metal box, but the animals would refuse to let go of the coins. This is because whenever the raccoon might have accidentally put the coin into the box and received the food reward, both classical conditioning and instrumental conditioning were taking place simultaneously. On one hand, as the Brelands expected, the raccoon's act of putting the coin in the box was reinforced by the reward they gave to the animal. On the other hand, since the food is also an unconditioned stimulus that triggers an unconditioned hoarding response for the raccoon, pairing it with the coin caused the animal to produce a similar conditioned response whenever it received a coin. The raccoon's conditioned response in this case might be to grab it and try to hide it in a safe place, rather than giving it up to a suspicious metal box. For the raccoons trained by the Brelands, classical conditioning had a more powerful influence on their behavior than instrumental conditioning.

Classical conditioning can produce undesirable outcomes for humans, too, when it collides with instrumental conditioning. For example, when someone had an unpleasant argument with their partner, they might very well know that it is useful not to see each other for a while just to cool down. This behavior might be favored by instrumental conditioning, because this potential punishment should deter them from seeing each other if they expect that the argument might erupt again. But, in reality, they might find it hard to wait, because classical conditioning tends to produce approach behaviors, especially when their gifts or photos work as conditioned stimuli. This is one of many examples in our daily lives where the tension between classical conditioning and instrumental conditioning leads to an approach–avoidance conflict.

Knowledge: Latent Learning and Place Learning

Almost everything psychologists have studied about learning in the last century belongs to classical conditioning or instrumental conditioning. However, you might think that there is something missing in the examples of learned behaviors we discussed so far—for example, how about the knowledge we spent so much time to acquire in various disciplines at school, such as history and science? Studying such materials seems quite different from classical conditioning or instrumental conditioning. It surely doesn't seem that everything we learned in so many years of school is merely a collection of conditioning. Of course, some of the behaviors necessary for studying, such as sitting at the desk for hours, might be learned through instrumental conditioning, if they are appropriately reinforced by good grades and praise. However, the main goal of education is knowledge. For example, knowing that the capital of Brazil is Brasilia, not São Paulo, might not be a product of classical conditioning or instrumental conditioning. In addition, the ability to apply knowledge flexibly is not unique to humans. We need to understand better the role knowledge plays in learning.

Classical conditioning always requires unconditioned stimulus, whereas instrumental conditioning always requires primary reinforcer or punisher. Stimuli such as food, water, and loud noises are highly relevant for the survival and safety of the animal and, accordingly, tend to attract or repel animals even before any learning takes place. Therefore, unconditioned stimuli and primary reinforcers are genetically and innately determined. By contrast, learning promotes self-replication of genes because it can expand the range of behaviors beyond genetically determined ones. Behaviors learned through classical and instrumental conditioning can help the animal accumulate more conditioned stimuli and reinforcers while avoiding punishment more efficiently. Indeed, many psychologists in the first half of the 20th century thought that no learning is possible without conditioned stimuli or reinforcement.

It was against this zeitgeist that Tolman and his colleagues began to demonstrate that animals could learn and acquire knowledge without any conditioned stimulus or reinforcement. One such example is the phenomenon Tolman referred to as latent learning. Latent learning can occur when the animal can explore freely in a new environment, such as a maze, before any reinforcement is introduced. If the animal is later reintroduced to the same environment and must learn the location where food is hidden, it can do this more quickly than naive animals that did not have the opportunity to explore the maze. This suggests that the first group of animals became familiar with the maze and learned something about its layout without any reinforcement. Such knowledge acquired through latent learning can be extremely valuable for the animal to select appropriate behaviors, when their physiological needs or parts of their environment change later.

Even before Tolman, Kenneth Spencer and Ronald Lippitt had shown in the 1930s that rats could flexibly utilize their previous knowledge according to their changing physiological needs (Spence et al., 1950). Their experiment was conducted using a Y-maze (Figure 6.3), which was baited

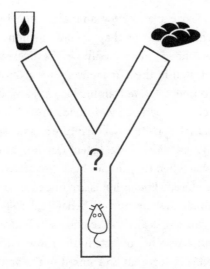

Figure 6.3. Experiment of Spencer and Lippitt.

with food in one arm and with water in the other arm. This experiment proceeded in two stages. In the first stage, rats were first introduced to the maze after they received food and water to their satiety so that neither was desirable to the animal. The animals would not show any interest in either water or food, and none of their behaviors during this initial exploration were therefore reinforced. After this procedure was repeated for several days, the rats were randomly divided into groups, before proceeding to the second stage. Animals in the first group were made thirsty by restricting their access to water, whereas those in the second group were made hungry by depriving them of food. These animals were then reintroduced to the same Y-maze they previously explored. Now, will they behave differently depending on whether they are hungry or thirsty? If they did not learn anything during the first stage of the experiment, all the animals should behave similarly. If the animals did not learn where the food and water are located, hungry and thirsty rats can only randomly guess where food and water are located, respectively. However, this is not what Spencer and Lippitt found. They found that hungry rats tended to choose the side with food, while thirsty rats mostly went to the side with water. This is a nice demonstration that animals can acquire knowledge about their environment without reinforcement and use that knowledge later when it is needed.

124 BIRTH OF INTELLIGENCE

Latent learning also explains how animals tested in Tolman's T-maze described in the beginning of this chapter could demonstrate place learning when the maze was rotated unexpectedly. Unlike in Spence and Lippitt's experiment, animals tested in the T-maze were not given the opportunity to explore their environment before training began. However, they could presumably form associations between various features of the T-maze with their surroundings, such as the positions of furniture and other salient landmarks in the room, through latent learning. Latent learning can take place for any sensory features, even when they do not have any motivational significance to the animal. Therefore, while animals are undergoing instrumental conditioning and learning the appropriate behavioral responses necessary to obtain food, they can also learn the relationship between the location of food and the positions of other objects in the room, such as the flowerpot. Once such knowledge is acquired and stored in the animals' memory, this can provide important information needed for the animal to select the path of navigation and behavioral responses necessary to obtain food, even when the maze is rotated or moved to a new location. This corresponds to place learning, and it works like a navigation software that can recalculate the route to the destination when the driver misses a turn in the original route.

In Spencer and Lippitt's experiment, latent learning extended the range of instrumental conditioning. Latent learning can also be combined with classical conditioning. For example, imagine that a naive dog is repeatedly presented with two neutral stimuli, such as a yellow flag and the sound of a bell. Next, we can expose the dog to classical conditioning in which the sound of a bell is repeatedly paired with food and becomes a conditioned stimulus. When the dog sees the yellow flag, how would he respond? Experiments like this showed that the dog would show a conditioned response, such as salivating, in response to the yellow flag, although this was never directly paired with food before. This implies that the dog had learned that the yellow flag predicts the sound of a bell, when they were both neutral. The tendency for animals to form an association between two neutral stimuli even before either of them is paired with an unconditioned stimulus is referred to as preconditioning. Preconditioning is an example of latent learning.

Preconditioning looks superficially similar to second-order conditioning in that each of them involves two separate associations. One of them is between two conditioned stimuli that are initially neutral to the animal, and the other one is between one of the conditioned stimuli and an unconditioned stimulus. However, there is a key difference in that the order of forming these two associations is opposite for preconditioning and second-order conditioning. In the second-order conditioning, the association between two originally neutral stimuli is formed after one of them has already become a conditioned stimulus by getting repeatedly paired with an unconditioned stimulus. Therefore, when the second-order conditioning begins, one of the two stimuli is no longer neutral to the animal and is already predicting the onset of the corresponding unconditioned stimulus. By contrast, preconditioning occurs when both stimuli are still neutral, and neither is yet a conditioned stimulus. In other words, second-order or high-order conditioning requires that classical conditioning has already occurred, whereas preconditioning can occur without any help of an unconditioned stimulus or a conditioned stimulus.

Through evolution, humans and other mammals have acquired the ability to learn appropriate actions in a variety of environments, and this is largely through the two major types of learning we reviewed in this chapter, namely, classical conditioning and instrumental conditioning. In most cases, learning is ultimately driven by unconditioned stimuli as well as primary reinforcers and punishers, all of which have direct implications for the survival and reproduction of the animal. Even with these two simple mechanisms of learning, genes would have found it worthwhile to build a brain and delegate the ability to select most of an animal's actions to it. However, if the brain learns new behaviors through classical conditioning only when there is a direct link between an unconditioned stimulus and another stimulus or through instrumental conditioning only when a certain behavior is directly reinforced or punished, this would not be the most effective strategy. Throughout the course of an animal's life, some previous experience that might have been completely neutral and irrelevant to the animal's well-being originally might become a critical source of information necessary to make the right choice later. Therefore, somehow, genes must make their brain agents seek new knowledge about the animal's environment. Even if some knowledge does not contribute to satisfying any immediate physiological needs, it might still play a critical role later to allow the genes to replicate successfully. The ability to accumulate a large amount of knowledge about the environment is even more important for animals like humans with relatively long lifespans. Curiosity of our species played a crucial role in enabling us to dominate earth and outcompete many other animals with simpler nervous systems.

References

Breland K, Breland M (1961) The misbehavior of organisms. Am Psychol. 16: 681–684.

Ferster CB, Skinner BF (1957) Schedules of Reinforcement. New York, NY: Appleton-Century-Crofts.

Skinner BF (1948) Walden Two. Indianapolis, IN: Hackett.

Spence KW, Bergmann G, Lippitt R (1950) A study of simple learning under irrelevant motivational-reward conditions. J Exp Psychol. 40: 539–551.

Thorndike EL (1911) Animal Intelligence: experimental Studies. New York, NY: MacMillan.

Tolman EC (1948) Cognitive maps in rats and men. Psychol Rev. 55: 189–208.

Tolman EC, Ritchie BF, Kalish D (1946) Studies in spatial learning: II. Place learning versus response learning. J Exp Psychol. 36: 221–229.

Further Reading

Ardiel EL, Rankin CH (2010) An elegant mind: learning and memory in *Caenorhabditis elegans*. Learn Mem. 17: 191–201.

Dayan P, Niv Y, Seymour B, Daw ND (2006) The misbehavior of value and the discipline of the will. Neur Netw. 19: 1153–1160.

Mazur JE (2013) Learning and Behavior. 7th ed. Sydney, Australia: Pearson Education.

Restle F (1957) Discrimination of cues in mazes: a resolution of the "place-vs.-response" question. Psychol Rev. 64: 217–228.

7

Brain for Learning

The brain is the organ in our body specialized in decision-making and action selection (Figure 7.1). The ultimate reason why the brain plays such a critical role in decision-making is because this responsibility was delegated by the genes for their replication. As we examined in previous chapters, it is inefficient for genes to specify the exact behavior of an animal in an unpredictable environment, because the most beneficial behavior might vary when the environment changes. Therefore, genes have developed a way to incentivize the brain to learn better behavioral responses than the genes can anticipate. Learning is essential for successful division of labor between the brain and genes.

The brain learns by changing its structure and function continuously through experience. Since animal behaviors are largely determined by the brain, the brain has to reconfigure itself when the animal receives unexpected sensory information or when its previous motor responses produced unexpected outcomes. How does this happen? This is what we are going to explore in this chapter.

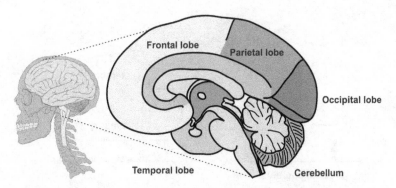

Figure 7.1. A schematic drawing of the right half of the human brain.

Source: Modification of images from Wikipedia. Skull drawing by Patrick J. Lynch under the Creative Commons Attribution 2.5 Generic license. Brain drawing by NEUROtiker under the GNU free documentation license.

Neurons and Learning

Sensory stimuli are ephemeral. Objects important for our survival, whether they are prey or predator, often move and tend to become visible only for a short period of time. Similarly, many important acoustic stimuli tend to be short-lasting. However, for the purpose of learning, even such brief sensory stimuli somehow need to leave lasting changes in the brain. Such changes might occur in individual neurons or synapses. Let us first consider how a brief stimulus might produce persistent changes in neural activity. When a physical stimulus causes enough perturbation in sensory receptors, such as the photoreceptors in the retina or hair cells in the inner ear, changes in the activity of these sensory neurons tend to dissipate and return to their baseline fairly quickly (Figure 7.2), after this signal is transmitted to more central locations in the brain, such as the cerebral cortex. In contrast to sensory receptors, neurons in the cerebral cortex tend to show more sustained responses, with their activity lasting sometimes even after the stimulus has disappeared. Even within the cortex, neurons in the sensory cortical areas, such as the primary visual or auditory cortex, show relatively transient activity, suggesting that their role is primarily in detecting and identifying an object. By contrast, neurons in the high-order cortical areas, such as the parietal cortex and frontal cortex that are often referred to as the association cortex, display more persistent activity. As a result, neurons in the association cortex can maintain information about past sensory stimuli that are no longer present, suggesting that they

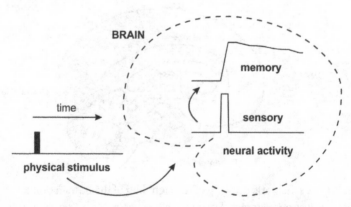

Figure 7.2. Neural activity related to sensory perception and memory in the brain.

might be more important for learning and memory. However, even for such neurons in high-order cortical areas, their persistent activity decays over time, usually within a few seconds. In addition, persistent activity in the cortex can get easily interrupted and overwritten by subsequent sensory stimuli.

So, does the brain lose the information about past sensory stimuli completely once the persistent neural activity related to the stimuli disappears? This cannot be the case, because humans and animals can remember important sensory experience for a much longer period of time than a few seconds. The mechanism that stores information about brief sensory experience for days or even years lies within the synapse, a contact point between a pair of neurons. It is estimated that the number of synapses in the human brain is approximately 100 trillion (10^{14}) to a quadrillion (10^{15}). Learning can occur through chemical changes in this large number of synapses. We can remember events that happened several decades ago, because that memory is stored in some of these synapses.

How can synapses play such a central role in learning? To understand this, let us remember that intelligent animal behaviors emerge as a result of communication among many neurons. As we reviewed earlier, for example, an escape reflex in cockroaches is initiated when the sensory neurons in their cerci changes their activity as a result of increased air movement. This signal must be ultimately transmitted to the cockroach's leg muscles via multiple synapses among sensory neurons, interneurons, and motor neurons. Finally, motor neurons must act on muscles via special types of synapses called motor endplates. What would happen if synapses between sensory neurons and interneurons are suddenly removed or substantially weakened? Or, if synapses between interneurons and motor neurons stop working? Obviously, the cockroach would no longer show its escape reflex, since the signals detected by the sensory neurons would not be transmitted to the muscles. This thought experiment makes it clear that signal transmission through synapses plays a central role for the nervous system to control the animal's behavior. In addition, changes in synapses can modify the escape reflex. For example, if neurotransmitters are no longer released from the presynaptic terminal or there are too few receptors in the membrane of the postsynaptic neuron, behaviors supported by such malfunctional synapses might fail. By contrast, if there is an excessive release of neurotransmitters or too many receptors in the postsynaptic neurons, synapses might become hyperactive, which could also lead to abnormal behaviors. These thought experiments demonstrate that the strength and type of coupling between presynaptic and postsynaptic neurons might be critical for optimal behavior. The strength of a synapse, often referred to as synaptic weight, can be defined as the amount of change in the membrane potential of the postsynaptic neuron caused by a fixed change in the activity of the presynaptic neuron, such as a single action potential.

Changing synaptic weights, which is referred to as synaptic plasticity, provides a means by which an animal's experience at a particular moment exerts lasting influence on its subsequent behavior after persistent neural activity evoked by that experience has completely dissipated. If no neurons are added to or removed from the animal's nervous system and if no synapses change their properties, a sensory stimulus would always generate the same behavioral response. By contrast, the repeated application of air puffs to the tail of a cockroach might increase or decrease the speed of its escape reflex depending on whether some of the synapses in the neural pathway for this reflex are strengthened or weakened.

Search for the Engram

If learning is mediated by plastic synapses, it might be possible to determine the physical location of synapses responsible for learning as well as the corresponding presynaptic and postsynaptic neurons. Exact locations in the brain where synapses change their connection strengths to store the information acquired during learning are referred to as the engram for that memory. Arguably, the engram is a holy grail in neuroscience, and many neuroscientists have sought to identify it. How can you find the engram? To measure the strength of synaptic connection between two neurons, one approach would be to impale presynaptic and postsynaptic neurons with two different electrodes. One can then electrically excite the presynaptic neuron with one electrode, while measuring the changes in the membrane potential of the postsynaptic neuron with the other electrode. When the presynaptic neuron is stimulated with the same amount of electric current, the size of the change in the postsynaptic membrane potential will increase and decrease according to the strength of the synaptic connection. For example, a stronger synaptic connection will lead to a larger change in the postsynaptic membrane potential, while a weaker connection will lead to a smaller change in the postsynaptic membrane potential. However, finding one synapse somewhere in the brain that changed its strength during learning does not provide strong evidence that this is the engram for that learning. This is because synapses might be strengthened or weakened for some other reasons unrelated to learning, including aging and disease. It is not trivial to show that the pattern of synaptic changes measured in a specific area of the brain is directly related to the content of information acquired during learning. Moreover, an engram might be distributed very diffusely throughout the entire brain. This was, for example, a conclusion reached by a famous neuroscientist named Karl Lashley after he failed to find an engram in numerous experiments during the first half of the 20th century.

Numerous studies in the last half century have used a variety of experimental techniques to validate the synaptic plasticity as an important mechanism of learning and memory. Until recently, however, it was not possible to measure ongoing changes in synaptic strengths while the animal is learning something specific during classical or instrumental conditioning. Instead, much of the early evidence was collected using recordings of neural activity from a thin slice of brain tissue placed in a dish supplied with oxygen and other nutrients to keep its neurons alive. Many such studies have shown that the strength of a synapse tends to increase when the presynaptic and postsynaptic neurons are electrically stimulated together (Bliss and Collingridge, 1993). This phenomenon is referred to as long-term potentiation (LTP). In the 1940s, Donald Hebb has proposed that such synapses can store information in the brain. Accordingly, synapses demonstrating LTP are also referred to as Hebbian synapses. Although LTP provides a possible biophysical substrate for information storage in the brain, it does not tell you where in the brain the learned information is stored. Given the large number of neurons and synapses in the brain, this is like finding a needle in a haystack. LTP was first discovered in the hippocampus. However, most neuroscientists nowadays believe that practically all the neurons in the brain and their synapses are plastic and therefore capable of modifying their properties according the animal's experience. Nevertheless, there are two structures in the brain that seem to be highly specialized in learning. They are the hippocampus and basal ganglia. These two anatomical structures are good candidates for engrams.

Hippocampus and Basal Ganglia

Even before the discovery of LTP, there was a lot of interest in the hippo-campus for its potential role in learning and memory. The possibility that the hippocampus might be critical for learning was first recognized in the case studies on Henry Molaison, perhaps the most famous patient in the history of modern neuroscience research (Annese et al., 2014). Better known as H. M., Molaison suffered from severe epilepsy for many years since he had a bike accident at the age of 7. In 1953, when he was 27, a neurosurgeon named William Scoville discovered that his epilepsy originated from the hip-pocampus. Accordingly, Scoville removed the hippocampus from both sides of Molaison's brain, which successfully treated his epilepsy. Unfortunately, as a result of this surgery, Molaison suffered from a new unexpected problem for the rest of his life. Namely, he could no longer form new memories about events that happened after the surgery (Scoville and Milner, 1957). This is referred to as anterograde amnesia. The observation that the loss of the hip-pocampus produces severe amnesia naturally led to the idea that this brain region is critical for learning and memory. As we will see in the following dis-cussion, however, the story is more complicated, as Brenda Milner and other psychologists found that Molaison did not lose the ability to learn new things completely. Rather, the loss of the hippocampus affected only some types of learning and memory.

In the last chapter, we saw that animals can change their behaviors using more than one learning strategy. Learning in humans can also take various forms. However, studies on human learning and memory adopted a different nomen-clature than those used to describe learning strategies in animal studies. The main reason for this discrepancy is that humans have language. Humans can share their memory and what they learned with other people using language. Of course, it is not possible to express everything in our memory and every-thing we learned verbally. Therefore, human memory can be divided into two categories, depending on whether its contents can be described verbally to other people or not. The type of memory that can be explained in words is referred to as declarative or explicit memory. Declarative memory is subdivided into episodic memory and semantic memory. Episodic memory is about a specific event that a person experienced at a particular moment in a particular place, such as what you ate for breakfast yesterday. By contrast, semantic memory is not linked to any such individual events. For example, the knowledge about the oldest restaurant in your city would be an example of semantic memory.

In contrast to declarative memory, memory that is not possible to express verbally and not available for conscious recall is referred to as procedural or implicit memory. For example, learning to ride a bicycle or play the guitar takes place through many trials and errors. The resulting skill tends to last for a long time and is not easily forgotten, but it is nearly impossible to explain in words precisely what it is that you learned. Contents of procedural memory are also difficult to retrieve piece by piece and tend to be remembered as a whole. They are also referred to as habits.

The findings from Brenda Milner's studies on Molaison demonstrated that there are indeed multiple memory systems in the human brain and that the hippocampus underlies a particular type of memory. She presented a variety of learning tasks to Molaison and examined whether Molaison's learning abilities were uniformly impaired for all tasks. From these studies, Milner found that Molaison did not lose his abilities to learn completely (Milner et al., 1968). Although Molaison could no longer form new episodic memories, his procedural memory was not different from that of normal subjects. One of the tasks Milner used to examine Molaison's procedural learning was the mirror-tracking task (Figure 7.3). For this task, a subject is required to draw a geometrical shape using a pen. It is not too difficult to do this if the subject can view the target shape and their drawing hand directly. However,

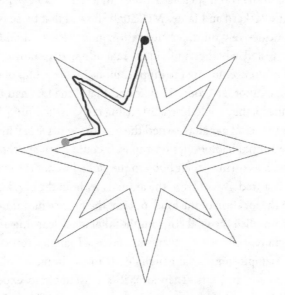

Figure 7.3. An example geometric shape used in the mirror-tracking task.

for the mirror-tracking task, the subject is allowed to view their hand only through a mirror. This makes the task much harder, especially in the beginning, since the real and reflected hands move in opposite directions. Nevertheless, when the task is performed repeatedly, the speed and accuracy for the mirror-tracking task improves gradually. If Molaison lost his abilities to learn completely, he would not show such improvement. To the contrary, Molaison's performance in the mirror task got better with repetition. Despite his nearly complete loss of the episodic memory, he could learn to draw a new shape using the visual feedback in the mirror and became faster and more accurate with practice. This suggests that the hippocampus was necessary for the episodic memory, but not for the procedural memory. The discovery that there are multiple, dissociable memory systems in the human brain has had a major lasting influence on subsequent neurobiological studies of learning and memory.

If the hippocampus is critical for episodic memory, then where does procedural learning take place? Many lines of evidence suggest that the area known as the basal ganglia might be specialized for procedural learning. Some of this evidence comes from studies in which rats were trained in a T-maze task. As we reviewed in the last chapter, when rats are trained to turn to the right for food in the T-maze, some animals learn that turning to the right leads to food (response learning), whereas others learn that they must go to a particular location in the room (place learning). In a remarkable paper published in 1996, Mark Packard and James McGaugh showed that these two different learning strategies rely on different brain regions (Packard and McGaugh, 1996). They tested whether individual rats adopted response learning or place learning after removing the hippocampus in one group of rats and the basal ganglia in another group. They found that if the rats had their hippocampus removed, they could learn only using response learning. By contrast, rats without the basal ganglia learned the task using place learning. In other words, if the animal had no hippocampus, it could learn appropriate motor responses, such as turning their body to the right, but not the exact location where food is stored. By contrast, the animals without the basal ganglia were able to learn the location of the food, but not the precise motor behaviors required to accomplish the goal. This implies that place learning and response learning might rely on the hippocampus and basal ganglia, respectively.

The hippocampus and basal ganglia exist in the brains of all mammals, including humans and rats. Therefore, it is reasonable to expect that the impairments in learning and memory resulting from the lesions in each of these brain areas might produce similar changes in behavior across different mammals. In fact, response learning in rats, which is impaired by the lesion in the basal ganglia and spared by the lesion in the hippocampus, is analogous to the procedural learning in humans, which is also spared when the hippocampus is surgically removed as in Molaison's case. By contrast, when the function of the basal ganglia is disrupted in human patients, as in Parkinson's disease, they often show little or much slower improvement in motor tasks that demand rapid production of sequential motor responses, again suggesting that the basal ganglia might be important for procedural learning. Therefore, specialization of the hippocampus and basal ganglia in different forms of learning might be preserved across different species of mammals.

Another interesting difference between declarative and procedural memory is that behaviors supported by procedural memory tend to be automatic. We are familiar with occasional failures in correctly switching between different types of behavioral control. For example, we sometimes get distracted and realize only after arriving home that we were supposed to stop by a store for grocery shopping. This might happen because our behaviors were temporally dominated by the basal ganglia, which tends to favor stereotypical sequence of motor responses. This would not be very different from the rats that relied on response learning during the T-maze task. The hippocampus might be critical if we need to select appropriate behavioral responses according to the most relevant goal in a given context.

Reinforcement Learning Theory

Humans and other animals can learn in more than one way. This suggests that multiple brain areas might be involved in implementing different learning algorithms. However, this makes it much harder to understand how different brain areas contribute to learning or to find the engrams. To advance our understanding of the brain mechanisms of learning, we need a rigorous theoretical framework that can be used to study the similarities and differences between different learning strategies. Such a theoretical framework can give us helpful tips on how to design new experiments and how to interpret the results from those experiments to improve our understanding of the brain functions related to different types of learning. This is why we now turn to reinforcement learning theory.

In Chapter 2 of this volume, we examined why it is helpful for animals and artificially intelligent robots to compute utilities. Choosing an action with the maximum utility function among a large number of potential options makes it possible to make choices consistently and rationally. However, choice behaviors can change through experience. This implies that utility functions for various options are not fixed. It is precisely the goal of reinforcement learning theory to understand how utilities must be altered by experience so that rational choices based on the utility functions can still produce the most desirable outcomes through learning (Sutton and Barto, 1998).

Both utility theory and reinforcement learning theory provide a mathematical framework to study decision-making, but they have different roots. The utility theory was developed in economics, whereas the reinforcement learning theory is largely the work of psychologists who study animal intelligence and computer scientists who study machine intelligence. They often use different terminologies. The hypothetical quantity that determines all the choices in utility theory is referred to as utility, but this is referred to as value or value function in reinforcement learning theory. Nevertheless, these two quantities play similar roles. Just like economists assume that the decision maker selects an action to maximize their utilities, it is assumed in the reinforcement learning theory that the probability of taking an action increases with the value function of that action. A big difference is how they treat learning. There has been relatively little interest in economics regarding the origin of utilities or how they might be learned. Utilities in economics can be any hypothetical quantities consistent with a set of choices. By contrast, psychologists have always been interested in how humans and animals change their behaviors through learning. Similarly, computer scientists are interested in how they can train machines to perform complex tasks. In this context, value functions can be viewed as the subjective estimate of future rewards expected by the decision maker. These quantities can be updated or learned through experience.

Reinforcement learning theory is versatile and can be applied to account for all types of learning we have reviewed, including classical conditioning. To account for how the dog's salivation changes through classical conditioning in Pavlov's experiment, we can postulate two separate value functions, one for salivating and another for not salivating. The likelihood that the dog salivates would increase with the former and decrease with the latter and so depends only on the difference between these two value functions. Therefore, without losing any generality, we can set the value function for not salivating at zero and just allow the value function for salivating to change over time throughout the conditioning experiment. This is because increasing the value function for not salivating has the same effect on the dog's behavior as decreasing the value function for salivating by the same amount. Now, the probability of salivation depends only on the value function for salivation. If the value function for salivating is greater than zero, it is greater than the value function for not salivating, so the dog is more likely to salivate.

A naive dog would not be constantly salivating in response to the presentation of a neutral stimulus before any conditioning occurs. So, we can assume that initially the value function for salivating is negative. However, as this initially neutral stimulus becomes repeatedly paired with food, the value function of salivating increases gradually as the same stimulus becomes a conditioned stimulus. In reinforcement learning theory, this gradual change in the value functions is driven by a quantity known as the reward prediction error. Reward prediction error corresponds to the difference between the reward or unconditioned stimulus expected by the animal and the actual reward received. The value function changes whenever there is any reward prediction error. If there is a positive reward prediction error, indicating that the animal received more reward than expected, then the value function would increase. This can be expressed by the following update rule:

new value function ← old value function + α × reward prediction error.

The coefficient α is referred to as the learning rate, and it determines what fraction of the reward prediction error would be incorporated into the value function. For example, let's assume that the subjective value of food used in Pavlov's experiment is 8, and the dog's learning rate is 0.2. Let's also assume that when a neutral stimulus, such as the sound of a bell, was presented for the first time, the value function for salivating in response to this stimulus was −2. When the dog receives food unexpectedly after this neutral stimulus for the first time, the reward prediction error would then be 10. As a result, the value function would now become 0 (−2 + 0.2 × 10). As the same stimulus is repeatedly followed by food, the value function for salivating would gradually increase, making it more and more likely that the dog would salivate after the onset of the same stimulus. This change would continue until the dog can predict the food completely and the reward prediction error becomes zero. The initially neutral stimulus has now become a conditioned stimulus.

Reinforcement learning theory can also explain behavioral changes observed during instrumental conditioning. The main difference between classical conditioning and instrumental conditioning lies at which value functions are affected by reward prediction errors. For classical conditioning, it is the value function for the conditioned response, which is the same as the unconditioned responses. In the example of Pavlov's experiment, since salivating corresponds to the unconditioned response for food, reward prediction error causes changes in the value function for salivating. By contrast, for instrumental conditioning, a reward prediction error modifies the value function of whatever action the animal had just produced immediately before unexpected reward was delivered. Accordingly, in the example of Thorndike's cat that successfully escaped from the puzzle box, it would be the value function for the action that unlocked the puzzle box, such as pulling the string and pressing the lever, etc. Finding a reward after a successful escape corresponds to a positive reward prediction error, and by increasing the value functions for the actions responsible for the escape, the cat would become better at escaping from the puzzle box. The fact that the reinforcement learning theory can be flexibly applied to a wide range of behaviors makes it a powerful unified theory of learning.

Pleasure Chemical: Dopamine

In addition to providing a parsimonious account of learning, the reinforcement learning theory also contributed to elucidating the brain functions related to learning. A good example of this is how it accounts for the activity of dopamine neurons. Dopamine is one of several neurotransmitters in the brain. However, it behaves a bit differently compared to more conventional neurotransmitters, such as glutamate and gamma-aminobutyric acid (GABA). Glutamate and GABA are used by excitatory and inhibitory synapses, respectively, and they are used by neurons in many areas of the brain, including the cerebral cortex. However, there are only two areas in the mammalian brain that contain neurons releasing dopamine as their neurotransmitter. One of them is the retina, and the other is in the brainstem that includes two neighboring areas called the ventral tegmental area and substantia nigra. In the retina, dopamine is thought to play an important role in light adaptation and to assist in preventing sensory signals from getting saturated due to too much light. Whereas the effect of dopamine-releasing neurons in the retina is largely limited within the retina, dopamine neurons in the brainstem send their axons to many different areas of the brain, including the entire cerebral cortex and basal ganglia (Lewis et al., 2001). Accordingly, dopamine neurons in the brain stem can release dopamine globally throughout the brain, and this is thought to be involved in several important aspects of learning and motivation. Dopamine is also implicated in multiple psychiatric and neurological disorders. For example, Parkinson's disease is characterized by the loss of dopamine neurons in the brainstem. Interestingly, it has been reported that the amount of dopamine is also reduced in the retina of patients with Parkinson's disease, which might underlie impaired visual functions of such patients. It is also hypothesized that abnormal activity of dopamine neurons might underlie some symptoms of schizophrenia. Moreover, addictive substances, such as cocaine and amphetamine, commonly elevate the concentration of dopamine in the brain. What makes dopamine so special?

An important clue about the function of dopamine neurons came from a series of experiments conducted by Wolfram Schultz in the 1990s. These experiments showed that the activity of dopamine neurons in the brainstem were closely related to the reward prediction errors in reinforcement learning theory (Schultz et al., 1997). In Schultz's experiments, monkeys were subjected to classical conditioning. Fruit juice was used as the unconditioned stimulus, and various visual images presented on a computer screen were used as conditioned stimuli. Schultz and his colleagues then monitored the action potentials from dopamine neurons in the brainstem using microelectrode. They discovered that dopamine neurons tended to increase their activity transiently when the animal received a drop of fruit juice unexpectedly (Figure 7.4, top). This might indicate that dopamine neurons function simply as a reward detector. Surprisingly, however, the response of dopamine neurons at the time of reward delivery was drastically reduced after classical conditioning. Once the animal learned that a particular visual image predicted the arrival of juice reward after a few seconds, dopamine neurons ceased to change their activity when the reward was delivered. Instead, they increased their activity transiently when the reward-predicting visual cue was presented (Figure 7.4, middle). These results suggest that dopamine neurons might signal reward prediction errors. Namely, after conditioning, they no longer respond to juice reward, because this is now fully predicted by the conditioned stimulus, and there is no reward prediction error.

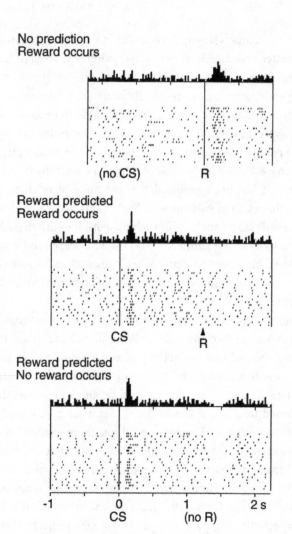

Figure 7.4. Activity of dopamine neurons related to reward prediction errors. Histogram and raster plot in each panel show the average activity of a dopamine neuron and the activity in individual trials, respectively. Top: Dopamine neurons display transient activity in response to the unexpected delivery of reward (R). Middle: When a reward is predicted by a conditioned stimulus (CS), transient activity of dopamine neurons follows the onset of the CS, but is absent after reward delivery, as expected positive reward prediction error. Bottom: When reward is omitted after CS, activity of dopamine neurons is depressed, as expected for a negative reward prediction error.

Source: Schultz W, Dayan P, Montague PR (1997) A neural substrate of prediction and reward. Science 275: 1593–1599. Reprinted with permission from AAAS.

What would happen if reward is omitted after classical conditioning? If a predicted reward is omitted, this produces a negative prediction error. Therefore, if activity of dopamine neurons reflects reward prediction error, then it should decrease when the expected reward is omitted. This is precisely what Schultz observed (Figure 7.4, bottom). These results indicate that the number of action potentials generated by dopamine neurons do not simply reflect the presence or magnitude of reward received by the animal. Instead, activity of dopamine neurons signals reward prediction errors. Subsequent studies by Wolfram Schultz, Okihide Hikosaka, and Geoffrey Schoenbaum have shown that dopamine neurons consistently signal reward prediction errors not only during classical conditioning, but also during instrumental conditioning. Therefore, dopamine neurons are involved in multiple types of learning.

Anatomical studies can show how the axon terminals of dopamine neurons are distributed throughout the brain, and the results from these studies shed further light into the role of dopamine in different types of learning. Although terminals of dopamine neurons are widespread throughout the cortex, they are maximally concentrated in the basal ganglia.

In particular, cortical inputs to the basal ganglia and projections from do-pamine neurons converge in a region called the striatum. This suggests that the basal ganglia might play an important role in updating the values of dif-ferent actions according to dopamine reward prediction error signals. For example, imagine that a rat discovers food every time it turns to the right arm of a T-maze. During learning, there will be a positive reward prediction error, accompanied by the release of dopamine in the striatum whenever the animal makes the correct turn in the T-maze and discovers the food reward. This process might gradually alter the weights of the synapses between cor-tical (presynaptic) and striatal (postsynaptic) neurons, underlying the cor-responding changes in the values of the actions chosen by the animal. This might be a possible mechanism of response learning and explain why the animal might switch to place learning when the basal ganglia are lesioned.

If dopamine neurons are broadcasting reward prediction error signals throughout the brain, this can also explain how drugs of abuse can become addictive. Almost all addictive substances, including nicotine and opioids, increase the level of dopamine in the brain. If dopamine release is interpreted by the brain as a reward prediction error, this would increase the values of actions that preceded the intake of addictive substances, hence making it more likely for the drug addicts to pursue the same behavior in the future.

For example, imagine a smoker has stored a cigarette in the second drawer of a desk in his office. If he smokes this cigarette and the level of dopamine increases in his brain, this would increase the value of opening the same drawer and all the subsequent behaviors ultimately leading to smoking. He would be more likely to repeat the same behaviors when he later returns to the same office and sees the same desk.

Although dopamine might be released during normal learning as well as while consuming addictive substance, they lead to very different outcomes. This is because there is an important difference between reward prediction errors generated naturally during normal learning and those produced artificially by addictive substance. During learning, reward prediction errors signal the need for adjusting the animal's expectation about the outcome of their behaviors, and therefore, they are gradually reduced as the animal becomes familiar with the environment and learns appropriate behavioral responses. By contrast, drugs of abuse bypass the normal brain functions involved in learning and cause dopamine to be released whenever such drugs are taken. Therefore, even if the users of the addictive substance fully learned that taking a particular drug produces pleasure, the amount of dopamine released by the drug will not decrease. It is possible that this might be one reason why it is extremely difficult for some people to discontinue the use of addictive substances (Redish, 2004).

Reinforcement Learning and Knowledge

In the last chapter, we have reviewed the evidence that rats can display the so-called latent learning, namely, the ability to acquire knowledge about their environment without any reinforcement and to guide their actions later using that knowledge. The reinforcement learning theory can account for the same phenomenon using the concept of mental simulation. In mental simulation, animals can predict the hypothetical outcomes of various actions based on their knowledge of the environment and adjust the values of corresponding actions by comparing such hypothetical outcomes to previously expected outcomes. As a simple example, imagine you learn from the morning news that an accident caused the subway you normally take to work to stop operating. If you could immediately change the course of action and take a bus or taxis instead without going to the subway station, this must be the result of mental simulation. If the values of different actions can be updated only after experiencing real reward prediction errors, then the news about the accident would not influence your immediate action, and therefore you would head to the subway station. By contrast, mental simulation would allow you to anticipate the consequence of such inappropriate action. The value of going to the subway station would be lowered just by mentally simulating the outcome of that action, allowing you to seek for alternative actions without directly experiencing any negative outcome.

Without mental simulation, any knowledge acquired about a new environment would be useless to a decision maker, because it cannot influence their actions. In reinforcement learning theory, the process of adjusting decision-making strategies through mental simulation and previously acquired knowledge is referred to as model-based reinforcement learning. By contrast, learning without mental simulation, like the behaviors observed in simple classical and instrumental conditioning, is referred to as model-free reinforcement learning.

Model-based reinforcement learning can account for place learning in rats trained in a T-maze. When a rat is placed in the same T-maze repeatedly and obtained food reward after turning to the right, model-free reinforcement learning would gradually increase the value of turning to the right. If the experimenter later changed the position or orientation of the maze inside the room, rats that relied exclusively on model-free reinforcement learning would continue to turn to the right. This corresponds to response learning. However, during learning, rats might also learn the spatial relationship between the maze and various landmarks in the room. When the maze was moved or rotated later, the rat might anticipate the outcome of turning to either direction in the maze by mentally simulating the outcomes of two alternative motor responses. Although turning to the right used to yield a desired outcome previously, mental simulation would quickly increase the value of turning to the left, leading to behaviors consistent with place learning. Therefore, although model-based reinforcement learning requires seemingly cumbersome and potentially time-consuming mental simulation, it might allow the animals to avoid unnecessary trial and error, especially when their environment changes suddenly. If the animals have appropriate information about the new environment, they can adapt much more quickly using model-based reinforcement learning than model-free reinforcement learning might allow.

Another important advantage of model-based reinforcement learning is that it allows animals to change their behavior flexibly without trial and error, when their internal physiological needs, such as thirst and hunger, change. For example, during the Y-maze experiment of Spencer and Lippitt that we reviewed in the previous chapter, all rats initially acquired the knowledge about the location of food and water but later chose different options depending on whether they were hungry or thirsty. This implies that the values of alternative motor responses were calculated at the time of choice differently according to the animal's physiological condition. Imagine that rats were initially hungry while exploring the maze and learning that food was in the right side of the maze while water was in the left side. For these animals, the value of selecting the right side of the maze would have increased more than the value of selecting the left side. Now, animals relying entirely on model-free reinforcement learning would return to the right side again at least once even when they are thirsty but not hungry anymore, since the values of different actions would be determined entirely by their previous experience. When the animals arrive at the food location and get disappointed by what they find because they are no longer hungry, they would experience a negative reward prediction error. Only then would the value of selecting the right side of the maze diminish, and the animal might choose the left side in the next trial. By contrast, animals capable of mental simulation would be able to update their value functions and select the action to approach water on the very first trial. If the animals have only one chance to make such a choice, only the animals equipped with model-based reinforcement learning would obtain the desired result.

The advantage of model-based reinforcement learning is that behavioral changes can occur without real reinforcement or punishment. Therefore, it is probably not too surprising that many human behaviors are shaped by model-based reinforcement learning. However, mental simulation necessary for model-based reinforcement learning can be potentially very time-consuming, and spending too much time on decision-making can be costly and even fatal. If we have enough information, and if there is enough time to run all the simulation necessary to estimate the outcomes of different actions accurately, then model-based reinforcement learning would produce more desirable results. Otherwise, model-free reinforcement learning might be a better option. Model-free reinforcement learning updates the values of different future actions immediately as soon as the outcomes of previously chosen actions are observed, and therefore do not require much calculations at the time of decision-making. This allows decisions makers to select their actions more quickly. Tasks that are often repeated successfully, such as taking a shower and cleaning the house, tend to be performed by habits acquired through model-free reinforcement learning. If we have to perform all our tasks using mental simulation and model-based reinforcement learning, this would be very exhausting, since the brain would have to spend increasing amount of energy as the complexity of mental simulation increases.

I would like to emphasize another important difference between model-free and model-based reinforcement learning. In model-free reinforcement learning, the value of an action needs to be updated only when the outcome of that action is observed. By contrast, the strength of model-based reinforcement learning depends entirely on how complete and accurate the decision maker's knowledge of the environment is. Therefore, for successful model-based reinforcement learning, the process of acquiring and revising the knowledge about the environment should never stop. It might not be always possible to know in advance which changes or events in the environment become relevant later. Although simple tasks like taking a shower can be handled by model-free reinforcement learning, observing seemingly minor changes in the environment, such as cracks in the bathtub, can play an important role in model-based reinforcement learning and might allow you to avoid an unpleasant accident later. Rats in the Y-maze fundamentally faced the same problem. They were able to select the food or water appropriately depending on their physiological needs, precisely because they gathered and stored the information about their locations, even when they were not immediately useful. Even if you can solve the problem you face now using only model-free reinforcement learning, it would be short-sighted not to update the knowledge of your environment when it changes.

Regret and Orbitofrontal Cortex

Blaise Pascal, a French philosopher, once said, "The human being is only a reed, the most feeble in nature, but this is a thinking reed." We can probably paraphrase this into the language of reinforcement learning as follows: "Model-based reinforcement learning and mental simulation never stop in humans." The process of acquiring new knowledge about their environment never stops for humans, and they are always running mental simulations based on new information from their environment. Even when there are no real reward prediction errors, they constantly adjust the values of different actions based on hypothetical reward prediction errors.

For example, on your way home after a hard day's work, you might suddenly remember a meeting with your friend and decide to change your destination to your favorite bar. This can be accounted for by changes in the values of going home versus going to the bar based on hypothetical reward prediction errors. Simulating the outcome of going to the bar would generate a hypothetical positive reward prediction error. Practically, all our thoughts can be interpreted as mental simulation for model-based reinforcement learning.

The significance of mental simulation in decision-making cannot be overemphasized. Nevertheless, just as eating anything too much is bad for you, it is also possible to have too much mental simulation, and this can interfere with optimal decision-making. For example, we often reflect on our behavior in the past and regret our actions. This process of reflecting on past behaviors could help improve our decisions in the future, but too much regret could hurt our mental health. You cannot go back to the past and change the actions you already completed. You cannot unsay the words you have already spoke. In reinforcement learning theory, regret occurs during mental simulation when the actual outcome from your action is worse than hypothetical reward you could have received by taking a different action. Sometimes, the opposite can also happen. Namely, as a result of mental simulation, you might realize that the actual outcome from your action was better than the hypothetical outcome you might have obtained from an alternative action. This is referred to as relief.

In reinforcement learning theory, regret and disappointment can be clearly distinguished. Disappointment occurs in model-free reinforcement learning when there is a negative reward prediction error, namely, when the actual outcome is worse than the outcome expected from previous experience. Of course, the opposite can occur, too. When the actual outcome is better than the expected outcome, this positive reward prediction error is referred to as elation. Elation and disappointment refer to positive and negative reward prediction errors during model-free reinforcement learning. By contrast, regret and relief refer to model-based reinforcement learning.

Regret is a strange and complex emotion, and its real function and benefit might not be obvious. Even when we know that regretting something will not change the outcome of our previous behavior, many of us often suffer from agony associated with regret, because we cannot stop thinking that we could have done better and avoided the negative consequences from our actions. The reason for this becomes obvious when we take the perspective of model-based reinforcement learning. When we make decisions, this is often done without having sufficient information to determine with certainty which action would produce the best outcome. Almost always, there is some uncertainty about the outcomes from different actions. We often obtain important information essential for our decision-making only after taking the action. This is when we might experience regret or relief. Regret and relief occur as a result of mental simulation, and therefore this implies that we were involved in model-based reinforcement learning. Humans experience regret and relief not because we do not understand that past actions cannot be undone. Instead, these emotions are common because humans are constantly engaged in model-based reinforcement learning to improve our behavior in the future.

An important study published in 2004 showed that activity in the orbitofrontal cortex (OFC) is closely related to regret (Camille et al., 2004). The OFC is a part of the prefrontal cortex, which lies in the most frontal sector of the human brain. For several decades, it had been thought that the prefrontal cortex played an important role in many high-order cognitive processes related to thoughts and emotion. Although there are several major subdivisions within the prefrontal cortex, such as the OFC, that can be distinguished anatomically and functionally, their precise functions were still not well understood. In the paper published in 2004, scientists examined the choice behaviors of a patient whose OFC was removed to excise cancerous brain tissue (Figure 7.5). The patients and control subjects in this study performed a gambling task designed specifically to test how their choices and emotions are influenced by hypothetical payoffs and regret. In each trial, a participant had to choose between two circular targets shown on a computer screen (Figure 7.5). Each target provided information about two alternative numerical scores and their probabilities in different colors. For example, the left target in Figure 7.5. indicated that if chosen, this target could result in the gain of 200 points with 20 percent probability and the loss of 50 points with 80 percent probability, while the right target could result in the gain and loss of 50 points with equal probabilities. Once the participants made their choice, an arrow appeared and began rotating inside the chosen target, and the final position of the arrow determined the outcome of that trial.

This task included two different conditions. In the partial feedback condition, after the participant made their choice, the arrow would appear only inside the chosen target, so each trial ended without providing any information about how many points the subject might have earned from the unchosen target. By contrast, in the complete feedback condition, arrows would

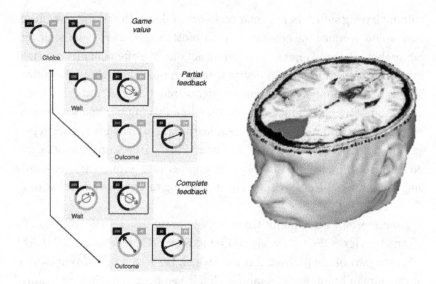

Figure 7.5. Behavioral task used to study the effect of regret on decision making (left) and the orbitofrontal cortex (right).

Source: Camille N, Coricelli G, Sallet J, Pradat-Diehl P, Duhamel JR, Sirigu A (2004) The involvement of the orbitofrontal cortex in the experience of regret. Science. 304: 1167–1170. Reproduced with permission from AAAS.

appear in both chosen and unchosen targets, and the participants were informed not only about the outcome of their choices but also about the hypothetical outcome from the unchosen target. In both conditions, the outcomes from both targets were unknown before the choice, so there was a reward prediction error in every trial, and the participants would experience either disappointment or elation. However, in the complete feedback condition, the subject also received information about the hypothetical reward prediction error and therefore could experience regret or relief. The participants in this experiment were asked to report their mood after each trial, and these responses were analyzed to examine how they were affected by real and hypothetical reward prediction errors.

Both the OFC patients and normal subjects who participated in this experiment reported that their mood worsened with the magnitude of negative reward prediction errors in the outcomes of their choices. This suggests that disappointment may not strongly depend on the OFC. Normal subjects also reported more negative mood when there was regret, namely, when the hypothetical outcome from unchosen target was better than the actual outcome from their choice. Negative hypothetical reward prediction errors were aversive to normal subjects. By contrast, the mood of OFC patients was not affected by the hypothetical outcomes. They did not report negative emotion, even when they learned that the hypothetical outcome from unchosen target was better than the outcome from their choice. Therefore, these results imply that the OFC might play an important role regulating emotion according to the information about hypothetical outcomes or regret.

Observation of behavioral and psychological changes following damage to a brain area provides valuable information about how different brain regions might contribute to specific aspects of cognition. This was true in the case of Molaison, who provided an important clue about the relationship between the hippocampus and episodic memory. The study mentioned above regarding the role of OFC in regret is another example. However, the ability to understand the brain functions solely based on studies of brain damage and lesions is limited, because they do not tell us anything about how a specific cognitive function was implemented in normal brain tissue. For example, if you cut off electricity at night, the entire house gets dark, which demonstrates that electricity is necessary for lighting in the house, but this method cannot tell us much about how the light bulb converts electricity into light. Similarly, lesion studies or studies of brain damage can tell us that the OFC might be involved in emotional and cognitive processes related to regret, but they do not provide much information about the precise nature of OFC functions related to regret. Since individual neurons exchange information using action potentials, it would be very helpful if we could monitor action potentials of individual neurons in the human OFC, but such experiment is presently impossible to do in healthy subjects. As we reviewed in Chapter 2 of this volume, there are two alternative approaches to overcome this limitation. One is to use function magnetic resonance imaging (fMRI) and study the functions of the human brain, and the other is to use more invasive methods, such as single-neuron recording technique, in animal models. Indeed, results from additional studies using these alternative methods have indicated that neural activity in the OFC is related to the hypothetical outcomes from unchosen options.

In one of these fMRI studies, scientists have used the same gambling task used to characterize regret in OFC patients and found that activity in the OFC did not change much with the choice outcome in the partial feedback condition (Coricelli et al., 2005). OFC activity was not affected even in the complete feedback condition, if the outcome from the participant's choice was better than the hypothetical outcome. However, OFC increased its activity when the hypothetical outcome from the unchosen target was better than the outcome from the chosen target (Figure 7.6A). This suggests that the OFC might be involved in the comparison between actual and hypothetical outcomes.

Regret Neurons

The results from studies of patients with damage in the OFC and fMRI experiments implicated the OFC in cognitive processes related to regret and model-based reinforcement learning. To test more directly how these results are related to the type of information processed by individual neurons in the OFC, experiments in my laboratory at Yale University examined the activity of neurons in the monkey OFC while the animals played a virtual rock–paper–scissors game again a computer opponent (Abe and Lee, 2011). As we will examine more closely in the next chapter, rock–paper–scissors is a competitive game that requires decision-making in a socially interactive manner. In our daily lives, we often use rock–paper–scissors to randomly choose a winner. In laboratories of experimental economics or psychology, this game can be used to study the dynamics of reinforcement learning and social reasoning. Since it would be much more challenging to train the animals to reveal their choices with their hand gestures, we trained monkeys to play this against a computer using their eye movements to indicate their choices.

In each trial, we showed monkeys a set of three green targets on a computer screen and required them to shift their gaze toward one of the targets (Figure 7.6B). These three green targets stood for rock, paper, and scissors, respectively. At the same time, the computer predicted which target the animal would be mostly likely to choose by analyzing the animal's choice and outcome history. For example, if the monkey tended to choose the rock target several times in a row and if the animal had just chosen the rock target in the previous trial, then the computer would predict that the animal would select the rock target again. Based on this prediction, the computer would select paper. Therefore, it was disadvantageous for the monkey to make a predictable sequence of choices that might be exploited by the computer opponent. For example, if the animal always chooses scissors, then it would lose constantly as soon as this pattern is detected by the computer opponent.

In our experiment, the animal received a drop of juice if they tied, but nothing when they lost. In the standard rock–paper–scissors game, the

A. Regret and human OFC

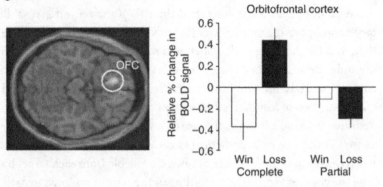

B. Rock-paper-scissor game against a computer opponent

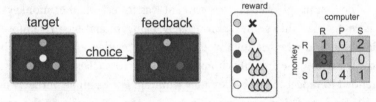

C. Regret signal in a single monkey OFC neuron

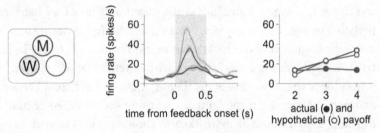

Figure 7.6. Neural activity related to regret in the orbitofrontal cortex (OFC). (A) Activation of the human OFC related to regret was identified in an functional magnetic resonance imaging study. (B) Computerized rock–paper–scissors task (left) and payoff matrix (right) used for neurophysiological experiments in monkeys along. (C) A single OFC neuron that gradually increased its activity according to the magnitude of hypothetical reward.

Source: (A) Reprinted by permission from Springer Nature. Coricelli G, Critchley HD, Joffily M, O'Doherty JP, Sirigu A, Dolan RJ (2005) Regret and its avoidance: a neuroimaging study of choice behavior. Nat Neurosci. 8: 1255–1262. Copyright (2005). (C) Abe H, Lee D (2011) Distributed coding of actual and hypothetical outcomes in the orbital and dorsolateral prefrontal cortex. Neuron. 70: 731–741. Copyright (2011), with permission from Elsevier.

payoff from winning would be the same regardless of the choice the players make. In our experiment, we varied the size of the reward across different targets and gave the animal two, three, and four drops of apple juice when they won by choosing rock, paper, and scissors, respectively. This changed not only the size of the actual reward received by the animal in a winning trial across trials, but also how much the animal could have received when the animal tied or lost. Therefore, we could examine how the activity of OFC neurons varied according to the size of actual reward received by the animal as well as the size of hypothetical juice reward that the animal could have received. We indicated the size of reward available from each target by changing the color of each target according to the reward assigned to each target after the animal made its choice.

The first purpose of this experiment was to test whether monkeys could learn to play this game appropriately using model-based reinforcement learning and whether they would show any evidence of regret. When we analyzed how the animal's choices changed across trials, we found that they tended to repeat their choices after winning. For example, if they won after choosing rock, they were more likely to choose rock again in the next trial. This is consistent with model-free reinforcement learning and therefore was not surprising. A more interesting question is how they behaved after they tied or lost. For example, if the animal lost after choosing scissors because the computer chose rock, what would the animal choose in the next trial? Animals relying entirely on model-free reinforcement learning would be less likely to choose scissors again but might be indifferent between rock and paper. However, if the animal was using model-based reinforcement learning, then it would be more likely to choose paper than rock in the next trial, given that it would have won had it chose paper. Indeed, we found that monkey's choices were consistent with model-based reinforcement learning. This indicates that monkeys might be evaluating not only the real outcomes of their choices but also the hypothetical outcomes from unchosen actions. Monkeys might also regret their behaviors when they learn the outcome might have been better.

The second purpose of our experiment was to understand whether and how the activity of individual neurons in the OFC might be related to regret. Hiroshi Abe, who was a postdoctoral researcher in my lab, recorded the action potentials of individual neurons in monkey OFC while the animal was playing rock–paper–scissors against the computer. Indeed, he found neural signals related to regret in the OFC. As expected from previous studies, many neurons in the OFC changed their activity systematically according to the size of the reward expected by the animal, suggesting that they might be involved in calculating utilities. More interestingly, many neurons in the OFC also changed their activity according to the hypothetical reward the animal could have received from one of the unchosen targets, after the animal lost or tied. These results imply that the OFC might contribute to model-based reinforcement learning by evaluating the hypothetical outcomes from unchosen actions.

As we reviewed in this chapter, multiple areas of the primate brain are involved in various types of reinforcement learning. Reinforcement learning theory plays a critical role in understanding how different computational elements of reinforcement learning might be implemented across different anatomical areas of the brain. Nevertheless, reinforcement learning theory itself is not sufficient to account for the diversity of brain size and morphology. Even among mammals, humans and other primates have much larger brains than other animals even after accounting for the difference in their body sizes. Brains of all mammals are learning machines, and many mammals, including rodents, are capable of model-based reinforcement learning. Therefore, there might be additional reasons as to why large brains benefit humans and other primates more than other mammals. Many scholars believe that this might have something do with the complex structure of primate society. In the next chapter, we will examine the nature of problems in social decision-making and how this might have contributed to the evolution of social brains.

References

Abe H, Lee D (2011) Distributed coding of actual and hypothetical outcomes in the orbital and dorsolateral prefrontal cortex. Neuron. 70: 731–741.

Annese J, Schenker-Ahmed NM, Bartsch H, et al. (2014) Postmortem examination of patient H.M.'s brain based on histological sectioning and digital 3D reconstruction. Nat Commun. 5: 3122.

Bliss TVP, Collingridge GL (1993) A synaptic model of memory: long-term potentiation in the hippocampus. Nature. 361: 31–39.

Camille N, Coricelli G, Sallet J, Pradat-Diehl P, Duhamel JR, Sirigu A (2004) The involvement of the orbitofrontal cortex in the experience of regret. Science. 304: 1167–1170.

Coricelli G, Critchley HD, Joffily M, O'Doherty JP, Sirigu A, Dolan RJ (2005) Regret and its avoidance: a neuroimaging study of choice behavior. Nat Neurosci. 8: 1255–1262.

Lewis DA, Melchitzky DS, Sesack SR, Whitehead RE, Auh S, Sampson A (2001) Dopamine transporter immunoreactivity in monkey cerebral cortex: regional, laminar, and ultrastructural localization. J Comp Neurol. 432: 119–136.

Milner B, Corkin S, Teuber HL (1968) Further analysis of the hippocampal amnesiac syndrome: 14-year follow-up study of H.M. Neuropsychologia. 6: 215–234.

Packard MG, McGaugh JL (1996) Inactivation of hippocampus or caudate nucleus with lidocaine differentially affects expression of place and response learning. Neurobiol Learn Mem. 65: 65–72.

Redish AD (2004) Addiction as a computational process gone awry. Science. 306: 1944–1947.

Schultz W, Dayan P, Montague PR (1997) A neural substrate of prediction and reward. Science. 275: 1593–1599.

Scoville WB, Milner B (1957) Loss of recent memory after bilateral hippocampal lesions. J Neurol Neurosurg Psychiatr. 296: 1–22.

Sutton RS, Barto AG (1998) Reinforcement Learning: An Introduction. Cambridge, MA: MIT Press.

Further Reading

Lee D, Seo H, Jung MW (2012) Neural basis of reinforcement learning and decision making. Annu Rev Neurosci. 35: 287–308.

McKernan MG, Shinnick-Gallagher P (1997) Fear conditioning induces a lasting potentiation of synaptic currents in vitro. Nature. 390: 607–611.

Padoa-Schioppa C, Assad JA (2006) Neurons in the orbitofrontal cortex encode economic value. Nature. 441: 223–226.

Square LR (2004) Memory systems of the brain: a brief history and current perspective. Neurobiol Learn Mem. 82: 171–177.

Whitlock JR, Heynen AJ, Shuler MG, Bear MF (2006) Learning induces long-term potentiation in the hippocampus. Science. 313: 1093–1097.

Xiong Q, Znamenskiy P, Zador AM (2015) Selective corticostriatal plasticity during acquisition of an auditory discrimination task. Nature. 521: 348–351.

8

Social Intelligence and Altruism

We face a countless number of choices daily. Some are relatively simple and handled effortlessly, such as choosing socks in the morning, and some are more difficult, such as choosing a spouse or a career. Sometimes, you may not know whether there is a right choice. Such difficult choices are often made in social settings. Humans are social animals, because most of our decisions are social. Of course, some of the problems we have in our lives require more advanced science and technology, and they will continue to improve the quality of our lives. Finding a source of renewable energy and cures for cancers are just a couple of examples. However, not all human problems will be immediately solved by technological advances. People will still have to decide how the product of new technology, such as energy and medical treatments, will be distributed. These are very difficult choices to make, and perfect solutions might not exist.

What makes social decision-making so difficult? In individual decision-making, the outcome of your choice does not depend on the behaviors of other people. By contrast, in social decision-making, the outcome of your action will depend not only on your action but also on the actions of others. Therefore, to get the best outcome, you must be able to predict the actions of others accurately. However, just as you try to predict the behaviors of others, they will also try to predict your behavior. This interactive process of trying to predict the behavior of others makes optimal social decision-making much harder than individual decision-making.

As a simple example, let's imagine two people playing the game of rock–paper–scissors. The outcome of choosing scissors in this game would result in a win, tie, or loss, if the other person chooses paper, scissors, or rock, respectively. Now, imagine that one of the players announces that they will select scissors. Should the other person believe this and choose rock or avoid choosing rock since this might be a feint? The problem of inferring the intentions of others based on signals they send becomes much more complex when people interact repeatedly, since this increases the number of possible strategies that they can use to influence the behavior of other to their own benefits. For example, if two people are playing the rock–paper–scissors game repeatedly, each of them would try to predict the choice of the opponent based on how they behaved in the past. Once they identified predictable patterns in the opponent's choice history or other available signals, then they might exploit this pattern to make their choice. However, the ultimate outcome is still difficult to predict because everyone would try to predict everyone else's next move. For example, let's imagine that you lost in the last trial because you chose rock and your opponent chose paper. If your opponent is adjusting their strategy based on model-free reinforcement learning we examined in the last chapter, they might be more likely to choose paper again. You should then choose scissors to maximize the chance of your winning. However, if your opponent already predicted your reasoning, then they would select rock to counter your strategy. You might also anticipate this and then change your choice to paper. This iterative reasoning might never end.

This is precisely what a character named Vizzini faced when he was engaged in the battle of wits in the movie *The Princess Bride*. To guess which of the two goblets his opponent offered might contain poison, his reasoning proceeded as follows.

> But it's so simple. All I have to do is divine from what I know of you. Are you the sort of man who would put the poison into his own goblet, or his enemy's? Now, a clever man would put the poison into his own goblet, because he would know that only a great fool would reach for what he was given. I'm not a great fool, so I can clearly not choose the wine in front of you. But you must have known I was not a great fool; you would have counted on it, so I can clearly not choose the wine in front of me.

What was the right answer for Vizzini? Is there a right way to choose when you play rock–paper–scissors repeatedly? Even for relatively simple social decision-making, such as rock–paper–scissors, we need a more formal and logical approach to determine what would be an optimal strategy. As we will see in this chapter, game theory emerged in economics and mathematics to analyze social decision-making. Not only is game theory useful to study competitive interactions in economics, it also provides extremely valuable insight into how it is possible for people to control their selfish desires so that they can cooperate and even become altruistic in trying to solve complex social problems. Therefore, game theory helps us understand the process by which selfish genes end up producing the brains that can choose their actions altruistically.

Game Theory

Game theory is a mathematical study of social decision-making and began in 1944 with the book titled *Theory of Games and Economic Behavior* by John von Neumann and Oskar Morgenstern (1994). In game theory, a problem of decision-making is often depicted by a decision tree or a payoff matrix (Figure 8.1). Each decision maker is referred to as a player, and the choice of each player is referred to as a strategy. In general, a strategy is a set of probabilities associated with alternative actions. For example, the strategy of always choosing rock in a rock–paper–scissors game would correspond to a set of three probabilities, 1, zero, and zero, for rock, paper, and scissors, respectively. A strategy that assigns the probability of 1 to one option and zero to all

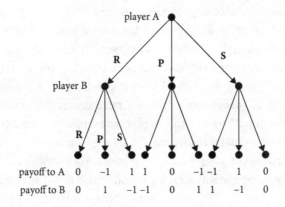

Figure 8.1. Rock–paper–scissors game can be illustrated using a decision tree (top) or a payoff matrix (bottom). R, P, and S indicate rock, paper, and scissors, respectively, and a pair of numbers inside each cell of the payoff matrix correspond to the payoff to the players 1 and 2.

the other options is referred to as a pure strategy in game theory. By contrast, a strategy that has multiple options with nonzero probabilities is referred to as a mixed strategy. The game theory formulated by von Neumann and Morgenstern is often referred to as the classical game theory and assumes that all the players have full knowledge of the decision tree or payoff matrix and make their choices to maximize their individual utilities. Therefore, the goal of game theory is to understand how such rational and selfish players should behave.

We can apply the game theoretic analysis to the rock–paper–scissors game. Rock–paper–scissors is an example of zero-sum game, which is a good model to study competitive social interactions. In zero-sum games, the sum of the payoffs to all the players is always equal to zero for any strategies. This implies that to maximize your own payoff, you have to minimize the sum of payoffs to everyone else. This is true if the sum of all payoffs is a constant other than zero, so zero-sum games are often referred to as constant-sum games. As we previously examined, trying to find an optimal strategy through iterative reasoning for rock–paper–scissors is futile, since this inevitably leads to infinite regress. Game theory attacks this problem from a different angle. First, it distinguishes between a best response for a single player and an optimal strategy for all players. A best response is a utility-maximizing strategy of a single player in response to the strategies selected by all other players in the game. For example, the best response against an opponent who always chooses rock is a pure strategy to choose paper. By contrast, an optimal strategy for all players requires the best responses for all players to be mutually consistent. For example, if you always choose rock while your opponent always chooses scissors, your strategy is the best response, but your opponent's strategy is not, so this is not an optimal strategy for the group. For rock–paper–scissors, there is only one optimal strategy, which corresponds to a mixed strategy of choosing rock, paper, and scissors equally often, namely, with the same probabilities of 1/3.

An optimal strategy in a rock–paper–scissors game has several interesting properties. First, if you use the optimal strategy, then the probabilities of winning, losing, and tying are all 1/3, regardless of the strategy adopted by your opponent. Namely, as long as you choose rock, paper, and scissors with the same probabilities, the probabilities of different outcomes do not change regardless of whether your opponent also uses the optimal strategy or not. Second, the outcome of the best strategy does not change even if you announce your real strategy to your opponent. If you do not use the optimal strategy and instead, for example, choose rock with a probability higher than 1/3, then you should hide this information, because your opponent might exploit it. However, if you are going to choose rock, paper, and scissors with the same probabilities, such information is of no use to your opponent.

There is no limit in the number of players or the number of actions that can be included in a game. So, the number of different games is infinite. In addition, some games are one-shot in that they are played just once, but any such one-shot game can be extended to create a new game where the same one-shot game is played multiple times. Given this, an interesting question arises. Do all games have optimal strategies? The fact that simple games like rock–paper–scissors have an optimal strategy does not mean that this is true for all games. The answer to this profound question was found by a mathematician named John Nash, who was the subject in the movie *A Beautiful Mind*. In a paper published in 1950, Nash mathematically proved that all games have optimal strategies (Nash, 1950). In other words, no matter how complex a game is, there is at least one optimal strategy for the group. To honor this accomplishment, an optimal strategy where every player is choosing the best response to everyone else's strategy is referred to as the Nash equilibrium.

Death of Game Theory?

Many problems that plague human society, such as war and pollution, are due to the inabilities of its members to deal with the problems of social decision-making efficiently. Game theory analyzes social decision-making mathematically. Therefore, when Nash proved that all games have equilibriums and optimal strategies, this was initially embraced by many social scientists as a solid foundation to search for the solutions to our social problems. This optimism was not shared by everyone, though. Many behavioral scientists quickly lost their faith in game theory, because its predictions did not match the behavior of real people very well. A clear discrepancy between game theoretical equilibriums and human behavior can be illustrated by a game called prisoner's dilemma.

Prisoner's dilemma begins when two suspects are questioned by the police or prosecutors in two separate rooms. Although the prosecutors believe that the two suspects are co-conspirators in a serious crime, the evidence they have is not strong enough to indict both for a large penalty. So, they offer each suspect the following plea bargain. First, if both suspects refuse to cooperate and continue to deny their wrongdoings, then based on the evidence already found, each of them will be sentenced for one year in prison. Second, if both confess their crime, they will still avoid the maximum sentence and get three years in prison. However, if one refuses to cooperate while the other person confesses, then the cooperator will be released immediately, but the person who refuses to cooperate will get the maximum sentence of five years in prison.

It is relatively easy to find the optimal strategy for this prisoner's dilemma game once the outcome of each choice is numerically displayed in the payoff matrix. Since each player would try to minimize the number of years in prison, the number of years in prison x should be entered to each element in the payoff matrix as −x. This is illustrated by the first payoff matrix in Figure 8.2, where two numbers inside each element of the matrix indicates the number of years in prison for prisoners A and B, respectively. The two options available for each prisoner are indicated by S and B for silence and betrayal, respectively. Given that rational players will try to maximize their payoffs, adding the same number to all the elements of the payoff matrix does not change the optimal strategies of the game. For example, the utility-maximizing choice would be the same when the utilities of two goods A and B are zero and 1, respectively, versus when they are 10 and 11. For simplicity, therefore, we can add five to everything in the original payoff matrix, which produces the second payoff matrix in Figure 8.2. Two options are now labeled as C and D for cooperation and defection, since they are equivalent to silence and betrayal. These two payoff matrices describe essentially the same game and therefore have the same Nash equilibriums.

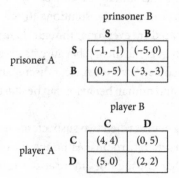

Figure 8.2. Payoff matrix of the prisoner's dilemma game before (top) and after (bottom) adding a constant to all payoffs.

If you are one of the suspects in this game, how would you decide? Do you think your choice will match the Nash equilibrium strategy given by game theory? To identify the Nash equilibrium for this game, we can ask what a player should do when the other player cooperates or defects. For example, let's assume that prisoner B cooperates and remains silent. In this case, prisoner A would be released immediately by defecting, but would get three years in prison by cooperating. Therefore, if prisoner A wants to minimize their sentence, they should defect. Namely, defection is the best response if the other player cooperates. Similarly, if prisoner B defects and confesses, prisoner A would get three or five years in jail by defecting or cooperating, respectively. Again, defection is the best response if the other player defects. Therefore, whatever prisoner B chooses, prisoner A should always defect. Since this game is symmetrical for two players, mutual defection is the Nash equilibrium for the prisoner's dilemma. When both prisoners choose their equilibrium strategies and defect, they will be sentenced to three years in jail. Ironically, this outcome is worse not only for one of the players, but for both, compared to when both of them cooperate and remain silent.

In economics, a particular outcome for a group of players is referred to Pareto-optimal, when it is no longer possible to improve the well-being of anyone without diminishing the well-being of someone else. Therefore, the Nash equilibrium in the prisoner's dilemma game is not Pareto-optimal. The outcome of mutual defection is worse for everyone than the outcome of co-operation; hence, this is a dilemma. The fact that the Nash equilibrium in the prisoner's dilemma game is mutual defection might explain why cooperation often fails in human society. For this reason, the prisoner's dilemma is commonly used as an important paradigm in social sciences to study cooperation.

According to game theory, the optimal strategy for the prisoner's dilemma game is mutual defection. However, this does not mean that people would behave necessarily as predicted by game theory when they encounter a situation like the prisoner's dilemma game in real life. Hundreds of papers have been published to provide answers to this question. However, the results were quite variable. In fact, none of these studies have found that people always cooperated or always defected. In other words, there was always individual variability during the prisoner's dilemma game. Moreover, the average proportion of participants who cooperated was also variable across different studies and could be as low as 5 percent and as high as 97 percent. On average, the proportion of people who chose cooperation was about 50 percent, and for about half the published studies, the proportion of cooperators was between 30 and 40 percent. So, although there was a lot of variability in the results from empirical studies of the prisoner's dilemma game, the prediction from game theory was clearly not supported by the data. Initial optimism about the game theory of von Neumann and Morgenstern did not last very long (Sally, 1995).

Iterative Prisoner's Dilemma

Game theory is a mathematical study of social decision-making, and the truth of its propositions depends only on their assumptions and logic. If all the players in a prisoner's dilemma game are fully aware of their payoff matrix and try to maximize their individual payoffs, then they should all defect. This can be proved, so it is a mathematical theorem. The fact that people do not always behave exactly as predicted by such theorems of game theory does not necessarily mean that the game theory is flawed. Instead, it indicates that the assumptions of the theory were violated in real-life experiments. If all the participants in the experiment on prisoner's dilemma were fully informed about the payoff matrix of the game, such discrepancy indicates that people did not act rationally and selfishly to maximize their own interests.

This poses an interesting and important question. If the brain evolved to facilitate the replication of genes, how can this process lead to behaviors that are not entirely selfish or even altruistic from the perspective of genes? If behaviors selected by the brain do not maximize the efficiency of gene replication, does this mean that brain evolution was at least occasionally free from the competition among different species? Alternatively, did cooperative brains and behaviors evolve because they ultimately benefit the genes responsible for their production? Cooperation in a society can often produce better outcomes compared to when its members selfishly seek to maximize their individual benefits, for example, by betraying their friends and families. This is analogous to what happens in the prisoner's dilemma game. Therefore, to avoid unnecessary conflicts and improve the quality of our lives in society, it is important to understand the strategies that genes might have used to encourage their brains to cooperate with other brains.

For idealized prisoner's dilemma games, each player is selfish and does not care about the interest of the other player. In reality, this assumption might be valid if the players of the prisoner's game had never met or exchanged any information about each other before and if they believed they would never meet again and therefore do not have any additional responsibilities for the outcome of their choice in the future. In such one-shot prisoner's dilemma game, every player makes only a single decision. During typical laboratory experiments on one-shot prisoner's dilemma game, participants are explicitly told that they will play this game only once. Nevertheless, the fact that people still cooperate sometimes in such experiments implies that the participants acted as if they still believed that they might encounter other players again.

Throughout human evolution, it is likely that our ancestors have had repeated interactions with the same people rather than only having had interactions with strangers. When the same group of people play a game with the same payoff matrix multiple times, this is referred to as an iterative game. Iterative games can have equilibrium strategies more complex than one-shot games. Therefore, if people have extensive experience with some iterative games, such as iterative prisoner's dilemma game, then it is possible that the human brains might have internalize the optimal solutions to such iterative games. This might bias people to select the optimal strategy for iterative games, even when they are explicitly told that they are going to play a one-shot game.

Nash already proved that all games have at least one equilibrium. Therefore, we know that all iterative games also have equilibrium strategies. So, what are the equilibrium strategies for the iterative prisoner's dilemma game? Unfortunately, the answer to this seemingly simple question is still not known. However, although we do not have a general answer to this question, we know that for iterative prisoner's dilemma games, cooperation can sometimes produce better results for individual players than defection. In 1980, a political scientist named Robert Axelrod held a tournament for computer programs playing an iterative prisoner's dilemma game with one another. The first winner in this tournament was the strategy called "tit-for-tat," which was submitted by a psychologist named Anatol Rapoport. The tit-for-tat strategy always selects cooperation for the first trial when it begins to interact with a new player, and then for every subsequent trial, it copies and repeats the choice of its partner. Therefore, the choice of a tit-for-tat player is history-dependent, and this has several benefits. For example, when it encounters a player that always defects, a player with the tit-for-tat strategy can protect itself from getting exploited since, except for the first trial, it will also respond with defection. However, unlike the constant defector, the tit-for-tat strategy can maintain cooperation with constant cooperators. Similarly, two players using the tit-for-tat strategy will always cooperate. The fact that the choice of the tit-for-tat strategy can vary according to the strategy of the partner allows this strategy to obtain the maximum average payoff when it faces many different strategies. The key for success of this simple algorithm is that it allows the players to cooperate selectively with other cooperative players. By contrast, an algorithm that always chooses to cooperate will be less successful, because it will be betrayed and exploited by defectors.

Pavlov Strategy

The tit-for-tat strategy is not the only strategy that enables cooperation in the iterative prisoner's dilemma game. The so-called Pavlov strategy, which was discovered later than the tit-for-tat strategy, can also produce cooperation, in part because, like the tit-for-tat strategy, its choice to cooperate depends on the past choice of its partner (Nowak and Sigmund, 1993). There is an important difference between the tit-for-tat and Pavlov strategies, though. The tit-for-tat strategy always copies the choice of its partner. By contrast, the Pavlov strategy makes the same choice as in the previous trial if its partner cooperated in the previous trial, but switches from its previous choice if the partner defected in the previous trial.

An interesting feature of the prisoner's dilemma is that the outcome of your choice is always better when your partner cooperates than when they defect, and this is true regardless of whether you cooperate or defect. Therefore, the fact that the Pavlov strategy changes its choice when and only when its partner defects implies that it repeats the same choice after a good outcome and switches after a bad outcome. This is quite different from the tit-for-tat strategy. For example, a player using the tit-for-tat strategy would choose to cooperate if their partner cooperated in the previous trial. By contrast, the Pavlov strategy would repeat whatever its previous choice was when its partner cooperated in the previous trial. If it defected in the previous trial, then it will defect again. If it cooperated previously, then it would cooperate. This is based on the principle of the so-called win–stay–lose–switch strategy. You simply repeat the same choice when it produced a good outcome before. The behaviors of the tit-for-tat and Pavlov strategies are also different when their partners defected. In this case, a player with the tit-for-tat strategy would also defect in the next trial, whereas the Pavlov strategy will switch its choice. In other words, the Pavlov strategy changes its choices when the outcome of its previous choice was bad. After the partner's defection, the Pavlov strategy would cooperate if its previous choice was defection, but defect if its previous choice was cooperation.

Given that the Pavlov strategy modifies its choice according to the outcome of its previous choice, this is more similar to Thorndike's law of effect and the principle of operant conditioning than Pavlov's principle of classical conditioning. Therefore, it is ironic that the strategy implementing the principle discovered by Thorndike is referred to as the Pavlov strategy. It might have been more appropriate to name it Thorndike strategy or reinforcement strategy.

It is easy to understand that the Pavlov strategy is more successful than the tit-for-tat strategy especially when it faces an innocent unconditional cooperator. In this case, the tit-for-tat player would happily continue to cooperate, whereas the Pavlov player can exploit such naive cooperators. However, the Pavlov strategy is not always more successful than the tit-for-tat strategy. For example, when faced against a constant defector, the tit-for-tat strategy will be able to protect itself from getting exploited since it will also always choose to defect. By contrast, the Pavlov strategy will constantly switch back and forth between cooperation and defection and therefore will end up with the lower average payoff than the tit-for-tat strategy.

Despite such weakness, the Pavlov strategy is better at forming cooperative relationship with various types of partners than the tit-for-tat strategy. Perhaps, this can be best illustrated by examining the behaviors of multiple players using the Pavlov strategy. When two players both use the Pavlov strategy, they can begin to cooperate continuously within three trials, regardless of how they previously behaved toward each other. For example, imagine that in the first trial, player A defected while player B cooperated. Then, in the second trial, both players would defect, since player A would make the same choice as in the previous trial while player B switches. Following a mutual defection, both players would now switch their choices, and therefore in the third trial, both players would choose cooperation. This would then continue forever. In contrast, the tit-for-tat strategist is not forgiving and cannot recover from a defection of its partner using the same tit-for-tat strategy. Once there is a defection between two tit-for-tat strategists, this will persist forever. The ability to start cooperating after temporary defection is important, because in real life communication is often noisy. Therefore, even everyone in a group intends to cooperate, their actions might be occasionally mistaken as defections. Pavlov players can recover from such errors much better than tit-for-tat players.

Both tit-for-tat and Pavlov strategies are learning algorithms, so they require memory. The tit-for-tat strategy needs to remember the previous choice of its partner, whereas the Pavlov strategy needs to remember both its previous choice and the previous choice of its partner. The tit-for-tat strategy is not forgiving, so the result from any error in this memory is catastrophic. For example, imagine that two players were constantly cooperating during an iterative prisoner's dilemma using the tit-for-tat strategy. This constant cooperation depends on both players remembering the previous cooperation of their partners perfectly. If one of them is mistaken and believes that its partner has defected, then it would choose to defect in the next trial although its partner innocently would cooperate. From this point on, both players would then begin to switch back and forth between cooperation and defection until another error occurs. By contrast, a pair of players using the Pavlov strategy can recover from such an error. As we previously examined, they are more forgiving and therefore can restore cooperation after a few trials even after occasional defections or memory errors.

We can learn two important lessons from the fact that the tit-for-tat and Pavlov strategies tend to enable cooperation in iterative prisoner's dilemma games. First, although the optimal strategy for some games like prisoner's dilemma is defection when it is played just once, cooperation might become an optimal solution when the same game is played repeatedly. Second, it is important to have the ability to change how to behave based on experience. In other words, learning becomes essential for iterative games. Sometimes, it might be enough to remember the behaviors of other players, but often as in the Pavlov strategy, it might be also necessary to remember one's own behavior. This suggests that reinforcement learning can be applied broadly to understand the dynamics of social behavior, in addition to individual decision-making.

As we saw in the previous chapter, there are multiple forms of reinforcement learning, such as model-free and model-based reinforcement learning. These different forms of learning algorithms can be applied to decision-making during repeated social interactions. For example, the Pavlov strategy corresponds to model-free reinforcement learning, since only the outcome of the player's previous choice determines whether that player would repeat the same choice in the next trial. By contrast, the tit-for-tat strategy is a type of model-based reinforcement learning, in that the player keeps only the information about the previous behavior of their partner and makes their next choice entirely based on this knowledge. If one's knowledge about other players is accurate enough to predict their behaviors, model-based reinforcement learning would always perform better than model-free reinforcement learning. However, without such knowledge, model-based reinforcement learning might be worse than model-free reinforcement learning. In the case of the iterative prisoner's dilemma, some model-free reinforcement learning algorithms, such as the Pavlov strategy, might be more efficient than model-based reinforcement learning algorithms with only limited knowledge about the behaviors of other players, such as the tit-for-tat strategy.

It is precisely because it is difficult to predict the behavior of other players that model-free reinforcement learning can often occur for many types of repeated social interactions. As social relationship become more complex, model-based reinforcement learning will require more sophisticated knowledge about the goals of other people and their decision-making processes. As such knowledge may not always be available, this can limit the benefit of model-based reinforcement learning. By contrast, model-free reinforcement learning requires only a limited amount of information about previous experience. We can illustrate this again using an iterative rock–paper–scissors game. The optimal strategy for the one-shot rock–paper–scissors game is also an optimal strategy when the same game is played repeatedly. Namely, if both players choose each of three options with the probability of 1/3 and do this independently across successive trials, this corresponds to a Nash equilibrium. This would be an easy task for a random number generator, but humans are very poor at producing a completely random sequence of actions. Instead, many laboratory experiments and observations of real-life behaviors show that people tend to use model-free reinforcement learning when they play iterative rock–paper–scissors game. Namely, they tend to repeat the same choices that were successful in the past. This tendency is stronger among children whose brains are not yet fully developed. Readers can test this by playing rock–paper–scissors games with children and adults and observing how often they tend to make the same choice after winning.

Cooperating Society

Prisoner's dilemma game is an excellent paradigm to study how cooperation might emerge and can be maintained when there are only two players.

However, cooperation in a real human society often requires coordination among many people. Can we generalize anything we learn from the prisoner's dilemma to larger games with more players? Indeed, game theory gives us important insights even if there are more than two players.

In economics, cooperation becomes an important topic when there are public goods. Goods that have utilities can be divided into private goods and public goods. Private goods can be consumed entirely by individuals without increasing or decreasing the utilities of other people. For example, if I eat some food in my house, this hardly affects the well-being of others. By contrast, consumption of public goods changes the utilities of other people. The effect of an individual's consumption on the utility of others is referred to as externality, so the concept of public goods is closely related to externality. Public goods have externality, which can be positive or negative. When someone consumes certain public goods with positive externality, this increases the utilities of others who did not purchase them. Examples of public goods with positive externality include social infrastructures, such as roads and bridges. By contrast, negative externality occurs when consumption of public goods produces harmful effects on the environment, such as air pollution. Public goods with positive externality tend to be underproduced, because people can enjoy such goods without paying for them and therefore tend to avoid producing and purchasing such goods. This is referred to the free-rider's problem. For example, let's imagine that everyone in a town has roughly the same need for a public library and is asked to donate money to build a new library. In such cases, people might be reluctant to donate, if they expect to use the library even without making the donation. One possible solution to solve the free-rider's problem like this is to make the government to collect mandatory taxes for public financing.

In contrast to public goods with positive externality, public goods with negative externality tend to be overproduced. For example, if some companies are allowed to avoid cleaning up harmful chemicals generated during the production of their products, they would be able to lower the prices of such products. This would increase their consumption, compared to when the companies have to cover the cost of cleaning up the environment. Like the public goods with positive externality, this might also require intervention of the government.

Is it always necessary to get the government involved whenever there is externality to prevent public goods from getting produced too much or too little? If we could solve the problem of public goods without the

government, that would be good news, since it would reduce or eliminate the cost of an unnecessarily large government. This question can
be studied using the public goods game. Whereas a prisoner's dilemma
game has only two players, a public goods game can have any number of
players. In a public goods game, each player is first endowed with a certain
amount of money. Then, each player independently decides what fraction
of their endowment to donate to a public pool. The total amount of money
collected in this public pool is then multiplied by some factor greater
than 1 and then the total amount of money in this increased public pool
is equally divided among all the players in the game, regardless of their
original donation. For example, let's consider a public goods game with 10
participants who all start the game with an initial endowment of $10. Let's
assume that the money in the public pool is doubled. If nobody donates
any money, the game ends immediately, and everyone keeps $10. By con-
trast, if everyone donates all the money they have, then each person will
end up getting twice the amount of money they had originally. The total
pool doubles from $100 to $200, and this will be shared equally among the
10 players. Therefore, it is clearly better for everyone if everyone donates
all the money, than no donations at all. This is analogous to the prisoner's
dilemma game in that full cooperation is better than mutual defection.
Unfortunately, the same dilemma exists in both games. As a result, the
Nash equilibrium in the public games is no donation, rather than the maximum donation.

To understand the reason for this tragic outcome, we should remember
that in a Nash equilibrium, every player's choice must be the best response
considering the choices made by all other players. Imagine that you are one
of the players in this game. What would you choose to maximize your self-
interest if all other players donate all their money? If you donate everything
in your initial endowment, your final payoff would be $20. However, if you
keep all your money and donate nothing, then you will still receive one tenth
of money in the public pool, which is $18. Therefore, your final payoff would
be $28. Your best response is to keep all your money, so maximum donation
is not a Nash equilibrium strategy. A main difference between the prisoner's
dilemma and public goods games is the number of players, but they share
an important feature. In both games, the Nash equilibrium is not a Pareto
optimum. The Nash equilibrium for the public goods games is no donation
for everyone. This is clearly not a Pareto optimum, since it is worse than the
maximum donation for everyone.

There is another important parallel between the prisoner's dilemma and the public goods game, in that defection and no donation are the only Nash equilibrium strategies, but this is true only when these games are played just once. Just as there was room for cooperation in an iterative prisoner's dilemma game, it is possible that cooperation might be the better strategy if the same public game is played repeatedly. For iterative public goods games, strategies that can learn from previous experience, such as the tit-for-tat strategy, can also perform better than the Nash equilibrium strategy for one-shot games, because it makes it possible for players to influence the future behaviors of other players.

Learning makes cooperation possible even for a large society. This has important implications in understanding the forces that could have shaped the direction of brain evolution for social animals, including humans. If defection always produced better results for individual animals interacting with one another even when such interactions are repeated many times, brains that choose cooperation would be at a disadvantage. We can also understand that unconditional cooperation is not the best strategy. Animals and their brains that blindly choose cooperation would be easily exploited and outcompeted by animals and brains that can form cooperative relationship more flexibly according to the cost and benefits of cooperation. Therefore, genes capable of building adaptive brains with the ability to cooperate selectively would be replicated more efficiently. This leads to the following questions. Have humans indeed acquired the ability to cooperate flexibly according to their experience? If so, what learning algorithms do they rely on? It appears that the evolutionary solution to the problem of cooperation in human society might rely on revenge.

Dark Side of Altruism

Revenge might be one of the most controversial types of human social behaviors. Many religious and legal texts throughout human history contain phrases seemingly justifying revenge, such as "an eye for an eye." Regardless of whether the true intention of such phrases is to encourage or limit such retaliatory actions, such texts rationalize revenge. At the same time, many religious and political leaders, such as Martin Luther King Jr. and Mahatma Gandhi, emphasized that people should refrain from responding to violence with violence. In his acceptance speech for receiving the Nobel peace prize in 1964, Martin Luther King Jr. said, "Sooner or later all the people of the world will have to discover a way to live together in peace, and thereby transform this pending cosmic elegy into a creative psalm of brotherhood. If this is to be achieved, man must evolve for all human conflict a method which rejects revenge, aggression and retaliation. The foundation of such a method is love." Is it possible to achieve such a utopian society? Which of these two conflicting principles will the human species ultimately choose?

One cannot deny the fact that humans are capable of ethical judgment. We often classify actions as right or wrong, although such judgment might be subjective. At the same time, ethical reasoning and judgment are functions of the human brain, and therefore are at least in part the product of brain evolution. Therefore, deciding whether to retaliate toward someone who has harmed you or your family is not only an ethical question, but also a topic that can be studied using the tools of game theory and evolutionary biology. As we have seen, adaptive strategies such as the tit-for-tat and Pavlov strategies produce better outcomes than unconditional cooperation or defection. This implies that such adaptive strategies could have emerged during animal evolution. If cooperation in human society mostly relies on such adaptive strategies, then refusing to cooperate might result in a short-term gain but will ultimately be a loss to the defector. This is because eventually other people will stop cooperating with the defector. In other words, a society in which most people behave according to the tit-for-tat or Pavlov strategy might punish its members who do not cooperate. In such a society, the level of cooperation might increase with the intensity of punishment against defection. If much of human evolution took place in an environment where our ancestors formed stable communities and frequently interacted with the members of the same group, then the strategy of punishing defectors might have been adopted as a default strategy in the human brain. Strong negative emotions we often feel toward injustice and the desire to revenge even when such unfair acts were directed to others might be a product of this evolutionary process.

In fact, researchers have previously tested whether revenge might be a default response of the brain. In this experiment, participants chose how much money to donate in an iterative public goods game. In addition, at the end of each trial, they were given an opportunity to penalize any free-riders who refused to donate money in that trial. The results from these experiments showed that many people were willing to punish free-riders, even when they had to pay for revenge using their own money. Such an act of punishing others who refuse to cooperate or deviate from other social norms even at the expense of personal cost is referred to as altruistic punishment. When people get angry and want revenge after they are treated unfairly, they are seeking altruistic punishment. In addition, revenge is sweet. The fact that people often anticipate and experience pleasure from successful vengeance might be a product of a brain mechanism that was installed during evolution to encourage altruistic punishment. Results from neuroimaging studies have given some support to this hypothesis. For example, some studies found that the brain activity closely related to reward and utilities, for example, in the ventral striatum, increase when the participants decide to punish defectors (de Quervain et al., 2004).

Relatively simple adaptive strategies, such as the tit-for-tat and Pavlov strategies, might be somewhat effective in facilitating cooperation, but they are unlikely to eliminate defection completely in a large society, since the strategies of defectors can also become very sophisticated. Therefore, more powerful measures, such as altruistic punishment, might be a necessary evil to maximize cooperation. If so, is altruistic punishment really the best possible solution? If the goal is to encourage cooperation as much as possible, how about giving large rewards to cooperators rather than punishing defectors? Sadly, a positive method of rewarding cooperators might be less effective than altruistic punishment. If a society tries to reward every cooperator, then the budget necessary to cover the total amount of such rewards would increase with the frequency of cooperation. By contrast, the budget for altruistic punishment decreases as the level of cooperation increases. No expenses are required when everyone cooperates. Therefore, altruistic punishment is more efficient than rewarding cooperators.

To facilitate cooperation using altruistic punishment, the punishment must be directed selectively at those refusing to cooperate. In other words, members of the society should be able to identify defectors. In laboratory experiments on altruistic punishment, defectors are often known to all participants. This may not be the case in real life. For example, although similar games might be played repeatedly, members participating in such games might change frequently. When the members of a group can select who can join their group, it would be beneficial for them to accept only those who are willing to cooperate, rather than allowing both defectors and cooperators indiscriminately. The ability to identify potential cooperators before they join the group would become more important as the group increases its size and as the games become more complex, since the benefit of cooperation is likely to increase accordingly. This is why we care so much about reputation. From the perspective of game theory and evolutionary biology, an essential element of someone's reputation is our expectation about their tendency to cooperate. However, the benefit of positive reputation also increases the temptation for deception. If a group has only cooperators, then both defectors and cooperators would benefit by joining such a group, although the existing group members would try to accept only true cooperators. Therefore, defectors capable of disguising and displaying false signals as if they are cooperators would be more successful than naive defectors that can be identified easily. Accordingly, the need to identify genuine cooperators co-exists and competes with the need for defectors to imitate cooperators, and an arms race between those two strategies would get increasingly more sophisticated. These problems are unique to brains that evolve in complex social structures.

Predicting the Behavior of Others

We constantly face difficult choices to make in a complex society, a problem that would become much easier if we could accurately predict the behaviors of others. The ability to predict what choices others will make is important, regardless of whether the relationship is competitive or cooperative. For example, in competitive zero-sum games like rock–paper–scissors, winning is easy if one can correctly predict the choice of the opponent. Similarly, it would be much easier to maintain cooperation within an organization, if it is easy to identify those individuals that are willing to cooperate. To predict how others will behave, it is necessary to know what they know and what they want. In other words, if you want to predict the behavior of someone, you need to understand their knowledge and preference. The ability to predict the behavior of others accurately based on their knowledge and preference is referred to the theory of mind. Theory of mind is essential to interact with other people efficiently, especially when we live in a complex society.

An essential first step in theory of mind is the ability to recognize the difference between self and others. In other words, it is necessary to distinguish between the knowledge and intention of oneself and those of others. It would be impossible to predict how others will behave without knowing the difference between oneself and others. For example, I would not be able to predict what you would do, if I did not distinguish between what I know and what you know. The ability to distinguish between these two types of knowledge can be tested using the so-called false-belief test. Also known as the Sally–Anne test, this is one of the most common laboratory tasks used to evaluate theory of mind among children (Frith, 2001). During this task, participants are shown two dolls, named Sally and Anne (Figure 8.3), and told the following story. First, Sally puts a ball in a basket and leaves the room. Then, while Sally is away, Anne moves the ball from the basket to a box. Later, Sally returns and is trying to find the ball. Where will Sally look?

The correct answer is, of course, the basket, since she does not know that Anne has moved it from the basket to the box. However, to produce this correct answer, the participants must dissociate their knowledge about the real location of the ball (box) from what Sally knows (basket). To predict Sally's behavior correctly, they must utilize what they believe Sally knows, not necessarily what they know. This task is called a false-belief task, because Sally's belief or knowledge is false, but it is still what you have to access to answer the question correctly. When this test is given to children that are less than 4 years old, most of them answer that Sally would look in the box where the ball is actually placed. This implies that theory of mind is not fully developed in young children below the age of 4. They do not have the ability to represent and evaluate the knowledge of another person independently of their own knowledge.

Humans tend to acquire full-blown theory of mind by about 4 years of age. How about other animals? Do animals other than humans have theory of mind? Can they understand the difference between what they know and what other animals know? It is much harder to test theory of mind in nonhuman animals, since they do not understand our language. Nevertheless, it would be absurd to conclude that other animals do not have theory of mind, simply because we cannot talk to them. If we applied the same logic, we would also conclude that foreigners unable to understand our language did not have any thoughts. Despite the difficulty in studying animal cognition, recent evidence suggests that some apes, including chimpanzees and orangutans, can pass the false-belief test (Krupenye et al., 2016). Chimpanzees can also understand the intention of human experimenters and even voluntarily help them acquire certain physical objects they are trying to reach (Warneken and Tomasello, 2006). In fact, chimpanzees and human infants often show similar altruistic behaviors in that they often spontaneously help others trying to get some objects. Therefore, theory of mind might not be unique to humans.

We should always guard ourselves against believing that only humans possess certain cognitive abilities, without sufficient evidence. This is because

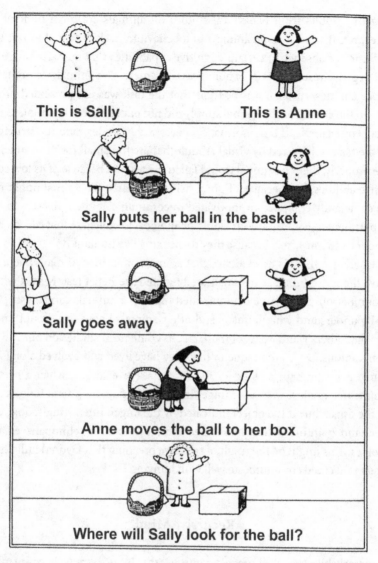

This is Sally   This is Anne

Sally puts her ball in the basket

Sally goes away

Anne moves the ball to her box

Where will Sally look for the ball?

Figure 8.3. A false-belief task known as the Sally–Anne task used to evaluate theory of mind.

Source: Frith U(2001) Mindblindness and the brain in autism. Neuron 32: 969–979. Copyright (2001), with permission from Elsevier.

negative results from behavioral studies on animals are often difficult to interpret. If we test some animals in a behavioral task designed to test the presence or absence of certain cognitive capabilities that humans have and get negative results, this does not necessarily mean that animals do not have those abilities. Instead, it is possible that the task was not presented properly to the animal or the animal simply did not pay sufficient attention to the task. For example, if the information necessary to understand the structure of the task is delivered by visual stimuli that are too small for the animal to see properly, then the animal would fail in the test not because of its low cognitive abilities, but because of poor vision. Similarly, the animal might not be sufficiently equipped or motivated to communicate their answers to the experimenter. For example, it would be illogical to conclude that cats do not understand music just because they do not sing like humans do.

Currently, there is no evidence that animals other than humans and apes have theory of mind, as demonstrated by the false-belief test. Nevertheless, a number of studies have demonstrated that other animals can at least partially understand what humans and other animals know and do not know or what others want. Many of these results come from studies on our canine companions. Dogs are unique in that they have lived and evolved alongside humans for perhaps as long as 30,000 years. For example, when a person points to an object with their finger in front of a dog, dogs tend to look not at the finger, but at the object indicated by the finger. Interestingly, dogs understand pointing better than other animals, including chimpanzees and wolves. This might be the result of selective breeding that favored individual dogs who could communicate well with humans.

Recursive Mind

A remarkable feature of human cognition is the ability to apply theory of mind repeatedly and recursively. By applying theory of mind recursively, I can imagine or understand not just what you might be thinking, but also what you might imagine that I might be thinking. Like countless images of you forming when you stand in front of a pair of large mirrors facing each other, my thoughts can include not just your thoughts about other people and objects in the world, but your thoughts about my thoughts and feelings. Of course, this can be further extended to your thoughts about my thoughts about what you might be thinking, and so forth. We all experience this endless stream of inferences in our everyday lives even when we participate in relatively simple social interactions, such as when we play a rock–paper–scissors game.

It is not easy to measure the depth of such recursive theory of mind, namely, how many times someone else applied theory of mind to make a choice. One of the tools developed to test this in a laboratory experiment is a beauty-contest game. In this game, each participant chooses a number between zero and 100. Then, all the chosen numbers are averaged, and multiplied by a factor, commonly 2/3, and the person who chose the number closest to this final number wins. If you are new to this game, imagine you are participating in this game with nine other people. What number will you choose to win?

This game allows us to estimate accurately how recursively each participant has applied theory of mind based on his or her chosen number. Let us consider possible strategies participants in this game might use. First, some participants might just randomly pick any numbers between zero and 100. This random strategy can be referred to as the zero-th order strategy. Some of the participants might even choose numbers much greater than 67, even though this is clearly not a wise strategy. It is extremely unlikely that everyone chooses the largest possible number in this game, namely 100. Even if this were to happen, the average of all the chosen numbers multiplied by 2/3 would never exceed 67. Second, some participants might try to estimate the target number by assuming that everyone plays this game using the zero-th order strategy. In this case, the average would be approximately 50, so such participants might choose a number close to 33, since $50 \times 2/3 = 33.3$. This strategy can be referred to as the first-order strategy. Namely, the first-order strategy is to choose 33, and this corresponds to the best response when we assume that all the other players use the zero-th order strategy.

Of course, we can imagine more complex strategies than the first-order strategy. If you assume that all other participants in this game choose their numbers using the first-order strategy, then you should choose 22, since the expected average multiplied by 2/3 in this case would be 22.2. This corresponds to the second-order strategy. These examples clearly show that the best response in the beauty contest game depends on what strategy one believes others would use. This creates a paradox. If you believe everyone would use the n-th order strategy, then you must use the $(n + 1)$-th order strategy. Conveniently, it is straightforward to calculate the answer given by the n-th order strategy in the beauty-contest game, which corresponds to $(2/3)^n \times 50$. One can then realize that the difference between the answers given by the n-th and $(n + 1)$-th order strategies diminishes gradually as n increases and disappears completely when n becomes infinitely large. Remembering that at the Nash equilibrium, everyone's choice must be the best response to everyone else's choice, this implies that one arrives at the Nash equilibrium for the beauty-contest game when n becomes infinitely large. In other words, the Nash equilibrium for the beauty contest game is for everyone to choose zero. More important, the beauty contest game entails a one-to-one relationship between the choice of each participant and the order of their strategy. In other words, you can infer directly the depth of recursive theory of mind for someone from the number they choose in this game.

The beauty contest game was invented by an economist named Rosemarie Nagel in 1995. It was named after the phrase used by John Maynard Keynes, the founder of macroeconomics, to refer to the irrationality in the behavior of stock markets. Keynes claimed that future stock prices are difficult to predict because people make their buying and selling decisions not just based on the real value of the companies, but mostly according to how much value they believe others would assign to the companies. Sometimes, the decisions might be based on the predictions about how some people predict what other people might predict. Keynes compared this recursive process to predicting the winner in a beauty contest. To predict the winner successfully, you would not choose someone you think is the most beautiful, but instead who you think the judges might think is the most beautiful.

Social Brain

Almost every choice we make in our modern society occurs in a social context. This is true not only when we are physically interacting and communicating with other people, but sometimes even when we are alone. Strictly speaking, reading and writing messages, reading books, watching television, or even listening to music are all social activities. Our brain continues to process information about the thoughts and emotions of other people through sound, images, and texts, even when they are not with us. Even when no sensory stimulus is delivering any social information to us, our mental activity is constantly filled with memories about our relationships and interactions with other people and our attempts to re-evaluate them. In addition, social isolation is painful. Feelings of loneliness constantly pull people toward various social groups.

If a substantial part of human activity takes place in social settings, the skills necessary to resolve various conflicts and problems arising from social interactions could have shaped the process of brain evolution. Namely, genes responsible for controlling brain development and learning would have changed gradually so that structures and functions of the resulting brain can make better choices in complex societies. Compared to individual decision-making, social decision-making requires animals to process more information at a greater depth, as when people apply theory of mind recursively. This is particularly true for primates, who tend to live in more complex societies than other animals with similar body weights. This might explain why primates tend to have larger brains compared to other mammals.

The proposal that primate brains have increased in size during evolution because a larger brain could confer primates with better abilities to process more complex social information is referred to as the social intelligence or Machiavellian intelligence hypothesis (Byrne and Whiten, 1988). It is easy to imagine why this might be the case. For example, during social interactions, one frequently needs to analyze the details of facial expressions of other people. This would keep the visual cortex busy. Similarly, to understand the sounds or words produced by others, the auditory cortex and other areas of the brain involved with linguistic analysis, such as Wernicke's area, must be recruited. To accurately predict the behavior of others and understand the intentions of observed behaviors, one needs to apply theory of mind, often recursively, and this might engage additional areas involved in social reasoning and working memory. Simply put, the entire brain might be recruited when we are engaged in complex social interactions. This could have induced neurons in many anatomical areas of the brain to increase their number and connections with other neurons.

The need to handle complex social interactions might have simply increased the overall size of the brain uniformly or given rise to special brain areas dedicated for social functions. This depends on whether unique and more complex computations are required for social interactions than for individual decision-making. If there are no fundamental differences in the types of computations that the brain must perform for individual versus social decision-making, it would be wasteful to have separate modules in the brain dedicated for handling the problems in the social domain. Indeed, there are many areas in the human brain that might be specialized for particular functions, such as Wernicke's area for language comprehension, and Broca's area for speech. The hippocampus might have a special role in consolidating long-term episodic memory. These special anatomical structures might have evolved, due to their anatomical and physiological properties appropriate for important cognitive functions, such as language and memory. Given that some cognitive processes, such as recursive reasoning and theory of mind, might be unique to social cognition, some brain areas in the human brain might be closely tied to social cognition.

Brain areas dedicated for special functions, such as social decision-making, is analogous to including circuits or modules dedicated to handling specific types of computations inside a computer, such as the graphics processing unit (GPU) for matrix operations related to fast image processing. The GPU technology, now central to advancing research in artificial intelligence and many other areas of science, was originally driven in large part by the video game industry that needed sophisticated three-dimensional image processing and animation.

In humans and other primates, there are several areas in the cerebral cortex specialized in the analysis of facial stimuli. This might not be too surprising, since faces provide rich information not just about the identities of different individuals but also about their health and psychological states. Rigorous neuroscience research on the brain functions related to face perception started in the laboratory of Charles Gross at Princeton University. In the early 1970s, when Gross's research was being undertaken, it was well known that neurons in the early stage of visual information processing in the cortex responded to relatively simple features of visual stimuli, such as their orientation. Gross was investigating the possibility that neurons in more downstream cortical areas, such as the inferior temporal cortex, might be responsible for analyzing and identifying more complex visual features or objects. During these experiments, he found that some neurons in the inferior temporal cortex are specialized or tuned for faces of monkeys and humans (Figure 8.4). These results led to the hypothesis that there might be anatomical modules in the primate brain specialized for face perception. This is also consistent with the fact that patients with lesions close to the border between the occipital and temporal lobes sometimes lose the ability to recognize faces. This symptom is referred to as prosopagnosia. When it became possible to measure the metabolic activities in living human brain using function magnetic resonance (fMRI) and positron emission tomography, it was confirmed that there are indeed several regions in the human cortex specialized for the analysis of faces. For example, an area referred to as the fusiform face area increase its activity when faces are shown to the

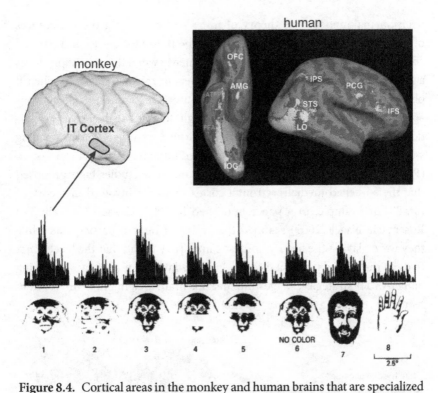

Figure 8.4. Cortical areas in the monkey and human brains that are specialized for face perception. Top: Inferior temporal cortex in the monkey brain contain neurons responding more strongly to facial stimuli, whereas multiple patches of the human brains show stronger BOLD signals when the subjects view human faces than when they view other nonface stimuli. Bottom: An example neuron recorded in the monkey IT cortex. This neuron increased its activity when face stimuli were shown to the animal, compared to scrambled faces or a hand.

Source: Top: Rajimehr R, Young JC, Tootell RBH (2009) An anterior temporal face patch in human cortex, predicted by macaque maps. Proc Natl Acad Sci. USA 106: 1995–2000. Copyright (2009) National Academy of Sciences USA. Bottom: Republished with permission of Society for Neuroscience. Desimone R, Albright TD, Gross CG, Bruce C (1984) Stimulus-selective properties of inferior temporal neurons in the macaque. J. Neurosci. 4: 2051–2062. Permission conveyed through Copyright Clearance Center, Inc.

participants during fMRI experiments (Kanwisher et al., 1997). Faces are not an exception, since other types of information important for social interaction, such as the dynamic pattern of body motion, can also activate anatomically distinct brain areas.

In addition to the cortical areas that might be specialized in socially meaningful stimuli, such as faces and bodily motion, some areas of the human brain might be closely related to other aspects of social reasoning and decision-making, such as theory of mind and estimating the preferences of others. For example, some neurons in the premotor cortex and parietal cortex of monkeys change their activity similarly when the animal produces a particular action, such as picking up a peanut from a table, and when it observes the same action performed by a human researcher. These neurons are referred to as mirror neurons and thought to mediate the process of understanding the meaning of actions performed by others. Neuroimaging studies have similarly identified the so-called human mirror-neuron system (Rizzolatti and Craighero, 2004). In addition, some studies have proposed that the so-called medial prefrontal cortex might be involved in theory of mind. For example, in a paper published in 2009, Giorgio Coricelli and Rosemarie Nagel (2009) scanned the brains of human participants while they were playing the beauty-contest game. They found that the level of activity in the medial prefrontal cortex increased when the subjects were using higher-order strategies, suggesting that this brain area might be involved in recursive reasoning and theory of mind (Figure 8.5).

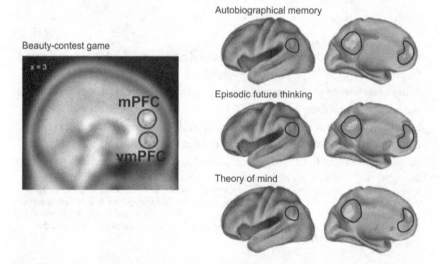

Figure 8.5. Areas of the human brain involved in social cognition. Left: The medial (mPFC) and ventromedial (vmPFC) cortex that increase their activity during recursive social reasoning. Right: Cortical areas activated during three different tasks related to autobiographical memory, episodic future thinking, and theory of mind.

Source: Left: Coricelli G, Nagel R (2009) Neural correlates of depth of strategic reasoning in medial prefrontal cortex. Proc Natl Acad Sci. USA 106: 9163–9168. Copyright (2009) National Academy of Sciences USA. Right: Buckner RL, Andrews-Hanna JR, Schacter DL (2008) The brain's default network: anatomy, function, and relevance to disease. Ann NY Acad Sci 1124: 1–38. Reproduced with permission from John Wiley and Sons.

Default Cognition: Anthropomorphization

The medial prefrontal cortex is part of a larger cortical network, commonly referred to as the default mode network. The default mode network refers to a set of brain areas that reduce their activity when participants are performing specific tasks instructed by the experimenter. When human participants begin to perform tasks designed to study specific cognitive processes, such as attention and memory, many brain areas with sensory and motor functions tend to increase their activity. By contrast, areas in the default mode network reduce their activity during the trials when the subjects are actively performing such tasks but increase their activity during the rest periods between trials. In addition to the medial prefrontal cortex, the default mode network also includes the hippocampus and posterior cingulate cortex. Although this may seem paradoxical at first, the reason why the default mode network increases its activity at rest might be due to mind wandering that occurs between tasks. Therefore, identifying the common contents and types of mind wandering experienced by participants of fMRI experiments would provide important clues about the function of the default mode network.

What do we usually think about when we do not have to follow specific instructions to perform a task? What are your favorite things to think about while you are waiting in line for your coffee? In such cases, we often think about our previous actions. In addition, most of these recollections revolve around social topics, such as our past interactions and conversations with our co-workers, friends, and family members. For example, you might be recollecting an encounter with a stranger in the subway this morning or might imagine the dinner you plan to have with your friends this evening. These two types of mental activities, namely, recollecting past events and imagining future events are closely related. This is not too surprising, since imaging the future is always based on our previous experience. Since we cannot predict what will really happen in the future, imagining the future often corresponds to recombining various elements of previous events that we expect to occur together in the future. In fact, scientists have found that amnesic patients, including those with damage to the hippocampus, such as Henry Molaison, whom we discussed in the previous chapter, are also impaired in their abilities to imagining the future (Haassabis et al., 2007). One of the authors of this study is Demis Hassabis, who was a graduate student at the University College London. In 2010, Hassabis founded DeepMind, which developed the AI Go program called AlphaGo.

If the activity of the default mode network increases during the rest period because participants are more engaged in recollecting past events or imagining new experience in the future, then asking the participants to perform either of those tasks should also increase the activity in the default mode network. Indeed, multiple experiments have confirmed these predictions. When participants were asked to recall their personal autobiographic memory or to imagine future personal experiences, the activity in the default mode network increased (Figure 8.5). Furthermore, the same areas of the brain also increase their activity when participants must use theory of mind, as when they perform a false-belief task or the beauty-contest game. These results support the idea that social cognition might be at the heart of human mind. Most of the activities people seek to avoid boredom correspond to seeking social stimulation. Reading books is analogous to conversation and watching TV and movies are virtual social interactions. Of course, the best way to escape from boredom is to spend time together with your favorite friends and colleagues. This might reflect our evolutionary history when being a part of a successful group was essential for survival and reproduction.

As long as we are alive, our brains never shut down completely. Even when we are physically inactive, our mind never stops wandering, and much of mind wandering corresponds to mental simulation of our social relationship. Therefore, it would not be entirely misleading to characterize the most unique and fundamental function of the human brain as social. This might have some undesirable side effects. Perhaps the most obvious side effect of setting the default mode of human brain as social would be anthropomorphization, namely, our tendency to treat any object resembling humans as a real human. Anthropomorphization is a hypersensitive response of the social brain to nonsocial stimuli. This is somewhat analogous to a golden retriever's pursuit of tennis balls, although they were originally bred to retrieve game during hunting. There is a strong tendency for people to presume a supernatural agent behind any natural disaster, such as flooding or earthquake. Sometimes, those disasters might be interpreted as god's punishment against our behaviors. Of course, there might be occasions where such superstitious beliefs might be adaptive. For example, if fear of ghosts in the middle of night encourages you to walk faster toward a safe destination, this might protect you from potential predators. Anthropomorphic belief that natural phenomena are controlled by an entity with emotions and other human-like characteristics, including vengeance, might provide some psychological and moral support at a time when scientific knowledge was too rudimentary to account for complex natural phenomena. Such beliefs about psychological entities that intend to reward and punish human behavior with supernatural forces do not disappear easily, even when scientific knowledge can account for natural phenomena accurately. This is because brain evolution is much slower than the rate of scientific and technological progress.

References

Buckner RL, Andrews-Hanna JR, Schacter DL (2008) The brain's default network: anatomy, function, and relevance to disease. Ann NY Acad Sci. 1124: 1–38.

Byrne RW, Whiten A (1988) Machiavellian Intelligence: Social Expertise and the Evolution of Intellect in Monkeys, Apes, and Humans. New York, NY: Oxford Univ. Press.

Coricelli G, Nagel R (2009) Neural correlates of depth of strategic reasoning in medial prefrontal cortex. Proc Natl Acad Sci USA. 106: 9163–9168.

de Quervain DJF, Fischbacher U, Treyer V, et al. (2004) The neural basis of altruistic punishment. Science. 305: 1254–1258.

Desimone R, Albright TD, Gross CG, Bruce C (1984) Stimulus-selective properties of inferior temporal neurons in the macaque. J Neurosci. 4: 2051–2062.

Frith U (2001) Mindblindness and the brain in autism. Neuron. 32: 969–979.

Hassabis D, Kumaran D, Vann SD, Maguire EA (2007) Patients with hippocampal amnesia cannot imagine new experiences. Proc Natl Acad Sci USA. 104: 1726–1731.

Kanwisher N, McDermott J, Chun MM (1997) The fusiform face area: a module in human extrastriate cortex specialized for face perception. J Neurosci. 17: 4302–4311.

Krupenye C, Kano F, Hirata S, Call J, Tomasello M (2016) Great apes anticipate that other individuals will act according to false beliefs. Science. 354: 110–114.

Nash JF (1950) Equilibrium points in n-person games. Proc Natl Acad Sci USA. 36: 48–49.

Nowak M, Sigmund K (1993) A strategy of win–stay, lose–shift that outperforms tit-for-tat in the prisoner's dilemma game. Nature. 364: 56–58.

Rajimehr R, Young JC, Tootell RBH (2009) An anterior temporal face patch in human cortex, predicted by macaque maps. Proc Natl Acad Sci USA. 106: 1995–2000.

Rizzolatti G, Craighero L (2004) The mirror-neuron system. Annu Rev Neurosci. 27: 169–192.

Sally D (1995) Conversation and cooperation in social dilemmas. Ration Soc. 7: 58–92.

von Neumann J, Morgenstern O (1944) Theory of Games and Economic Behavior. Princeton, NJ: Princeton Univ. Press.

Warneken F, Tomasello M (2006) Altruistic helping in human infants and young chimpanzees. Science 311: 1301–1303.

Further Reading

Camerer CF (2003) Behavioral Game Theory: Experiments in Strategic Interaction. Princeton, NJ: Princeton Univ. Press.

Lee D (2008) Game theory and neural basis of social decision making. Nat Neurosci. 11: 404–409.

Lee D (2013) Decision making: from neuroscience to psychiatry. Neuron. 78: 233–248.

9

Intelligence and Self

Can we understand who we are completely? Is it possible for a physical machine like the human brain to understand how it works completely? The significance of self-knowledge and self-insight has been emphasized by numerous philosophers, perhaps best illustrated by the maxim "Know thyself." This maxim was used by many ancient Greeks, including Socrates. In ancient China, a philosopher and general named Sun Tzu wrote "If you know the enemy and know yourself, you need not fear the result of a hundred battles." As Sun Tzu emphasized, self-knowledge or knowledge about oneself has clear practical benefits, since understanding what I need and what I can do is important for planning of our future. The efforts to understand human nature also permeates all our knowledge-seeking missions, including social and natural sciences as well as humanities. Humans might be unique in this regard. Biologically, humans and apes have similar brains and share most of their genes. Behaviorally, humans are not the only social species, since many other animals, including insects, form complex groups. Nevertheless, no other animals are as curious about themselves as humans. Self-awareness and self-knowledge might be the highest form of intelligence.

Life is a process of self-replication, and intelligence is the ability to make decisions beneficial for self-replication. In addition, although there is a great variation across different species, all life forms are fundamentally social. Even the most isolated life form becomes social when they reproduce, which creates potential conflict in resource sharing until the parents and offspring are separated. As the society grows in its size and complexity, the amount of information necessary for social decision-making and the importance of learning increases. The ability to cooperate and help others to avoid unnecessary conflict in human society, the ability to make appropriate inferences about the intentions of others and theory of mind become essential. This raises the possibility that the privilege of self-knowledge and self-insight might be a byproduct of understanding others in a complex society. However, self-knowledge is still fundamentally different from making predictions about other animate and inanimate objects in the environment.

In this chapter, we will examine what might happen when intelligent life forms try to understand themselves.

Paradox of Self-Knowledge

Self-knowledge or self-insight is a type of knowledge, and this knowledge can be used to predict the outcomes of various behaviors during decision-making. The nature and complexity of decision-making determines the type of knowledge necessary for decision-making. Self-knowledge is necessary for social decision-making. When many people begin to interact with each other in a complex society, knowledge about the cognitive processes and decision-making strategies of other people is necessary to make accurate predictions about their behaviors. It is then inevitable that inferences about the knowledge of others become recursive, and this naturally leads to self-knowledge. If I try to understand your thoughts about me, this indirectly but still inevitably leads to understanding myself. Therefore, the knowledge and insights of humans about themselves might have emerged as a byproduct of brain evolution that took place in a social environment, where accurately predicting the behaviors of others was essential. Ironically, just like self-replication of genetic materials is always imperfect, self-knowledge cannot be complete. Copying genetic materials is a physical process, so is constrained by laws of physics, especially the second law of thermodynamics. Biophysically, arriving at some form of self-knowledge might not involve any replication of physical entities, but self-knowledge can lead to logical paradoxes.

In self-knowledge, a person who seeks the knowledge becomes the object of the knowledge itself, and thoughts and ideas can begin to refer to themselves, creating self-reference (Figure 9.1). Self-reference can be challenging, as famously illustrated by the liar's paradox. The liar's paradox is created when someone says, "I am lying," or writes "This sentence is false." If the liar is lying, then the statement must be false, so the liar is not lying, leading to a contradiction. If the liar is telling the truth, then the statement must be true, so the liar is not lying. This is also a contradiction. The sentence cannot be true, but it cannot be false either, so it's a paradox.

The liar's paradox leads to contradictions, because it includes self-reference. Another famous paradox resulting from self-reference is Russell's paradox, also known as the barber's paradox. This example is a proposition that a barber in a town shaves all those, and only those, who do not shave

Figure 9.1. *La trahison des images* (The treachery of images, 1928~1929) by Rene Magritte, including a sentence *Ceci n'est pas une pipe* (This is not a pipe). *Source:* Copyright, Herscovici/Artists Rights Society, New York.

themselves. There is a paradox because one cannot easily determine whether this barber can shave himself, which includes self-reference. If the answer is yes, that is, if the barber shaves himself, this contradicts the proposition that he only shaves those who do not shave themselves. If the answer is no, that is, if the barber does not shave himself, this is also a contradiction, since he does not shave someone who does not shave himself. Therefore, there is a contradiction regardless of whether the barber shaves himself or not.

Propositions or sentences with self-reference can easily become a paradox. When multiple decision makers begin to interact in a social setting and begin to make inferences about the behavior of others recursively, similar problems can occur because this can also lead to self-reference. When the inferences of one person begin to cover the inferences of another person recursively, we can create somewhat complex, but seemingly benign sentences like the following.

Ann believes that Bob assumes that Ann believes that Bob's assumption is wrong.

The situation described by this sentence is not fundamentally different from the inferences we sometimes make about the thoughts of others, as when we play a rock–paper–scissors game. To understand that this sentence leads to contradiction, you should try to answer the following question. Does Ann believe that Bob's assumption is wrong? If the answer is yes, then from Ann's perspective, Bob's assumption that "Ann believes that Bob's assumption is wrong" must be right, but that implies that Ann does not believe that Bob's assumption is wrong, which leads to contradiction. On the other hand, if the answer is no, then in Ann's view, Bob's assumption that "Ann believes that Bob's assumption is wrong" is wrong, which implies that Ann does believe that Bob's assumption is wrong. This is also contradictory to the original sentence. Therefore, the original sentence contains contradiction either way. This sentence was presented by Adam Brandenburger and H. Jerome Keisler (2006), so is referred to as Brandenburger–Keisler paradox.

As these examples show, the use of any word that can refer to something, such as *know* or *believe*, can potentially create a logical paradox, when it is directed back to the subject. The liar's paradox reminds us that it is not always easy to distinguish between true and false. Russell's paradox reminds us that it is not always possible to classify everything into two mutually exclusive groups based on their properties. Brandenburger–Keisler paradox reminds us that recursive reasoning in a social relationship could lead to an infinite regress.

It would be physically impossible for a machine to duplicate itself entirely without any errors. Similarly, it might not be possible for humans to understand themselves completely without logical contradictions. Nevertheless, mutations are necessary for evolution, and physical machines can evolve precisely because they replicate themselves imperfectly. The essence of life is not perfect self-replication, but rather nearly perfect but still imperfect self-replication. Therefore, perhaps, we should not be disappointed even if complete and consistent self-knowledge is not possible. The ability to apply theory of mind recursively is beneficial, since it allows people to predict the behavior of others, thereby improving and stabilizing social structures. If self-knowledge emerges from the recursive theory of mind, its most important function might be to help us predict our own behavior. Nevertheless, we should be mindful of limitations of such self-knowledge. Self-referential statements, like "I am not lying," are interesting topics for logicians and philosophers, but they do not help us with decisions we face in our daily lives.

Logical paradoxes and contradictions are not the only negative consequences of self-knowledge. Trying to predict our own behavior based on self-knowledge can produce other unexpected effects. For example, if our predictions about our own future behaviors are too optimistic, such prediction might become a self-fulfilling prophecy, because the act of making such predictions itself can make the predicted behavior more likely to happen. On the other hand, if the predictions about our own behavior are too pessimistic, then they can become self-defeating prophecies. If I predict that I will get hungry before 6 PM today, then this would encourage me to eat some food before 6 PM, allowing me to avoid the anticipated hunger. Such self-defeating prophecies are therefore not accurate, but they are still useful and difficult to eliminate completely.

Problems created by self-knowledge include the notion of free will, which refers to the ability to control one's own behavior. The problem of free will is an important part of our desire to understand ourselves. However, this is separate from the question of whether our universe is deterministic and therefore is not a question about the physics of how the brain works. Once we realize that the notion of self is a byproduct of recursively applying theory of mind and that self is not a physical object existing independently of our mental simulation, there is no reason to expect coherent answers to the question of free will.

Metacognition and Metaselection

Self-knowledge emerges from a large pool of learning strategies developed by the genes and brains to improve their abilities to make decisions through evolution. People do not choose their actions by following just one rule or by using just one strategy. Instead, how they make choices varies across different contexts depending on the level of necessary knowledge and time pressure. Therefore, we often face a problem of metaselection, namely, a choice among different styles of learning and decision-making. The prefix *meta* is used when a concept is applied to itself and therefore might imply self-reference. For example, in computer science, the term *metadata* is used to refer to the data that contains information about other data.

It's easy to find examples of metaselection in our everyday lives. For example, let's imagine you are trying to choose a destination for a vacation. You might have many different options. If you like nature, you might be interested in visiting some national parks, such as Yellowstone, whereas if you like museums, then you might want to visit cities like London or Paris. When it becomes really hard to choose among many different options, you might decide to get some help from a travel agency. However, this creates a new problem if there are many travel agencies to choose from. Each travel agency might have specialties on trips to specific geographic areas or even different package tours. Now, you must choose one of these travel agencies that can help you choose the destination for your vacation. This is metaselection.

Obviously, the type of information you should consider during metaselection is completely different from the information needed for the original choice. When you are trying to choose a vacation destination, you might consider such factors as the distance to the destination, the cost of flight, the types of possible activities, and food. By contrast, when trying to select a travel agency, you must consider things like friendliness and reputation of the agents and their commissions. Similarly, the criterion used by the brain when choosing between different decision-making strategies or different learning algorithms would be quite different from how those individual strategies or learning algorithms operate. In general, during metaselection, one needs to evaluate the performance or reliability of different decision-making strategies or learning algorithms. More generally, the cognitive process applied to other cognitive processes can be referred to as metacognition. Therefore, metaselection is a type of metacognition. Similarly, self-knowledge is a product of metacognition.

Metacognition is an integral part of human intelligence, and we might rely on it more than most people might realize. An important function of metacognition is to evaluate the accuracy and validity of all the judgments we make. For example, let's imagine that someone asks you who the producer for the Beatles was. Although the correct answer is George Martin, you may not give that answer as soon as it comes to your mind, especially when you are afraid to embarrass yourself by answering this question incorrectly. You might want to think about it for a few more seconds before you give an answer. You would probably hesitate more before answering a question if you are less certain, and this sense of confidence is a part of metacognition.

Another metacognitive process familiar to us is the feeling of knowing. The feeling of knowing refers to knowing in advance whether your memory has the information necessary to answer a question before you find the information you are looking for. Studies on feeling of knowing rely on the fact that there are two different ways to retrieve information from memory, namely, recall and recognition. Recall refers to the process of retrieving the requested item from memory without being shown possible answers. For example, answering a question such as "What's the name of the tallest mountain in the world?" requires recall. By contrast, recognition refers to the ability to identify a correct answer when it is shown among other distractors. Recognition is easier than recall. Even if you couldn't recall the name of George Martin, you might be able to recognize him as the Beatles' producer once you are presented with his name together with the names of other music producers. Therefore, recall is the ability tested in a fill-in-the-blank question, whereas recognition is the ability tested in a multiple-choice question. If you have a feeling of knowing about the correct answer when you are given a fill-in-the-blank question, you would be confident that you could answer it correctly when the same question is given as a multiple-choice question. Indeed, studies have shown that feeling of knowing predicts the accuracy of your answers, indicating that people can trust their feeling of knowing. Studies based on brain lesions and neuroimaging experiments in humans have shown that feeling of knowing relies on the function of the medial prefrontal cortex (Modirrousta and Fellows, 2008).

Researchers studying the feeling of knowing typically ask the participants to describe verbally how strongly they believe they know the answer to a question. Similarly, to study confidence, researchers often ask how certain participants are with the answer they already gave. However, these questions are vague, and their answers are subjective and qualitative. More important, any methods based on human language are difficult to apply to study cognition in other animals. Fortunately, more objective and quantitative approaches to study confidence and other types of metacognition exist. One such method is called postdecision wagering (Persaud et al., 2007). Although you may not be familiar with the name of this method, people often use it to challenge someone with a claim that is difficult to believe. For example, let us imagine that someone predicts that it will rain tomorrow. We can ask this person how sure he or she might be, but the truthfulness of the answer would still be difficult to evaluate. Instead, we can use the postdecision wagering to determine the confidence of this person more objectively. For example, we can propose a series of gambles that has the following format. The person predicting rain gets x dollars if it rains tomorrow but must pay $100 if it does not. For example, let us imagine that the predictor gets $100 dollars if it rains, namely, x = $100. If the predictor accepts this gamble, it implies that they believe that their prediction is correct with a probability of at least 50 percent. When the subjective probability that it might rain tomorrow is above 50 percent, the expected value of this gamble is positive, so the gamble would be profitable. By contrast, if the same probability is less than 50 percent, the expected value would be negative, so the offer would not be accepted. Let's imagine that this person accepts the original gamble. We can then offer another gamble, for example, with x = $25, if we want to find out whether the same person believes the prediction with more than 80 percent confidence or not. In other words, this person would not accept such a biased gamble unless he or she is at least 80 percent certain that it would rain tomorrow. If the predictor is completely certain about their prediction, they would accept the gamble even if x is infinitely small. Postdecision wagering can be used in experiments on nonhuman animals (Kornell et al., 2007). In fact, scientists have investigated the activity of individual neurons in the prefrontal cortex and other association cortical areas whose activity is related to the level of confidence during decision-making in monkeys and rodents (Kiani and Shadlen, 2009).

As illustrated by postdecision wagering, confidence about one's own knowledge plays an important role in metaselection. Similarly, for choosing between different strategies of decision-making and learning algorithms, their reliabilities or performance must be accurately evaluated. For example, if you are experiencing relatively large reward prediction errors constantly, this suggests that your model-free reinforcement learning algorithm is not working reliably and might indicate that you might be better off to giving more weight to model-based reinforcement learning. By contrast, the success of model-based reinforcement learning depends on whether the decision maker has accurate knowledge about their environment. If this knowledge is accurate, then the predictions about how the environment would change after taking various actions should be relatively accurate. For example, if I am very familiar with the subway system of a city, then I should be able to predict what the next station will be without looking at the map. Conversely, if I frequently fail to predict the next station, it implies that my knowledge of the subway needs to be revised. When the actual state of the environment after an action is different from the predicted state of the environment, as when you fail to predict the name of the next station, this discrepancy is referred to as a state prediction error. Therefore, if one experiences state prediction errors frequently, it might be better to switch to model-free reinforcement learning. Of course, if someone just entered a new environment, it is possible that they might experience both reward prediction errors and state prediction errors continuously. In this case, there might not be a good solution other than trying to learn about the new environment as quickly as possible. When you move to a new environment, at least in the beginning, no reinforcement learning algorithm would be reliable. Reliability of all learning algorithms would gradually improve, but which algorithm would be more reliable for

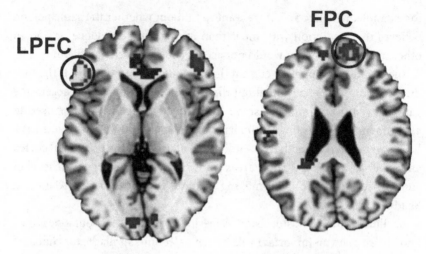

Figure 9.2. Lateral prefrontal cortex (LPFC) and frontal polar cortex (FPC) implicated for meta-selection during reinforcement learning.

Source: Lee SW, Shimojo S, O'Doherty JP (2014) Neural computations underlying arbitration between model-based and model-free learning. Neuron 81: 687–699. Copyright (2014), with permission from Elsevier.

a given problem might change unpredictably, depending on many factors, such as the complexity of the environment and the number of alternative actions. Recently studies have shown that functions related to evaluating the reliability of different reinforcement learning algorithms might be localized in the brain regions known as the lateral prefrontal cortex and frontal polar cortex (Lee et al., 2004; Figure 9.2). Given that the medial prefrontal cortex might be involved in feeling of knowing, these results suggest that various components of metacognition and metaselection might be implemented in specific subdivisions of the prefrontal cortex.

Cost of Intelligence

Life frequently requires trade-offs. It is probably an eternal truth that accomplishing anything valuable requires sacrificing something less important. For example, the benefits of large brains are numerous. Animals with big brains can learn more from their environment and, using this knowledge, choose behaviors that will produce more desirable outcomes. However, it is also expensive to maintain big brains, and therefore animals with larger brains will have to find, eat, and digest more high-calorie food. Therefore, animals will not be able to afford large brains, unless having big brains make it possible to earn enough calories and other nutrients. This might be analogous to the fact that major companies can maintain a large research department only if they develops profitable new techniques and products. Larger brains have other disadvantages. For example, it is very time-consuming to grow a large brain, because this requires an astronomical number of accurate connections among many neurons. Such a long and complex process of development is also more likely to result in errors, which might then prevent the adult brain from functioning properly. In humans, a prolonged period of brain development implies that children must stay under their parents' protection much longer. For mammals, again especially for humans, giving birth to a baby with a large brain increases the risk for both mother and baby.

Trade-offs exist for learning and decision-making as well. For example, *C. elegans* can begins to lay eggs only three days from fertilization. It is impressive that during that short period of time this animal can produce more than 300 neurons and connect them appropriately so that they can produce all the necessary behaviors for survival and reproduction. Such speed and simplicity have a cost in that learning in *C. elegans* is limited to relatively simple forms, such as habituation and classical conditioning. By contrast, due to their more sophisticated brains, mammals can change their behavior through operant conditioning in addition to habituation and classical conditioning. They can also acquire abstract knowledge of their environment and use it to select their actions, using model-based reinforcement learning. Moreover, humans and apes can use even more sophisticated methods, such as theory of mind, to make decisions in social settings. Not surprisingly, there is a cost in having access to many complex methods of learning and decision-making. For example, as self-knowledge emerges from recursive application of theory of mind, this begins to introduce logical paradoxes that can interfere with adaptive behaviors. Negative emotions and mental illnesses are also byproducts of sophisticated learning algorithms.

All learning algorithms used by humans and other animals require certain types of error signals, which can produce unpleasant consequences. As we reviewed in Chapter 7 of this volume, model-free reinforcement learning relies on reward prediction errors. The essence of model-free reinforcement learning is to adjust the value of each action according to whether its outcome was better or worse than previously expected. Therefore, it would not be realistic to prevent all negative reward prediction errors without shutting down model-free reinforcement learning entirely. Psychologically, such negative reward prediction errors manifest as disappointment. If you do not experience any disappointment or negative reward prediction errors, this suggests that your expectation of future rewards might be too low. This would prevent you from taking many actions that are potentially beneficial. Model-free reinforcement learning will also occasionally produce positive reward prediction errors or elation. Although you would not experience disappointment and elation simultaneously, they are like two sides of the same coin, in that you cannot have one without the other. This is true for regret and relief that arise from model-based reinforcement learning. For the success of model-based reinforcement learning, different counterfactual outcomes from alternative actions must be evaluated through mental simulation. Some of those simulated outcomes might be better than the outcomes you have previously experienced. Therefore, regret is an inescapable byproduct of model-based reinforcement learning.

When the brain runs mental simulation and begins to create a story based on imagined actions and counterfactual outcomes, it is critical to keep such stories separate from the reality. This is a risk unique to brains relying on model-based reinforcement learning and does not apply to animals solely relying on model-free reinforcement learning. When we try to adjust the values of alternative actions based on mental simulation, the simulated events that did not occur in reality might still be stored in memory. It is important, then, to distinguish the memories of real experience and imagined experience. The ability to determine how specific memories were formed, including whether they were from real or simulated experience, is another example of metacognition, and this is referred to as source memory. Since source memory is memory about memory, it is also metamemory. Source memory is essential for normal social life. For example, try to imagine that you loaned $500 to a friend of yours. Perhaps, several days later, you might remember that you imagined having loaned some money to your friend. If your metamemory or source memory is accurate, then you would remember that this was just your imagination and that you did not actually lend money to your friend. However, what would happen if you cannot distinguish between what you imagined and what really happened? Without source memory, you might erroneously think that your friend borrowed the money from you and you might demand payment.

Failures in source memory that blur the boundaries between reality and imagination result in such psychiatric symptoms as delusion and confabulation.

These symptoms are common in many types of mental illnesses, including dementia and schizophrenia. Source memory can sometimes fail even in healthy individuals, too. For example, we might occasionally get confused as to whether something we experienced in our dreams really happened or not. Although you don't have to be alarmed by such occasional failures in source memory, patients with borderline personality disorder have more difficulty in distinguishing between the contents of their dreams and reality (Skrzypinska and Szmigielska, 2015). In addition, difficulty in source memory can be related to other symptoms of these patients that related to interpersonal problems. Thus, although model-based reinforcement learning and mental simulations can improve our decision-making strategies in complex environments, this also requires the ability to keep our memories about real and imagined events separate. Mistaking events imagined during mental simulation for real events could potentially produce behaviors much worse than relying only on model-free reinforcement learning.

Another challenge related to model-based reinforcement learning and mental simulation is to decide how much mental simulation is enough before selecting an action. For difficult life-changing decisions, the number of important factors that need to be considered can be unyieldingly large. In large organizations, such as companies or governments, many people can participate in the process of decision-making and share the contents of their mental simulations during meetings. This increases the number and range of different scenarios that must be simulated, making it more difficult to reach a consensus about the best course of actions in a timely manner. We are all familiar with excessive mental simulation. Excessive mental simulation about past negative experience is referred to as rumination, which is a common feature of depression. Despite these side effects, it is mental simulation that allows us to select more appropriate actions based on the knowledge of our environment. Regardless of how much knowledge we have about the environment, we would not be able to predict the outcomes of alternative actions accurately and behave wisely without mental simulation. This might explain why depressed individuals can sometimes perform better in complex decision-making tasks that require analytical thinking.

As we discussed already, disappointment and regret are negative emotions related to model-free and model-based reinforcement learning, respectively. Another negative emotion we sometimes experience is envy. People experience envy when they discover their conditions are worse than those of others. All three of these negative emotions have something in common. Namely, we experience such negative emotions when the outcome of our action is worse than what we thought it would be. Therefore, much like disappointment and regret, envy is an error signal for learning, indicating that there might be a need to change your behavior. If someone else in the same group has obtained better outcomes than you, this suggests that you might not have discovered the best possible behavioral strategy. Envy is a biological signal indicating that you might be better off adopting someone else's strategy at least until you accumulate enough experience and knowledge.

What distinguishes envy from disappointment and regret is the source of our expectations. Disappointment or negative reward prediction error is a part of model-free reinforcement learning. By contrast, regret is a product of mental simulation and comes from model-based reinforcement learning. Similarly, we experience envy when we realize that what we obtained is inferior to what others received. We get envious for fundamentally the same reason we experience disappointment or regret, which is an error signal for reinforcement learning. Reinforcement learning operates by minimizing such error signals. When individuals can observe the actions of others in a group, this provides another possible means to discover most appropriate behaviors in a new situation. Imitation and observation learning can potentially eliminate trial-and-error learning. Moreover, it does not require extensive knowledge of the environment either and therefore can sometimes provide a more efficient way to learn appropriate behaviors than model-based reinforcement learning. Envy provides important error signals for such social learning.

Imitation and observation learning play a particularly important role during early human development. In a complex society with a sophisticated hierarchical structure and advanced technology, trying to learn everything using learning algorithms based on trial and error, such as model-free reinforcement learning, would be extremely slow and inefficient. Similarly, a long period of education would be required before model-based reinforcement learning algorithms can begin to recommend appropriate actions. Imitation and observation learning provide an easy alternative solution to such time-consuming learning algorithms. For example, imagine that you are in a foreign city and need to buy a train ticket from a self-service ticket machine. If there are no instructions written in a familiar language, you might want to observe what other people do and just follow what they do. When many people face the same problem as in this example, someone might have already invested all the time and effort necessary to discover a good solution to it, allowing others to imitate the same solution. Imitation and observation learning provided an important biological basis for the complex cultures humans developed. Nevertheless, humans are not the only species capable of imitating others. In addition to primates, some birds also demonstrate the ability to observe and imitate the behaviors of other animals. In some cases, this led to some elementary cultures among animals.

The cost of equipping our brains with various functions necessary to select the most appropriate actions is substantial. This includes negative emotions that are essential for different types of learning algorithms. Moreover, to combine advantages of different learning algorithms, the brain also requires the metacognitive ability to evaluate their reliability. Such metacognitive processes can become self-referential and, therefore, might require protection from logical paradoxes. Model-based reinforcement learning requires a means to control the amount of mental simulation. Unfortunately, as the number of different learning algorithms and cognitive processes increases, so does the number and potential side effects of negative emotions. In addition to negative error signals we discussed already, other negative emotions, such as fear and anxiety, are also related to specific types of learning and decision-making. Although we do not enjoy them, these negative emotions are just as necessary to improve the quality of our lives, as our abilities to feel physical pain. In a rare condition, referred to as congenital insensitivity to pain or congenital analgesia, patients can lose the ability to feel physical pain completely. This is a very dangerous condition, because without pain, patients with congenital analgesia often fail to respond properly to injuries and other illnesses. Similarly, various negative emotions are warning signs that are genetically programmed to promote behaviors ultimately consistent with the goal of genetic replication.

References

Brandenburger A, Keisler HJ (2006) An impossibility theorem on beliefs in games. Studia Logica. 84: 211–240.

Kiani R, Shadlen MN (2009) Representation of confidence associated with a decision by neurons in the parietal cortex. Science. 324: 759–764.

Kornell N, Son LK, Terrace HS (2007) Transfer of metacognitive skills and hint seeking in monkeys. Psychol Sci. 18: 64–71.

Lee SW, Shimojo S, O'Doherty JP (2014) Neural computations underlying arbitration between model-based and model-free learning. Neuron. 81: 687–699.

Modirrousta M, Fellows LK (2008) Medial prefrontal cortex plays a critical and selective role in "feeling of knowing" meta-memory judgments. Neuropsychologia. 46: 2958–2965.

Persaud N, McLeod P, Cowey A (2007) Post-decision wagering objectively measures awareness. Nature Neurosci. 10: 257–261.

Skryzpinska D, Szmigielska B (2015) Dream-reality confusion in borderline personality disorder: a theoretical analysis. Front Psychol. 6: 1393.

Further Reading

Hamilton JP, Farmer M, Fogelman P, Gotlib IH (2015) Depressive rumination, the default-mode network, and the dark matter of clinical neuroscience. Biol Psychiatry. 78: 224–230.

Hofstadter DR (1979) Gödel, Escher, Bach: An Eternal Golden Braid. New York, NY: Basic Books.

Minzenberg MJ, Fisher-Irving M, Poole JH, Vinogradov S (2006) Reduced self-referential source memory performance is associated with interpersonal dysfunction in borderline personality disorder. J Personal Disord. 20: 42–54.

Tomasello M, Call J (1997) Primate Cognition. New York, NY: Oxford Univ. Press.

10

Conclusion

Questions for Artificial Intelligence

Advances in psychology, neuroscience, and computer science in the last half century have phenomenally expanded our understanding of intelligence. Nevertheless, our knowledge of human intelligence is still quite limited. It is difficult to predict how certain limitations and weaknesses of human intelligence will make us vulnerable as the rate of change in our society continues to increase. Traditional value systems and conventional wisdom often fail due to technological innovations, and this is likely to result from the advances in digital devices and communications as well as biomedical technology. To adapt to such rapid changes in our societies, it will be increasingly more important to understand the limitations of human intelligence. A better understanding of human intelligence is also critical for accurately predicting how to best accommodate future artificial intelligence (AI) technology and how this might alter the relationship between humans and machines. In this final chapter, I will discuss how insights into the evolution of intelligence we discussed so far might enable us to better predict the impact of more powerful AI on human civilization.

In the beginning of this book, I emphasized the need to distinguish between intelligence and IQ. Intelligence is the ability to make good decisions and to solve a variety of problems that life faces in its ever-changing environment. The best solution in each circumstance depends on the needs and preference of an organism. This implies that the most appropriate form of intelligence would change depending on the environment of the organism. Therefore, it is not meaningful to reduce intelligence of a life form to a single number.

Assigning a number to a complex function, such as intelligence, is sometimes convenient, and this is why we have a ranking for everything. We rank not only music and sport teams, but also companies and universities, although such rankings are always subjective. Similarly, characterizing such a complex function as intelligence with a number is misleading. This gives the false impression that we can compare biological intelligence and artificial intelligence on the same scale. It is simple to compare the heights of two people, but this does not capture all the differences in the countless physical characteristics of the human body. Similarly, IQ focuses on a single aspect of human intelligence and can be used to rank different individuals accordingly. For example, we can capture some aspects of spatial perception or word memory using IQ scores. However, they do not reflect the entire intelligence of a person.

The widespread use and popularity of IQ was closely related to the industrialization that swept across the globe during the 20th century. However, as the range of AI application increases, unique abilities of individuals will become more important than IQ and other standardized measures of intelligence. IQ scores are designed to quantify cognitive abilities most relevant to economic productivity. However, as computers and AI become more sophisticated, the nature of human labor necessary to maximize the economic output in our society will fundamentally change. In the past, for example, an enormous amount of time and effort was necessary to accumulate, store, and retrieve the knowledge essential for economic activity and legal processes to support it. As a result, experts in areas that require extensive training, such as medicine and law, were rewarded generously. IQ test and other standardized exams were commonly used to identify appropriate candidates for such professional training. It is likely that the value of such standardized tests and exams gradually diminishes as AI begins to assist or even replace experts with such specialized knowledge and experience.

Throughout this book, I have emphasized the biological and evolutionary roots of intelligence and, hence, contiguity between animal and human intelligence. Humans and other primates share many common features of their intelligence. Nevertheless, human intelligence is most clearly distinguished from intelligence of nonhuman primates and other animals in two aspects, namely, social intelligence and metacognition, which we covered in the previous two chapters. These two aspects of human cognition overlap less with the abilities of other animals compared to more basic learning algorithms, such as classical and instrumental conditioning, so it is not surprising that we still do not understand the precise nature and biological mechanisms of social and metacognitive intelligence very well. Accordingly, the most valuable insight about the impact of emerging AI technology on human civilization might come from better understanding of our social and metacognitive abilities. It is not a coincidence that social intelligence and metacognition underlie precisely the type of activities humans enjoy most, such as sports, music, arts, and science. As man-made machines and AI increase their contribution to the production of various goods for people and free up human labor, the value of entertainment and personal development will continue to increase. Human society is likely to devote more and more resource in these two domains, demanding more precise understanding of human intelligence.

More and more studies are focusing on social and metacognitive abilities of humans. I expect that neuroscience and computer science will play the most important roles in these two important research areas. Human intelligence is a product of our brain, so a better understanding of brain development and function is essential for rigorous theories of intelligence. Currently, the precision of instruments, such as magnetic resonance imaging, that can be used to measure the activity of living human brains is quite limited. Development of noninvasive techniques that can probe and even control the neural activity of human brains precisely will significantly accelerate the progress in this area. Computer science and AI research also have close ties with neuroscience, since they provide valuable mathematical framework to analyze complex behavior and their underlying physical mechanisms. As exemplified by the recent machine-learning revolution, continuing advances in digital and computing technology will not only change the industry, but also our understanding of human intelligence. A better understanding of social and metacognitive intelligence will also help find causes and potentially even cures of many devastating disorders in brain functions, which will improve the quality of our lives.

Although social intelligence and metacognition might distinguish humans from other animals most clearly, there is no reason to think that they cannot be realized by AI. As AI technology advances, social and metacognitive intelligence will become an increasingly more essential part of AI. However, this does not mean that we are getting close to the technological singularity or that AI will begin to replace humans in all areas of intelligence. This will not occur any time soon because intelligence is a function of life defined by self-replication. As we have seen throughout this book, life has invented several major solutions during evolution based on the principle of principal–agent relationship to improve the efficiency of self-replication. Examples of the principal–agent relationship include the division of labor between germ and somatic cells and between the brain and genes. As long as computers do not physically reproduce themselves, humans will remain the principal and control the behaviors of computers with AI, just like the brain is unable to replicate itself and, as result, continues to function as an agent for the genes.

Individual AI programs are written to solve a relatively narrow set of specific problems, and they must perform more efficiently than humans in their applications. Otherwise, there would not be any economic demand for AI technology, and they would exist only as an object of entertainment or research. Therefore, competition between AI and human performance is not a threat to human society, but rather a necessary condition for AI. Brains evolved as sophisticated learning machines, and this was a solution, not a threat, to the principal-agent relationship between brains and genes. Similarly, advances in AI technology itself would not pose a threat to humans. AI will become a real threat to us if it has a set of its own independent values and utility functions antagonistic to those of humans. Otherwise, AI is fundamentally one of many tools that humans have invented to increase the efficiency of their labor.

Can we take for granted, then, that humans will always remain the principal in our relationship with machines with AI? The answer might be yes, but there is one catch. If we want to remain as the principal in our relationship with AI, we should not create machines that can reproduce themselves without human intervention. Real self-replicating machines must be able to complete all the functions necessary to replicate themselves, including the collection of its parts and final assembly. Making copies of the software that controls such machines is only a very small and easy part of self-replication. Therefore, a computer virus is not an artificial life. The developmental process that produces an adult human from a fertilized egg is extremely complex and includes learning. Similarly, a self-replicating machine must possess all the means necessary to survive and reproduce physically in an uncertain physical environment. An intelligent machine that can replicate itself would be a life form, even if it was originally created by humans. AI of such an artificial life form with the ability to replicate itself would be genuinely intelligent and might be a threat to our species. This would not be fundamentally different from the encounter with an alien civilization that is more advanced than ours.

It is difficult to predict how and when humans might ever be able to create artificial life. This process would be quite different from how digital computers and AI technology advanced in the last several decades. Many questions remain unanswered regarding the technology of artificial life and how this might affect the relationship between humans and human-made machines. For example, will machines with AI that currently work as agents for human users gradually acquire artificial life with more advanced technology? If so, what are the conditions for such transformation? How will this transform human civilization? These are difficult questions, and we do not know the answers yet. However, some day, we might have AI that can understand and answer these questions better than humans. If that happens before humans create artificial life, we should ask such a powerful AI, before it acquires its own life, how AI with artificial life will change human life.

Index

Figures are indicated by *f* following the page number

For the benefit of digital users, indexed terms that span two pages (e.g., 52–53) may, on occasion, appear on only one of those pages.